T0283540

MAYOR OF
**THE
TENDERLOIN**

MAYOR OF THE TENDERLOIN

DEL SEYMOUR'S JOURNEY
FROM LIVING ON THE STREETS TO FIGHTING
HOMELESSNESS IN SAN FRANCISCO

ALISON OWINGS

BEACON PRESS
BOSTON

Beacon Press
Boston, Massachusetts
www.beacon.org

Beacon Press books
are published under the auspices of
the Unitarian Universalist Association of Congregations.

© 2024 by Alison Owings

All rights reserved
Printed in the United States of America

27 26 25 24   8 7 6 5 4 3 2 1

This book is printed on acid-free paper that meets the uncoated paper
ANSI/NISO specifications for permanence as revised in 1992.

Text design and composition by Kim Arney

*Library of Congress Cataloguing-in-Publication
Data is available for this title.*
Hardcover ISBN: 978-0-8070-2057-9
E-book ISBN: 978-0-8070-2058-6
Audiobook: 978-0-8070-1708-1

For Del
and every person in his orbit

CONTENTS

PREFACE

ONE CHILLY EVENING some three decades ago, in an industrial section of San Francisco, I saw a man curled in a doorway. The sight so alarmed me, that having just heard a prediction the weather would turn bitterly cold, I rushed up, tapped the man on the shoulder, and gave him the warning. He looked at me blankly, in retrospect perhaps a gracious response considering I offered nothing more than words.

I walked on—and over the years, on and on—as such sights amid others more distressing, became familiar. Never again did I tap a stranger on the shoulder. Instead, I often looked away.

Then one morning on a sidewalk in San Francisco's Tenderloin, a neighborhood often described in published accounts as "seedy" or "gritty" (ciphers for filthy and drug-infested), where I usually walk quickly, my steps slowed. A stick-thin woman lay on her back, legs spread, appearing unconscious. Because the Tenderloin is where about half the city's officially tallied 7,754 homeless people live,[1] the sight of someone in her condition had become common. This time, though, I looked closer, noticing that her T shirt moved slightly. *She's breathing*, I thought. Several other people sat on the sidewalk near her, chatting. *They must know her. They'll call 911 if necessary*. Again, I walked on. My later shame came in realizing why I had paused, if only briefly.

It was not because of a fellow human's distress. It was because of the single word printed in capital letters on her T-shirt. It read RESPECT.

The plague of homelessness is soul-robbing to us all.

Indisputably, it also overwhelms us.

How in the United States could some two-thirds of a million people (the latest abominable statistic as of this writing is 653,104) have no home, something beyond a car or tent or friend's couch?[2] The question of what well-funded federal and private institutions could and should do for them has morphed into the discomfiting question of what we individuals with a home could and should do.

For years, I took the question personally but defensively, rejecting options I felt incapable of following, such as inviting a stranger into my home. Other options felt like puny bandages: awkward gifts of a little money, a little food. For a long while I considered using my oral history experience (and my wariness about stereotypes) to interview a countrywide range of homeless people, now commonly called unhoused or unsheltered people, then publishing the results. But, feeling daunted by the very idea, yet compelled by it, I wavered.

In 2015, amid this dilemma, my husband reserved tickets to a friend's play in the Tenderloin about its drug scourge. The theater also offered a pre-matinee walking tour of the neighborhood for a $15 donation. Why not? We signed on. At the appointed hour outside Cutting Ball Theater on Taylor Street stood a gaggle of white people, including us, and a tall, lanky, energized "light-skinned older brother" as one of his friends describes him. The man, who several times did a head count and checked his watch, dressed with urban elan. He wore a fedora, a suit, polished dress shoes, and a T-shirt advertising Tenderloin Walking Tours. This was our guide, Del Seymour, then sixty-eight.

Soon he led us down Taylor Street while saying, in a manner that suggested the retelling of a familiar story, he had spent many crack-addicted years in the Tenderloin but had gotten clean. We nodded and followed. At the intersection of Turk and Taylor Streets, he pointed out a block that once was a drug trafficking hub. To help stem the problem, he said, cars may no longer park there. The stretch looked like any scruffy urban street to me, but in Del's memory a different picture clearly prevailed. Gesturing toward the few pedestrians, he said he had often slept where they walked, then added, "I could have gotten a PhD in sidewalks." That sentence, ablaze with pathos and humor, launched this book.

Our friend's play was great but now of secondary interest. As soon as I got home, I did basic internet searches and from a few newspaper articles learned more about Del Seymour: success as a young contractor and electrician, then longtime addiction and homelessness, then not only recovery but also steps toward what resonated as redemption. He planned to start an organization to give free job readiness classes to help marginalized people get out of or avoid homelessness themselves. Clearly, Del knew the subject from—the phrase is inescapable—the ground up.

I phoned him. We met for lunch in Berkeley, a sociological midway point between the Tenderloin and my then home in Marin County. He rejected the restaurants I'd eagerly scouted—Turkish, Burmese—and opted for the plainest, where he ordered soup. Soup kitchen familiarity, I thought. (He later reproached me for using the phrase "soup kitchen," which I had not known to be objectionable. "Dining hall" is more respectful.) Over minestrone and crackers, I told him my plan, to write a book about homelessness from the point of view and experiences of one person: him. "Okay, sure," he said.

Slow-forward nearly a decade, many years longer than I thought this book would take. Del's inchoate plans for a free job-training program he called Code Tenderloin kept evolving as he did, catapulting him from the type of street person I once avoided to a community leader dubbed Mayor of the Tenderloin.

In those years, in many ways Del never changed—sending me emails at three in the morning, for example. His opinions on some matters evolved, but his basic outrage about people who take advantage of others never wavered.

This project was not without hurdles. Soon after our formal interviews began, I learned Del considered certain subjects off-limit. "I don't do family," he said. He emphatically did not want to name his father or brother. Then I learned something that gave me pause. One article described Del as "an ex-pimp." Prostitution long has so upset me, I had to convince myself pimping was not only part of Del's past but also informed his present and related to homelessness. Unbeknown to me at first, pimping is clearly a source of anguish to Del. In person, phone calls, and emails, he vehemently voiced concern and anger. "What's the salvation part of this?" he demanded. I attempted to explain my wanting to get a complete picture of him. Finally, as we both agreed he was trying to help a generation of young at-risk women, in effect daughters of the prostitutes he pimped ("the girls I ran," he sometimes put it), we tiptoed on.

Through Del, the Tenderloin became in my eyes an intriguing, wrenching, hopeless, hopeful, lively, and sometimes dangerous place (although I never felt threatened there). I write these words days after eight people were shot and wounded on the Tenderloin block where Del pointed out his PhD in sidewalks.

Neither of us expected the interviews to take so long, in years or minutes.[3] "Last question," I once announced after an hour-plus session. "Hallelujah," he replied. Yet I could always learn more, and Del seemed willing to expound, if not on all subjects.

I interviewed two of Del's daughters, as well, plus a variety of people from his past, including his last crack dealer. The only person who stood me up was one of Del's former prostitutes. When I told Del she never showed, he said she had some "issues." "Such as?" I prompted, annoyed at the wasted time. "Federal indictments."

Del's years of homelessness proved a tangled skein the farther back he reluctantly reached. He preferred to talk about his post-homeless era, being understandably proud of it. Were his memories and recollections accurate and truthful? From what I could check—and there was much I could not—they mostly were, if with caveats. Del tried to help with fact-checking, but at one point his filing system was a pocket of crumpled money and random business cards, among other effluvia. He produced no work resumes. Furthermore, his accounts often included hyperbole: that city is "100 percent white?" I noted minor contradictions too: When homeless he "always" had money—or he had been too broke to buy a beer. He never used a sleeping bag—or he had used a sleeping bag.

A friend of Del's told me with a raised eyebrow Del's memories could be "fluid."

Finally, though, I believe Del meant to be truthful, partly for his own good. He also relished being contrarian, which to me implies a certain honesty. Rather than utter the politically correct phrase "housing first," for example, he maintained such policies could be unfair to landlords. (Housing with supportive services was another matter.) Yet wherever we drove or walked, he would say something like, "See that parking lot over there? That could be housing." One day, when I joined him in a church effort to hand out sanitary supplies, he pooh-poohed my admiration of "tiny homes" as an interim approach. "Would you want to live in one?" he demanded. Beats curling up on the sidewalk, I thought, but his mood silenced me. Years later, he posted on Facebook an article touting tiny homes as a response to homelessness, adding, "SF let's do this."

When I finished my first draft of this book, I went way against standard practice and encouraged Del to read the entire text for errors. He accepted the offer, went over the pages carefully ("like an outside reader," he said), cited only a few mistakes or omissions, both mine and his, and never suggested any sugarcoating. Even pimping stayed.

Apart from questions about veracity that I could never answer, I often wondered what stories Del withheld. My sense is, many involved women. Others, considering his praise of hustling, must have involved money. Others certainly included unsavory aspects of his addicted years; during a videotaped panel discussion, he mentioned waking up in his own waste. He never told me that, nor did I inquire further.

My major journalistic frustration centered on Del's inability to pin down dates: by year, decade, even century. "I don't do dates" proved a mantra similar to "I don't do family." One file I labeled "Timeline" lists more than thirty incidents, with my printed-out pages marked by arrows moving each event from its first presumed year to another. Had he had this engineering assignment in Bangkok before that one in Minnesota? When did he live in the refrigerator box? When was he invited—once clean—to this or that corporate board? I do know when he quit one, because it happened in our own timeline. He told me he refused to be in any organization that did not give second chances.

To many questions, Del shrugged. Crack, he said more than once, does not help memory. Rap sheets he provided confirmed his slim body (6 feet tall, 135 pounds) and dates of San Francisco arrests from 2000 to 2004. Typically, he later lost his copies of these and asked for copies of mine. Stymied by attempts to answer a basic journalistic "W" question, "When?," I abandoned a traditional biography. Instead, I opted to write about this unconventional person in an unconventional way, crafting Del's dramatic life in scenes, arranged in a narrative that replicates much of his life, slipping forward, sliding backward, stabilizing.

It is my hope these scenes comprise an inspiring whole: conveying the life of Deleano Joseph Seymour while providing a guide to how people—homeless or not—can help battle this societal horror. I also hope housed readers will ponder: Who *is* that person sleeping in the doorway? As Del said over and over, sometimes able to hide his tears, "That old Black man could be me."

CHAPTER 1

THE APPROACHING FALL

DEL WENT DOWN HARD.

One day in or around 1986, while living in Oakland, working for Bay Alarm Company or as an electrician or maybe both, Del drove into San Francisco's Tenderloin.

Until then, Del said, he had never been in San Francisco at all, other than a single trip years earlier to visit a Chicago childhood friend. This time his plan was less specific.

"For some reason, I came over to the Tenderloin. That was it. End of story," he said and laughed. The some reason, he elaborated, was partly curiosity and partly attraction to "the party life, the freedom to do whatever the hell you want to do, to live a completely wild lifestyle, because basically, up to about that time, I was a firefighter. Military. I was pretty straight." Yes, he had been a party guy too. "Socially party. Not criminally party. I was working the prostitutes and all that. It was just fun. It's gangsterism."

The appeal of what he also called "the street life" included a cliché he deemed accurate: "Sex, drugs, and rock and roll. Let's put it like that."

Putting it like that, however, lacked detail Del later divulged to a male podcast host. "When I got out on Turk and Taylor [an infamous Tenderloin intersection], I'm thinking they're shooting a movie because there could not be a neighborhood like this in the civilized world. Where's the sound trucks? Where's the camera? People walking around naked, people walking around doing sex acts on themselves, people with needles. . . . People in drag and people smoking dope and people hitting people in the head with pipes. All within two or three minutes, I saw that whole thing. By eight o'clock that night, I was in that movie. Within twenty-four hours I was a blown-out drug addict."[1]

At the cusp of forty, Del Seymour's drug of choice was singular: crack cocaine.

To characterize his fall, Del typically invokes either of two honed statements. "I put a crack pipe in my mouth for eighteen seconds. It took eighteen years to get it *out* of my mouth." The other is, "I drove into San Francisco on Highway 280, and within thirty days I was living *under* Highway 280."

Because Del has mastery of cadence and because the dual misery of addiction and homelessness is central to his saga, both of his statements warrant a dash of deconstruction. Did it take eighteen seconds for his first hit? An initial crack high can be almost instantaneous. Perhaps it was slower for Del, and perhaps he really was counting off the seconds. As for the eighteen years parallel, his fateful drive into the Tenderloin seems to have happened in 1986, although Del has also mentioned 1989. If, piecing together various accounts, the year he finally got clean was 2010, his addiction and homelessness may have lasted a more alarming twenty-four years. But "eighteen seconds and eighteen years" has a memorable ring.

What about the timing of his descent under the highway? Del also said the transition to homelessness took three months, but "thirty days" may stick in one's mind better.

Why not lean on cadence? When Del took his plunge, he likely did not consult a stopwatch or a calendar. Then there is the matter of memory. He has insisted he retains little memory of his childhood and said he has even fewer memories from addiction. "It's like being in a blackout." Details of the years being "Del the straight-up dope fiend" are gone. "People never in heavy addiction don't understand anything I'm talking about. You don't remember names, places, anything."

Yet the central assertion stands: crack controlled his life for eighteen years, at least.

"A typical crack user will take a hit of crack maybe fifty times a day. Minimum. If you stand here long enough," Del noted, while overlooking a Tenderloin street, "you'll see somebody come and take four or five hits right here, within five minutes. Soon as you take the first hit, you're technically on a run. That run's not going to stop until you have exhausted *all* means of money or you're just exhausted and fall asleep. That'll be *days* later."

Do not believe anybody about getting "dope sick" from stopping crack, he said. "That's a particular term for heroin use. No other drug causes dope sickness." Practical Recovery, a treatment services program, echoes Del. It states on its website, "Withdrawal [from crack] usually causes more psychological discomfort than physiological discomfort, and is rarely, if ever, medically serious."[2]

Crack users do not even talk about withdrawal, said Del. "Just addiction. [If] you go to jail, you don't have it, it's no big. You just go to sleep. And wish you had some." You would not be twitching. "Not at all." You could, though, be broke. "I may start off in the morning with three hundred dollars," he continued. "I'm messing around with girls or getting high or whatever and wind up at noon, have no money. Then I run into some kind of hustle and have another two hundred dollars. By the end of the night, I'm sleeping in the tent. And went through two thousand dollars."

With few exceptions, all Tenderloin hotels (in particular single-room occupancies or SROs) condoned crack use, Del said, so he often stayed at one of them. But if he had enough money to be more comfortable, he rented an upscale hotel room, perhaps at the nearby Hilton. "Mostly, it was probably to get high, to get into a nice room so I could do my drug thing." Never with a man, he said more than once, but with "whatever girl I was with at the time."

Even today, the lure that slammed Del into homelessness shimmers to the point he cannot, or will not, talk much about it—especially about missing it. "If you're a real drug addict, and I'm a real drug addict, you'll *always* miss it." Del knows himself well. "I've kind of blocked all that out, because that's part of my recovery. People recover differently. In general, I say, get to a certain depth but no further. Don't go into 'Who was the first person you used with?' Because then your mind will wake up that addict who's been asleep. The addict says, 'Since you woke me up talking about this shit, let's go get one!'"

Crack not only reputedly offers a high greater than powdered cocaine, but a crack high laced with sex can be extraordinary. Websites such as addictionresource.com, meant to help addicts overcome dependency, may inadvertently promote it by stating, "The . . . crack sex drive . . . incredible in the short term."[3] Does everyone read on to subsequent warnings about risky behavior?

ONE COLD, FOGGY, AND MISERABLE NIGHT in the midst of his addiction, Del set his sights on finding a free warm place to sleep. He and his friend Cuba had waited hours at the large St. Vincent de Paul shelter in the Tenderloin to get a bed. They had vouchers in case people didn't show but at about 11 p.m. gave up. Instead, they decided to take a bus to a slightly larger shelter called Next Door and try for what Del called "sympathy" beds. The option, since discontinued, let the staff decide whether last-minute stragglers could spend the night if beds were available.

Just as Del and Cuba were about to board their bus, a man with a backpack got off. In exiting, one of the backpack straps snagged, the pack opened, and, in Del's telling, "there was a rainstorm of $20 bills." He and Cuba leapt into action, grabbing all they could. The man protested.

"But what could he do? We were two bad-looking guys."

Cuba, his nickname from having arrived in the United States on the 1980 Mariel boatlift, gave the man back a fistful of bills with a look that said, "Take this and be happy." The man scrambled off. The rest of the money, some $400, Del and Cuba split. With it, each rented a room in an SRO for a week and had enough money "for food and dope," Del added.

The tale reminded him of a similar miserable night. "When I got tired of the streets, I'd call Nasser." A longtime friend, Nasser financially supported a mosque and owned many SROs, a mainstay in the Tenderloin. That night, Nasser told Del he himself had no room available but directed him to an SRO his uncle ran on nearby 6th Street. Nasser said he would call his uncle to expect Del. But when Del arrived, he was met by a desk clerk who, apparently unbeknown to the uncle, kept three rooms on his own, renting them out by the hour. Unhappy about having one taken out of commission, he reluctantly gave Del a key. Del went upstairs, let himself in, and encountered a man who insisted the room was his. Arguing and shoving ensued. Del said he would call Nasser and the uncle to ask who had rights. Defeated, the man stormed out.

While settling in, Del noticed the wastebasket and its contents, including six $100 bills and crack. "For some reason, people hide stuff all the time in trash cans, thinking the police won't look there." They do, he said. So did Del. After taking what he wanted, he emptied the rest.

Before long, a knock sounded on the door. Del opened it. The previous occupant came in "real nice," saying he was sorry about the earlier misunderstanding. He might have left something in the room, perhaps in the wastebasket. Could he look? Del informed the man he'd emptied it, that maybe the guy should go check the SRO's garbage bin. The man, again defeated, left. "Deep down he knew."

In Del's opinion, the man was no scared guy with a torn backpack but a fellow "gangster." If he had behaved nicely at the outset, rather than arguing and shoving, Del said, he would have given him back everything and asked only "to break me off a piece" of the crack rock for himself. Instead, the man got nothing. There is a price to be paid for not observing Tenderloin protocol.

CHAPTER 2

THE TENDERLOIN AND A GOOD NIGHT'S SLEEP

A Contradiction

S AN FRANCISCO'S TENDERLOIN may have been named for Manhat-
tan's Tenderloin, whose name in turn may have come from police
lore. One theory has it that infamous New York policeman Alexander
"Clubber" Williams, the nineteenth-century "czar of the Tenderloin,"
took so many bribes he eventually announced it was time to skip chuck
steak and eat tenderloin. Del's research, however, convinced him San
Francisco's Tenderloin got its name from butcher shops that supplied
beef to fancy Nob Hill hotels.

His Tenderloin ("the TL" to locals) comprises a historic downtown area initially counted as some thirty square blocks but which
expanded reckonings now put closer to fifty. Whatever the size, it
includes a social petri dish, the number of languages spoken tallied at
30 on the low end to 112 on the high. Within its confines exists a large,
extraordinarily labile tech community amid unsheltered and often
traumatized have-nots, along with passed-out drunks and "people in
their addiction," as a delicate phrase puts it. Walking quickly around
them and their waste may be children accompanied by their essential
escorts: volunteers from the Safe Passage program. "I only get up at
6 a.m. for the kids," said a Tenderloin woman who helps guide them
to and from daycare or school (as do employees of Code Tenderloin,
the free job-training program Del founded). Amid this admixture

operates a plethora of community groups, theaters old and new, up-start art galleries, drag show venues, a Japanese vegan restaurant, and a glammed-up hotel with a pricey rooftop bar. It overlooks sidewalks lined with tents and with discarded drug paraphernalia, which reflect marked changes in drugs of choice. In addition to used needles, much current drug detritus includes crunched, burn-marked foil, a sign of one of several ways to take fentanyl, by some estimates a hundred times stronger than heroin. According to San Francisco's Department of Public Health, 2023 was especially deadly: 806 people in the city died from drug overdoses, mostly fentanyl and its sometimes intentional or unexpected mixture with other drugs.[1] A *San Francisco Chronicle* map of drug deaths shows that few areas of the city were spared entirely, but the majority of deaths were concentrated in the Tenderloin.

It is difficult to gauge how many of those people were in the category of sheltered or unsheltered homeless, but one fact is certain: the mythically stunning mecca of San Francisco is home to thousands of people who have none.

"I had many, many years of homelessness," Del noted, adding that did not mean he was outside every night. He estimated he has stayed at some fifty hotels, mostly SROs. Over the years, the majority became squalid drug dens, at least by reputation. Although many have since been cleaned up, Del's experience was with the squalid versions. "Got put out of every one of them because I was good at breaking whatever the rules were. I did exactly the opposite of everything on the rule book, because the rules are no fun."

As Del sometimes slept in a Dumpster, the next night in a proper hotel, then on a bus, then in an SRO, crack determined his finances. "Because my income was daily, my maintenance was daily. If I got some money, I could only buy a room for a night. If I didn't get out of that room and the next morning go out and hustle for another night in that room, then I was on the bus the next day. Or in the shelter." He grimaced.

Shelters were Del's least favorite places to sleep (or try to sleep). "The shelters are a hotbed of drug sales and usage. The bathrooms are like a high school bathroom. The place smells like an institution, smells like a jail. And it's a jail environment." One problem, he said, is that because staffers are underpaid, they in turn resent their jobs and do not offer a dignified welcome to people who especially need it. Furthermore, long-term shelter residents rule. "It's very territorial, exactly like prison. The guards, which in this case are monitors, let the inmates, in this case shelter residents, the longest-tenure guys, run the whole facility. They're what they call the shot callers. Unless you know them or you've been there long enough to be a shot caller, it's a miserable place. The guy in the next bed may be playing his boom box all night, because he's been there a long time, so no one's going to say nothing to him."

Whether rested or not, people generally must leave by 6 a.m., a rule Del finds cruel and absurd. These are people without homes. Where can they go at that hour?

DURING HIS ADDICTION, Del often cased the city for a doorway where he might spend the night. The best had several attributes. "Isolation from the wind. Low foot traffic. No other homeless around. Those are three things." He paused briefly, remembering. "Dry. And . . . where I would offend nobody. And where I didn't have to get up *too* early. I'd find a good place that screened out three ways, and I could stay there until maybe seven o'clock. Until foot traffic."

Of many doorways Del slept in, he said sometimes he got permission but mostly did not. The search alone was exhausting. "It would take you hours to find a doorway. Then I finally found a couple preferred doorways. I would travel to them. I never told anyone where I was."

Although now housed for years, Del's scanning impulse has not left him. "When I walk down the street, I'm still shopping. Not that I would ever need it."

Once Del reached his doorway of choice, he needed something to sleep on. "I had to go find my bedding every night, which was cardboard. Always cardboard. It cushions." No, Del said (contradicting another remark to the contrary), he did not use a sleeping bag. "I never had a sleeping bag in my life. See, that puts you in a bad, bad position. I couldn't've got out if someone came up to attack me. It's like being in a straitjacket. You're completely at their will. You're defenseless. That's *crazy!*"

He claimed no physical fear—"I ain't afraid of nobody; I'm from Chicago."—and he armed himself. "I carried a gun a lot of times." He had a 9mm pistol he usually kept in a shoulder holster ("I love shoulder holsters"). The pistol was loaded, but Del said he never fired it. He rejected knives: "a waste of time."

During his doorway nights, Del maintained, he never actually slept, whether armed or not. "I'm resting. I use the word 'sleep,' but . . . no one had to wake me up, because I had a motion detector in my brain. If you came *any*where near me, I would recognize you."

Another wake-up call was weather. Rain, he maintained, was not much of a problem. "I'm pretty creative. I always made a way. I never really got wet." But cold, yes. "It gets cold in San Francisco about four or five in the morning. Nights, the winds are pretty down, but about four o'clock the winds come up, from the ocean. That's when it freezes. So you're good until about four, then you got to get up and find someplace to go. We used to have doughnut shops open all night. Or all-night restaurants. We had Wendy's that was open, we had Louisiana Fish that was open. You go in there and buy whatever you could with the minimum amount of money you had. You didn't want to waste any money because you're not really hungry. You're just cold." Whether from the memory of those nights or being a person with virtually no body fat, Del remains attuned to cold, bundling in layers throughout the year, sometimes turning up a thermostat in a relatively warm room.

"One of the biggest, most popular tricks is get on BART [Bay Area Rapid Transit] and ride BART the rest of the night. The first BART [train] at the Tenderloin is at five minutes after four. Powell Street or Civic Center. You ride out to Walnut Creek [in the East Bay], then you come back, and you get off and you ride up to Richmond. You come back and ride out to Fremont. You ride till about ten o'clock in the morning, till it gets warm."

"Another trick we have," he started, as the past again became the present, involved long Bay Area bus rides. A favorite route took him from San Francisco to Palo Alto. "It was about a three-hour ride. So you got three hours of warmth and refuge from the cold and wind and elements."

Even on buses, though, Del would not really sleep. "You don't want to sleep around people. You can't. You would nod. When you're homeless, you learn how not ever to go to sleep." For real sleep, "you would have to be in your own room somewhere."

Falling asleep on public transit such as BART was a big no-no. "That's showing a weakness. You're around completely strange people. You got to be animalistic. An animal would never lay down around animals from other species. That's what you're around, other species [of] people. You're around the police. You don't want to be sleeping with the police coming, because they'll throw you off the train. It's against the law to sleep on BART."

When the day warmed up, Del sought real rest. "Usually I would find a nice park somewhere and go to sleep, on the grass." If he were trying to slow or stop his addiction, he chose a place as far as possible from fellow addicts, but that consideration came later. For daytime sleep, he appreciated San Francisco's open swaths of Crissy Field and nearby Fort Mason. "You could crash completely because there was a lot of normal people around. People walking their dogs and walking their babies. There was no threat." He amended that to a "low instance of threat": "You wake up and people be trying to take your shoes off, trying to steal your bag." Other times Del woke to find gifts. "There'd be a bag with a sandwich. Sometimes money. It would happen more often than not." But the grassy park beds were inconsistent, good one day, not the next.

More reliable were institutions such as the Tenderloin's Glide Memorial Church, where Del often lined up for a free meal. (One of many people he got to know in line was Chris Gardner, who later wrote the best-selling book *The Pursuit of Happyness.*) Del also sometimes slept at Glide (as a last resort, in a Glide doorway). Yet, as he said more than once, his homelessness was not constant. SROs a few nights, maybe jail the next, maybe a Dumpster the following night, then a regular hotel or, if desperate, a shelter.

They do offer what Del said people without homes need even more than clean socks: showers. But shelter showers could be risky. "You're trapped. You'll be attacked. You got to do the shower on the buddy plan. You got to have someone you know and trust to stand there while you're taking a shower, because you're vulnerable. Where you going to put your stuff? Where you going to put your wallet? Your watch? Your cell phone?"

Del did not mention another element: person-to-person proximity. A visit to the Next Door shelter on Polk Street, on the western border of the Tenderloin, illustrated the problem. Next Door shelters an impressive 334 people a night.[2] Quarters are tight, and snoring is an issue, as are smells. During one visit, cots were barely two feet apart, at least on the men's floors. Next Door is run by Episcopal Community Services, a San Francisco–based organization focused on a variety of programs to help people who are either homeless or nearly so. Unlike other shelters, Next Door allows residents to bring their pets. Any animal that is not well-behaved, however, is taken to a downstairs kennel.

One day a pit bull and a German shepherd snarled at each other between cots, catching the attention of program director Kathy Treggiari, an intrepid force facing daunting odds. She glanced at the dogs warily but said nothing. A veteran social worker from Massachusetts, her accent as strong as her opinions, Kathy's job frustrations went well beyond snarls.

Her primary concern involved the increasing trend of people arriving at Next Door in need of much more than a bed, which itself involved getting a reservation through another agency. According to city criteria, she said, "People need to self-care. The problem is, there's no one at the door saying you can self-care, you can't. So, we continue to see all sorts of folks coming in that are medically fragile, that are very sick, that can't self-care. But there's no place else for them to go."

Starting around 2012, Kathy talked often with a colleague in the city's Department of Public Health about the dilemma. "We had very little in the way of medical providers coming in here." Next Door needed a full-time nurse. Instead, the staff called the fire department for help. "We have Engine Three a block away that was getting seven hundred to eight hundred calls a year from here. My people are not medically trained. If there's a seizure, we call 911. If there's what looks like an OD, we call 911. They were here from one to three times a day. That's big bucks."

Finally, thanks in part to the Tenderloin's then supervisor Jane Kim, who stayed anonymously overnight at the shelter and soon publicized its extensive medical needs, the Department of Public Health assigned Next Door a full-time nurse. Engine Three, said Kathy, was "thrilled." But the nurse was immediately overwhelmed. Next Door needed far more than what one forty-hour-a-week nurse could provide, especially because it is open around the clock, unlike most shelters. By 2016, two health workers helped the nurse with such tasks as filling prescriptions and taking notes. Kathy painted a challenging situation.

"The Department of Public Health is out of San Francisco General Hospital. So, you have this homeless outreach team out on the streets, picking up people from the hospital. They're not trained on who can self-care, who can't. The hospital's saying they can toilet, they can get in and out of a wheelchair, they don't need assistance. What we're finding is that's not necessarily true." Yes, she said hesitantly, the hospital sometimes dumps people.

"The medical needs of the folks we're serving are going to get worse, not better. We all know that." At the time, the head of San Francisco's Department of Homelessness, Jeff Kositsky, asked Kathy what she would want at Next Door if she had all the money in the world.

She paused, then softly repeated her answer: "I'd like to see seniors together, so they can support each other. I'd like to see couples together. I'd like to see medically fragile people together. Right now, you could have someone with severe mental health issues, diagnosed, undiagnosed, medicated, unmedicated, and with a senior, and with someone who's actively substance using. You get that kind of mix."

People bring with them "anything from diabetes to cancer, to being terminal, to just getting out of surgery." Next Door's nurse has "seen people come in with catheter bags."

Before the nurse was assigned, Kathy's supervisor found himself delivering a baby. "No one knew this woman was so severely mentally ill. No one knew how pregnant she was or *if* she was pregnant, because she was so incoherent. He delivered a baby in the bed. That sounds great, but it wasn't. He was traumatized for days afterwards."

People also "absolutely" bring in their addictions. "Active drug using. We are a harm-reduction model that the city mandates, which we believe in." To Kathy, the now common term "harm reduction" means working with an addict to cut down on drug usage step by step, rather than demanding a cold turkey approach. She adamantly opposed "dry shelters." If someone gets ejected for smelling like alcohol, what happened to staff time spent trying to find the root of the person's problem? "They relapse and we kick them out? That doesn't make sense, and it's such a waste to maybe start all over again, maybe not get them back in for another six months. To me, harm reduction is realistic. [If someone comes into Next Door] who is actively using, staff here are very adept at knowing folks and saying, 'Hmm, you're a little bit too high right now. What are the chances of your going upstairs, not causing a ruckus, and sleeping it off?'" She added, "I want to emphasize, harm reduction isn't 'anything goes.'"

Whatever conditions residents arrive in, an increasing commonality is old age, coupled with lack of mobility. For them, "we have canes, walkers, wheelchairs." Some shelter seekers are in their nineties.

As in other shelters connected to city governments, beds get allotted according to various criteria, such as whether a person is on GA (General Assistance, or welfare) or is a military veteran. Kathy missed her more manageable situation back in Massachusetts, where she directed a hundred-bed shelter. "We did an intake on every single person who walked through the door. What's your medical history, what's your housing history, what's your mental health history, what's your income, what's your employment. Not to vicariously know about the person, although it's an intrusive process, but to begin working on 'What's your path out of homelessness?' It's a no-brainer. I come here where, if you don't have a case manager, we don't know who's walking through our doors. That's the shocker for me."

Regarding people with mental health issues, she added carefully, "They're not getting the kind of case management I would say is useful."

"Since 2009, we have absolutely fought for, begged, used our own [funding] to try to beef up our case management opportunities here [and hire more licensed behavioral health specialists]. . . . They will do crisis intervention, they will do some therapy, basic case management, but, for the most part, they're absolutely not meeting with everyone."

Next Door does offer dinner, limited personal storage space, and a library, as well as the rare privilege of pet companionship. When further crises—such as a spate of rough winter weather—challenge San Francisco's unsheltered population, necessitating a temporary shelter, perhaps in a church, Kathy Treggiari has organized that too. "We got *really* good" at it, she said, smiling. "Take 'em mats, take 'em blankets, then go into the church. It's only in the winter—to take sixty to a hundred additional men in out of the cold and the rain."

After sending her "seasoned staff" to help with the temporary shelter, she noticed an entirely different reaction from the clients, as she called them. For one thing, they had few complaints. "A lot of it was the food, because you have all these different churches that bring in five-course meals. A lot of it was a calmer staff. A lot of it was just a smaller environment. People feel safe, people feel heard." Neither the clients nor the staff could quite believe the others were the same people they had met before at the less calm Next Door.

Obstacles and challenges, administrative and physical, bureaucratic and mental, remained enormous, both for her and for people seeking shelter at Next Door. Despite the shelters' drawbacks and restrictions, some 90 percent of San Francisco's over three thousand shelter beds were occupied during one count in the summer of 2023, according to city government data. (Some were set aside for emergency situations.) And about five hundred people were on a waiting list to get a bed.[3]

In a sideways remark that seemed to slip out, Kathy said, "It's a lot of effort for one lousy bed." She added, "I will, till the day I die, say being homeless in a shelter is an abnormal way to live."

CHAPTER 3

THE BIRTH OF CODE TENDERLOIN

IN FEBRUARY 2014, when young British software designer Shash Deshmukh visited San Francisco for the first time, he was shocked. "In London we get fed a lot of things about how San Francisco is brilliant for startups and why we should all move there. It's this utopia." He had come to town to participate in Launch Festival, a tech conference for companies like his nascent one, Paperfold, "a visual email app for mobile devices," as his website described it.

"The first thing that hit me about San Francisco [was] obviously the homelessness." There, in the middle of Market Street, he said, a significant portion of the public seemed to him to have no home. He said British authorities would consider the situation a war zone and send in the army.

The difference between tech festival and street reality continued to rattle Shash, a soft-spoken and self-effacing graduate of Oxford University. He cringed at seeing a "do-good" poster in the office of a tech friend who worked for a billion-dollar enterprise. The poster heralded the company's fund-raiser for a homeless shelter—based on how many home runs the San Francisco Giants hit. Pictured was a sad-looking family presumably hoping for grand slams. "It's insulting. It tells you about the thinking behind these companies. The problem is not that serious to them. It's a marketing thing to make them feel good."

Street scenes made Shash even more distressed. "On my way to my Apple event, I'm walking over bodies, basically. That's not right." He managed to arrange an appointment with a mayoral assistant at a Tenderloin café. Even the walk to meet her troubled him. "Every single place where the window meets the ground was full of homeless people. What I saw is tech people, like me, wearing their badge and having their laptops with them, sort of crawling to get into the place, then opening the door and pretending everything is absolutely fine, literally breathing a sigh of relief. The empathy gap made me a little angry, actually."

If he lost his home in England, Shash said, his "state of worry would be a lot lower in approaching civic organizations for help. America is about going out there and doing things by [yourself] and winning. But if that doesn't work, you've got to save face and pretend you're winning? Or not ask other people for help? I think not being dependent on other people is a big American trait."

Americans in need, including unsheltered populations, he felt, are given the equivalent of a flashlight in the dark. "Run *only* as fast as you can see without falling over." In England, he said, government help comes without shame.

Expressing his concerns to the mayor's representative, Shash said they had an honest conversation. As an outsider, how could he help? She named various groups he might contact. While he mulled that approach, he also decided to attend a conference TEDx talk titled "Teach Our Girls How to Code: A Former Pimp's Call to Action." The speaker was Del Seymour.

The TEDx video of the talk shows Del wearing a gray fedora, a gray suit with a colorful pocket square, and a dangling scarf. His open jacket reveals a yellow T-shirt reading Tenderloin Walking Tours, the bare-bones enterprise he had started a couple of years earlier. He paces the small stage, waving his hands, his dominant left adorned with two gold rings, one on his index finger. The young audience seems locked on Del's words, as he implores them to help the Tenderloin community. "You folks need to meet *my* folks, because you folks are going to be down here, and you need to deal day to day with my folks. You need to feel our pain. We need to feel *your* pain. We need to understand you. You need to understand us."

He urges his audience not to brand Tenderloin residents as lawless but instead to help them get straight jobs. "We got girls standing on the corner of Turk and Taylor selling crack. Been there for years because

they don't know how to get off that corner. The only difference between you and the little girl with braids on Turk and Taylor? You can
code and she can't."

"They want Nikes, just like you," he continues. "They want Pampers, just like your kids. And they got criminal records. Mainstream
employers therefore will not hire them. They can't go to Gap. They
can't go to Sears. You ever see these little girls at Apple stores? No."
Pacing the stage, pointing, gesticulating, Del issues a challenge. "Go
down on Turk and Taylor. I'll make the hookup for you. Get one girl
and bring her into an incubator like this. Show her how to do *something*.
Invest in *one girl*. Solve *her* problem. And when you solve *her* problem,
you'll solve her kids', her mama's, her grandkids', her brother's, her
halfway dude's, her neighbors.' You'll solve a whole bunch of people's."
Del all but pleads, "All the minds in here, all the integrity, all the resources—come on, folks. Invest in our future. You can break the chain."

Shash was the first person to approach Del off the stage.

They soon met privately, Shash quizzing Del about his plan to start
a job readiness training organization. The basic idea, Del explained,
was to get real jobs for people such as those he spoke about, people
who for whatever reason—discrimination, addiction, homelessness,
despair—felt incapable of earning a decent living legally. They needed
encouragement and practical help. Del's name for the organization he
pictured was Code Tenderloin.

The name had nothing to do with software coding, he explained,
as he subsequently repeated countless times. "'Code Blue on floor 2'
or 'Code Red in the emergency room' means there's a problem in that
hospital. 'Code Tenderloin' means there's a problem in the Tenderloin
because we're not working." In his estimation, unemployment in the
Tenderloin ranged from 50 percent to 80 percent.

He and Shash met repeatedly. Some discussions focused on basic
needs of the people Del had in mind, said Shash, such as "classes to
prepare them for specific things, like interview prep. Del was saying
they need to have skills the startups need." The two also worked on
another element: exposing would-be Code Tenderloin students to new
opportunities. Shash had seen a similar approach in his university years,
a program taking inner-city London schoolchildren to Oxford to become familiar with the environment, so they might consider applying.

In his San Francisco visit, Shash spent what he had—time, enthusiasm, and coding skills but no money—developing a tech-oriented scenario for Del's idea. Then he headed back to England and his investors, who wondered what he had been doing.

TO MAKE CODE TENDERLOIN VIABLE, Del needed everything, including teachers, students, and classroom space.

To recruit teachers, he turned to a like-minded neighborhood activist, Neil Shah, who rounded up volunteers, such as April Trinh, who taught on her days off from work, and Natalie Perales, a college student. Initially, Del planned to do much of the teaching himself. Who else knew better how to get out of homelessness?

To recruit students, he simply went "on the streets," as he put it. His search did not take long. Virtually all candidates wanting a straight job were homeless. Almost all had criminal convictions. What Del offered for free was a program meant to launch them into not only jobs but also careers. The felony factor remained a concern, but he tackled that too, finding employers open to hiring vetted candidates. One later Code Tenderloin online ad referred to removing barriers, stating, "Previous history with difficult issues including substance abuse, mental health, education level, personal finances or criminal record does not disqualify you from securing work." Classes would include what became a standard: mock job interviews.

For the initial set of classes, several days a week for four weeks, Del signed up about ten people. Funding for such incidentals as modest snacks offered at the first classes came from contributions to the walking tours he had been giving for a few years. "I'm broke," he said matter-of-factly. One line he repeated to various audiences was "Sue me, because I've got no money." His stylish-looking outfits came from thrift stores.

A fact kept fairly private within Code Tenderloin was how much he helped students anyway, giving them money not only for transportation and cell phones but also for food, childcare, and sometimes even rent. "Everything to make them competitive," said Del one day. "Whatever they need. And we do that not only until they get a job but at least a month after they're on the job, so they can save those paychecks and get permanent housing." Additionally, students in difficult circumstances, sometimes with babies in tow, were found places to stay, including with Del. The word got out: people at Code Tenderloin care. One woman who phoned looking for a class was asked whether she was safe, whether she was hungry.

For classroom space, the three owners of a new scrappy nightclub/restaurant/performance space in the Tenderloin called Piano Fight—whom Del befriended on his walking tours—donated day use of two rooms used in the evenings for ragtag theatrical productions. (This made for arresting scenery backdrops during classes.) The trio also offered Del day use of Piano Fight's main floor area.

Del met there with a constant array of visitors, among them potential students and possible funders, sometimes a journalist or two, as well as people who needed help outside the formal classes he was developing.

"At Code Tenderloin," he mentioned one day at Piano Fight, "we have two different populations. We have the job readiness program, and then we have what they jokingly or lovingly or haltingly call 'Del's clients.' I've had three of them in here this morning. Those are my folks I deal with one on one. I don't [have] the highest expectations of them as I would in the job readiness course. But if I know about a job I think they can fill, I have no right to say, 'No, you need to go to this course first.'" Del got one such person a job at UPS. "I'm really concerned about his first paycheck, because he's newly clean."

Meanwhile, Del kept fund-raising. Eventually Code Tenderloin won a few small grants. With some of the money, he reimbursed Piano Fight for his costs. "I don't abuse stuff. When I'm in here by myself, I try to keep my footprint as small as possible. Lights or air conditioning I only do when I got students here for class. We're using twelve hours a week of HVAC and lights and water and napkins and toilet paper. We figured out that would be about $500 a month." He considered the Piano Fight trio "community partners, very socially conscious young men that actually donate the space. We just cover our expenses."

Unlike periods in his earlier life, Del became assiduously law-abiding, reciting IRS rules about what is and is not deductible. He put Tenderloin Walking Tours, as well as Code Tenderloin as its subsidiary, under the oversight of a San Francisco arts organization. Before long, between tours and the classes, he forged a connection to an entity he especially wanted to reach: high tech.

Back in 2011, city supervisors, urged by Tenderloin supervisor Jane Kim, passed what was called the "Twitter tax break." Whether San Francisco officials on their own lured high-tech companies, including Twitter, to move to the down-at-the-heels Mid-Market Tenderloin area by offering a tax break or whether the action followed fears, even threats, that the companies would move out of town, is still debated. Essentially, tech companies got a pass on paying a 1.5 percent payroll tax on new employees for six years. The first to take advantage of the offer was Zendesk, whose name prompted no alliterative phrasing. Thus did Twitter get the spotlight and the bulk of local anger. After the company refashioned two former Market Street furniture showrooms for its new headquarters, hundreds of people took to the streets to protest the "corporate tax giveaway." To them, high tech, with its high salaries, became public enemy number one and a symbol of inequality.

Not to Del Seymour. He envisioned jobs, especially for the people of Code Tenderloin ("my folks"). Tech, though, was not his world. He needed connections.

An early crucial one came from Supervisor Kim. Del's walking tours—which were attracting press coverage—caught her attention. She introduced him to several tech firms. He, in turn, introduced tech people to "hook-ups in the Tenderloin."

The connections took off. Del and community outreach personnel in such successful firms as Dolby, Twitter, and Zendesk got to know one another. The firms hosted Del and Code Tenderloin students, so they might see a future place to work, while Del took tech employees on walking tours to see the neighborhood.

In general, San Francisco–based techies comprise a mixed group in terms of background, the stereotype holding that a good number have Asian (Indian or Chinese) ancestry. But the overall impression some people might get walking the TL, as Del and other Black old-timers do, is that a majority of newcomers, whether in tech or not, are white. He said the old-timers told him for years, "Del, the white folks is coming in and taking over the Tenderloin." After denying it, he finally answered them, "Yeah, I know."

Before long, however, that seemed less a concern to Del than other entities partially taking over the Tenderloin: violence and drugs. Code Tenderloin would respond to them too.

CHAPTER 4

SUCCESSES AND SETBACKS

DEL CLAIMED REPEATEDLY that no matter what effort he expended for Code Tenderloin, efforts that started at roughly 4 a.m. when he woke up, to 8 or 9 p.m. when he usually crashed, he would prefer to sit in his rocking chair on his back porch (he had neither) watching *Oprah*. But he said he felt hooked by Code Tenderloin's success, an "almost addiction." He could not picture stopping "until every person in the Tenderloin that wants to work is able to work." Think of basketball, he said. If he played and the ball never went in the hoop, he would quit, but "the ball's going in right now with Code Tenderloin. So it's hard to stop. You get a few that miss, but it's also sort of seductive intimately. You're not meeting people on a superficial basis. You're meeting people who are revealing deep things."

Perhaps nobody was more surprised about a certain person who decided to take Code Tenderloin classes and turn his life around than one Alonzo Fluker. Del described him as "my last dealer."

When introduced at the Tenderloin corner where he then did most of his business, Alonzo, a hefty African American in glasses and loose-fitting clothes, carefully shifted to his left hand the cupcake he was eating, to shake hands properly with his right. In a basso profundo, he rumbled a few words of greeting.

Later, drinking green tea during a long conversation in his parked car near the same corner, Alonzo said that watching Del's walking tours gave him an idea. "I thought maybe I could get a job doing a walking tour. I kept asking him. I think he didn't believe me or something."

At the time, Del voiced his opinion Alonzo might be good as a tour leader, among other jobs. "He could be a retail clerk. He loves people. He loves talking. He could be a vendor at the baseball park. He's a very, very outgoing guy." But Del remained unconvinced Alonzo was ready for a straight job.

Alonzo, though, kept moving in that direction. He felt it was up to him to change his life. "You can't better yourself until you deal with your own problems. If you're always looking for somebody to bail you out, it ain't going to work." When Del started Code Tenderloin, holding classes in Piano Fight, steps away from Alonzo's corner, Alonzo paid closer notice. "I noticed programs starting up in there. I told Del I really need to get a job fast." As an interim measure, Del introduced Alonzo to his colleague Neil Shah, who walked Alonzo to a nearby program called Solutions. It trains people to get jobs such as desk clerks in the hospitality industry.

Alonzo made it. When he got his first check—sixteen hours, clearing $170—he was so excited, he went to show Del the pay stub. He treated himself, too. "I bought me a beer, I know that." The reward went beyond the amount. "It was good because it's like you're part of society now. You pay some taxes and stuff like that. It's the beginning of more checks."

Actually, the modest pay made Alonzo lose his SSI. "They say I make too much money. I don't really make that much, but it's too much money for them. Which is okay. I'm getting more than I was getting when I was coming out here and taking a chance every day. I don't have to worry about losing everything. That's a *big* relief."

What helped Alonzo further was Del accepting him into Code Tenderloin job training, which led to a job as night security manager at a senior citizens home. In a typical night, he saw few coworkers, but he lit up describing his work environment. "I couldn't have better people to work with. It's one for all and all for one. I love it because that's how I am."

Alonzo was such a success story, Del invited him to speak at a Code Tenderloin pizza-and-cookies celebration at Piano Fight in September 2016, an event meant to garner more volunteers and funders. Wearing a large striped T-shirt, Alonzo ambled up to the dark stage and gave a short wave. "Hi, everybody." He would keep it short and sweet, he said: Del had "changed my life" by getting him a job.

He was "kind of embarrassed" to be up there, he said, pushing his black-rimmed glasses back up his nose. "This program works. It worked for me." In an unusual addendum, he gave thanks to the people who operated the Piano Fight building and therefore made Code Tenderloin possible. He could not have imagined five months earlier his life being like it had become. "People like me need help." At that, he shrugged, looking self-conscious. He said he knew jobs did not come knocking on doors, yet Del had knocked on his door.

A voice came from the audience. It was Del, standing, pointing, his cell phone as usual in his left hand, saying Alonzo needed to take credit, that *he* had knocked on the door. After more jostling between the two and audience applause toward both, Alonzo became emotionally intimate. He is a sensitive person, he said, and had never been in a work world like the one he had entered; he was going through a *lot* of changes, for the better, and learning to be more professional. "I'm not even near stopping."

Because of how Code Tenderloin helped him, he said, he recommended the program to everyone. He even brought in one of his "partners from the streets," someone now working a straight job. That brought another burst of applause. Then came Alonzo's conclusion. At fifty-four years of age, he said his life has been hard and is sometimes lonely, but added, "If I can prevent one person from going through the things I went through, I think I'd be ready to go to heaven." This time, the applause lifted him off the stage.

LATER, IN HIS CAR, as Alonzo surveyed people he recognized walking by, including a woman "who does not live here," he reflected on his old life on a Tenderloin corner. "I never wanted to come outside *then*, but there was days I *had* to. The best thing could have happened to me [is] when I wake up and say, 'Oh, I ain't got to go downtown.'

"I miss the money. It ain't like it was that great, but it was something." It was more than he earned in his straight job. "I need money so bad it ain't funny. But that's my fault. I should have never been living outside of my needs anyway. I have to adjust to what I get. Anything you're not working for, you don't deserve. Don't nobody really treat drug money like they treat working money. You can't do the same things with working money you can do with drug money. You can go out and buy a car every day with drug money. You see people with three-hundred-dollar tennis shoes on. You can't buy that stuff when you working a job."

How can he tell if someone is selling drugs? Alonzo scoffed. "If they're wearing three-hundred-dollar tennis shoes, you can tell." He pointed to his own enormous footwear. "These cost thirty-five dollars. I bought them at Ross."

NOT EVERY PERSON who went through Code Tenderloin training was a poster child for the organization. Del recounted some misses. One promising young woman, who became a Code Tenderloin spokesperson, embezzled $1,400, at the time a good chunk of the budget. "It didn't kill us, but I felt so terrible that someone would do that to us. People who are trying to do for them. Before she embezzled the money, we put her in a hotel for a couple weeks. We gave hundreds of dollars to help her and her kid get clothes and food. Then she did this. One of our star students. And ironically she stabbed some people this morning."

The woman lived across the street from Piano Fight, and Del, pointing out the window to a parked police car, said, "She went on a stabbing spree, before I got here." Piano Fight's custodian witnessed the police action and told Del. "They brought her out hogtied."

Apart from Del's disappointment in the woman's behavior, she had featured in various Code Tenderloin videos. Now he had to edit her out. "That's the population we serve, but that doesn't mean anything." Consider Bernie Madoff, he said, who embezzled from his relatives as well as his community.

Del figured, "About one-fourth of our students are incarcerated. We got them on work release." One, he said, had been "selling dope in front of the Piano Fight since she was fourteen. I got her a job at the Gubbio Project [a program offering daytime sleep in churches].

She's been there four months now, hasn't missed a day, hasn't been late." He said she came up to him recently with a message that moved him deeply: "Del, thank you so much. I finally got a place I can show my kids where I work."

Over the years, Del managed to moderate his disappointments as "part of business." For example, a veteran asked for help paying tuition at the California State Maritime Academy. "He needed just two more courses to complete his maritime license." The man looked and spoke well. Del went to Swords and Plowshares, a self-help group started by Vietnam War veterans in the Bay Area, and facilitated a loan. "He completely disappeared on us." A young woman, newly released from serving a prison sentence involving a stolen car, talked big to Del (and anyone else who would listen) about her plans. "At first I thought she was talking bullshit; then I caught a glimmer of hope." Maybe she had potential. "She talked good. She seemed to handle our business well. We made commitments to each other." Del offered her work taking over his planned walking tours of Union Square. Then she too disappeared.

He figured she could have been rearrested, maybe hospitalized. "She could be on a run or went back to her family or met some guy who's the dream of her life. Whatever. I felt deserted, but I understand who I'm dealing with. How can I feel deserted about someone and within a month put this much trust and faith and belief in her? That was on me to feel."

Some Code Tenderloin volunteers, Del added, hold delusions about the students. "I have to make that very clear. Don't get jaded if someone disappears or drops out or comes in here so loaded they can't stand up. The person you thought was a class A student comes in tomorrow all cut up and beat up. This is what we deal with. This ain't Stanford."

CHAPTER 5

THE OFFER

"**O**KAY, I'M IN SACRAMENTO. Homeless. There's a Stand Down." The military term means to give soldiers a break from battle. The Veterans Administration adopted the term for a project to help homeless or troubled soldiers back home. A homeless Vietnam vet himself, Del knew all about the project.

"I'm pulling into the Stand Down, driving my shopping cart. Stand Down at the Boy Scout camp, on the bank of the Sacramento River. It's a crazy place too, because of rattlesnakes. I'm walking in, wearing an old nasty, pissy army jacket. These guys are putting up the temporary lights they do at carnivals and stuff. A pickup truck parked there says International Brotherhood of Electrical Workers. As I pass it by, I'm looking at these electrical workers of the union I used to be in. I make a comment to one of the guys. I'm drunk." Del now shouts, "'Oh yeah! I used to be in that union!' The guy says, 'Well, what are you doing now?'"

"'What am I doing now?' Fuck that. 'Can't you *see* what I'm doing now?' I took that as him already putting me down. It was confrontation."

Instead, the man asked Del his name, pulled out a business card, and handed it to him. "Said, 'Here. Come see me Monday morning. You know where the union hall is.'"

"I said, 'No, I don't know where no damn union hall is.' He said, 'Well, find out and come see me Monday morning.'"

Rather than respond or even read the card, Del turned his attention to more immediate matters. "My mind was on trying to get in line to get a meal and get me a bed because this was a three-day event. The next day, I'm hanging around. Some workers were still putting up the lights and the generators because we needed heat and everything. The union does this as a volunteer for the Stand Downs every year. I said, 'Hey! Remember when I came through there yesterday and this guy gave me a card?'

"They say, 'Yeah.'"

"I said, 'Who is that guy?' I hadn't even read the card. He says, 'That's Chuck Cake. He's president of the union.'" Actually, Cake was business manager of IBEW Sacramento Local 340, the number-two person in charge.

The sentiment of the other men to Del was, absolutely, go see Cake.

By Monday morning, when the Stand Down at the Boy Scout camp ended, Del felt mixed emotions. He had learned Sacramento's International Brotherhood of Electrical Workers (IBEW) union hall was some ten miles away. "He told me to be there at seven o'clock in the morning. The Sacramento buses don't start till eight, for some stupid reason. I parked my shopping cart, started walking. The only way to get there at that time. I'm still dressed in the same pissy clothes I hadn't changed in weeks. I looked like the worst bum on the street. But I'm going out there to *prove* that this guy was *bullshitting* me like everyone else in life. Just to prove to myself there ain't good people in the world. Why am I in the situation I am if there are good people in the world?

"I'm walking. You cross Highway 5 and you're round the hill. It's way out in the country. Then you got the union hall, and it's a sit-alone, gigantic building." Del was exhausted, but his quest was not over.

"There's a parking lot on the IBEW side with about a hundred slots, and a hundred of them are filled. All brand-new F-150, F-350 pickup trucks, with the ladder racks. All these are union guys out here to try to get a job, because they only give out a certain amount of jobs every day." The lengths of the jobs varied, Del knew. "They try to offer you short jobs, like a day job or two-day job. You'll take that, and you go to the back of the book. You may lose a nine-month job or two-year job. Depending on how your finances are, if you're broke, you'll take that short job. But if you had enough sense to save up from working eighty hours a week last year, all that overtime, you need to save that money up so you can come back to be selective about the jobs you take.

"But all these guys want to go to work today. This ain't no social club."

Somewhere along Del's long trek to the union hall, his mindset changed from defiance to hope. At the sight of the competition, though, hope slammed him in the face.

"I'm saying, 'This guy actually had the gall to have me come out here, and all these people with these brand-new pickup trucks, dressed for work.' I've got tennis shoes on. All of them good, sharp, and had a good night's sleep, smell good, got cologne on. Here I am smelling like piss. Coming across the hill. I got as bent as I can get. I walked an hour and a half, two hours. Straight, at a hard pace. And I says, 'I can't believe I *fell* for this, man! I'm sharper than this! I *knew* better.' Because IBEW is a very racist union. They just started cleaning up now. I got into the union through a government discrimination lawsuit. The federal government sued IBEW, so I was one of the people they were *forced* to pick to train. One of the few African Americans nationwide. Because there were zero Blacks in the IBEW." Del later said he became a union electrician in 1963, after the Department of Labor filed the lawsuit against IBEW's offshoot, the Communications Workers of America.

Knowing the union's history and that Sacramento "had some racist parts of it," Del was convinced the man with the business card had conned him.

"I'm *terribly* embarrassed because I look like a bum. A *real* bum. With a scraggly beard, all that. At that time I had hair, and it was all kinky. So I'm going to walk down here, embarrassed as I am. People'll probably offer me a quarter and tell me to get out, because I look like a homeless . . . not *looked* homeless, I *was* a homeless man." He now laughed.

The interior of the union hall, Del recalled, was enormous, with huge windows, a seating area, and glassed-in counters where hiring was done. "I go up, ready to be beat down," he said, by the "hardnosed prima donna" guys in charge.

"I said, 'Is Chuck Cake here?'"

Del yelled in imitation, "'No, he ain't here!'"

"I said, 'Oh. Well, you expect him?'"

Another yell. "'He's in New York! Be back next month.'"

"I said, 'Son of a bitch.' Now it's confirmed. He got my ass. Man, how stupid I was to come all the way out here. I *knew* he was bullshitting me. He knew Friday he wasn't going to be here. You don't just go to New York. I've got all this stuff on my mind. And the guy says, 'Who are you, anyway?'

"My name is Del Seymour."

"'Oh, Del! Man, don't let anyone see you, but go outside in the parking lot, come in the back door.' I says, 'Okayyy.'" Del drew out the word in the telling. "I leave the union hall and kind of slink around to the back door and come in. He says something like, 'I was hoping you would show up.'

"I said, 'And?'

"He says, 'You need to go to work? You got to be there in an hour.'

"'Work!'

"'Yeah. Didn't Chuck tell you?'

"I says, 'No. He told me to be here.'

"He says, 'Well, yeah. He's got you a yearlong job.'

"'What?' I'm looking at these hundreds of people out here waiting to get what I got. Any one of them. He said, 'Go get your truck and pull around the back.'"

"I said, 'Truck!'" Del started laughing so hard recalling the moment, he pounded one foot on the floor.

"The guy said, 'You don't have no truck?'

"I said, 'No.'

"He says, 'Son of a bitch! I'm going to have to drive you all the way to Folsom.'" The job included remodeling Folsom High School. "He says, 'Just go get your tools and meet me outside.'"

"Tools!" Del laughed again.

"The guy said, 'Oh *no*. Don't tell me you don't have no tools.'"

"I said, 'No, man.'

"And he says, 'Man, man. This is *crazy*.' He goes in the other room and comes out with like a five-hundred-dollar tool belt, with all the tools in it. He said, 'These are *my* tools. The first paycheck you get, you bring me my tools back.' He said, 'Let me go get my truck.'

"He took me out to Folsom High School and took me to the foreman, said, 'This is Del Seymour. He's one of Chuck's guys. Put him to work.' And he says, 'He lives in Sacramento somewhere. One of you guys take him every night and bring him back every morning. Get someone that lives around where he lives so he'll have a way to get back and forth.' And he said, 'Del, I want my tools back. You understand? Don't play with me.'" He added that in two weeks Del had to pay his union dues.

Del assumed the man earlier telephoned the foreman, who in turn informed the crew Del was "one of the guys that Chuck rescued from the Stand Down, to give him a pass and help him out."

According to Chuck Cake decades later, IBEW took part in Sacramento's Stand Downs in 1992, 1993, and 1994. "I felt an immense sorrow for these people," he recalled in a telephone call. "They were homeless, had rotten teeth, and they needed so much help."

As Del was promised, at the end of his first day's work, a crew member drove him back to Sacramento. "I was staying on the streets. So I went back to my box."

Literally. Outside a downtown branch of the Bank of Sumimoto, Del slept in a refrigerator box. It was sturdy, comparatively roomy, and folded up well. In the mornings, he stashed it behind bushes at the nearby Sacramento K Street Mall, he said, sketching the scene on a notepad. At dark, he retrieved the box to spend the night near other people in his situation. Each morning around 5 a.m., a Sumimoto guard woke them to get up and move before people started coming to work. Del admired the guard's combined job adherence and compassion. "He was handling the interest of his bank and the interests of needy people."

The morning after the Chuck Cake intervention, Del commuted from his box to work, then in the afternoon from work to box. Within the week, he was no longer homeless. "Union gives us the right to pull money from our employer within two or three days. So I got an advance, and I got me a room. And I eventually got an apartment, with my girl. I remember that apartment, right down there by Sutter's Fort."

"That was it. I worked at Folsom High School for a year. Then I worked at Safeway. We did all the Safeway resets for a year." Again, a government directive was involved. "The federal government came out, says two wheelchairs have to pass in the aisle in any supermarket. So we had to do massive resets of supermarkets all over. Which may sound like nothing, but wires run in every one of those counters. You got to move the counter over and then you got to remove the wire, cut into the concrete to replace the wire. Or the refrigeration lines. It's *massive* jobs. Multimillion-dollar jobs in every store. We did the gay Safeway on Church and Market [in San Francisco]. We did all the ones in Sacramento."

After finishing those jobs, what then?

Del no longer was in his exuberant storytelling mode. He spoke quietly. "I went back in addiction."

FOR A WHILE IN SACRAMENTO, Del lived in motels. Deleana Seymour, Del's oldest daughter, recalled, "One thing he always managed to do was figure out a way to make some money. [At one motel] they kept him on, gave him a place to stay and a little bit of money. Doing the handyman stuff. He was also taking care of an elder lady he made friends with."

One day, Deleana went there herself, to deliver very sad news. Del's sister Ethelear had contacted her to say his maternal grandmother Beatrice had died. "He was really, really, really, really close with his grandmother because that's who raised him." Deleana felt it was up to her to tell her father in person, if she could find him. "This was another pretty bad time, his Sacramento time. He was doing a *whole* lot in Sacramento. A *whole* lot of drugs."

"Nobody knew where he was. I knew the vicinity because I had been down there a couple times." Learning he stayed at a motel on Fulton Avenue ("a bad area"), she went there and found her father. "I had to tell him that, basically, his mother, to him, had died."

The news became even more excruciating. Deleana told Del his estranged brother had made and completed all the burial arrangements. Del's grandmother was already in the ground.

"The worst part, I think, for him," Deleana said, "was he had to talk to [his brother]. It turned into the ugliest conversation. He was sobbing. It was an anger sob, though. Partly he was hurt because his grandmother passed away and he couldn't participate in any part of it. His brother just took it over and decided he didn't need to know because he hadn't been there."

Deleana's sister Regina, listening to the account, nodded. "He was very angry about that."

"Yeah." Deleana blew out a deep exhalation.

Del's anger lasted a long, long time.

Except for his grandmother, Del had few close family ties. His unnamed father he termed "a gangster" who "did real gangster things," perhaps involving gambling. His mother was addicted to heroin. He remembered his grandmother Beatrice taking him as a child to visit her in jail, and that someone there bought him a treat of chocolate milk. With his sister Ethelear, one year older, he had a sometimes trying relationship into adulthood. As for his five-years-older brother, the fracture began in childhood. Once, to get rid of Del tagging along, the brother told him an uncle awaited Del back at the apartment with a toy fire engine. Del, besotted with everything related to firefighting, ran home. No uncle, no fire engine. No fraternal closeness.

Del does not even like his own name, meant to honor "this asshole Franklin Delano Roosevelt. That's why I use 'Del.'" Of Roosevelt, Del continued, "His politics were not my politics. The way the war was run, the way he handled the beginning integration of African Americans into society. His fighting that. His wife was wonderful. They could have named me after her, I would have been happy."

Del said he makes sure the name, if seldom used, is pronounced De-LANE-o, not DEL-ano.

DURING HIS SOUTH SIDE CHICAGO YOUTH, Del had two anchors. One was Hales Franciscan, a Catholic boys school, where he wrote a column for the school paper ("In the Know with Delano") and joined the respected drama club, the Spartan Players. He played Polonius in *Hamlet* and a half century later smiled in remembrance, then recited: "Neither a borrower nor a lender be, / For loan oft loses both self and friend."

Yet Del later told a podcaster, Hales was "as archaic and brutal and wrong as it could be." He cited beatings by nuns and priests. "Looking back on it, they were sexual beatings, because the priest would pull your pants down and whoop your bare ass with a paddle." But he scoffed at the notion of dropping out. At the time, no Black community anywhere in the country, he said, including Chicago, would allow a child not to finish high school.

Del's other anchor was work. His goal from the start, he said, deliberately using slang from his youth, was "Get out the projects." He lived in three: first Dearborn Homes; then Altgeld Gardens, known in part because Barack Obama worked there as a community organizer; and, finally, Stateway Gardens, built in the mid-1950s and demolished about fifty years later. Its eight concrete buildings, most seventeen stories, contained not a stick of wood, Del said. Warehouses, he called them.

When did Del not work? He once claimed, over breakfast of eggs and gravy in a Tenderloin coffee shop, his back at a wall to keep an eye on the street, he could write down his jobs in small letters on a corner of the table, cover every inch, and not finish. He worked as an A&P grocery clerk; he delivered telegrams; he delivered newspapers, including to Mayor Richard J. Daley, who called him "my boy" and promised him a fireman or policeman job when he turned eighteen. Del so admired Daley, among a slender list of politicians who have gained his approval, that he took up wearing a Daley-style fedora.

At work, however, "I wasn't always honorable," Del said of what happened one weekend. While helping clean empty offices at the Department of Motor Vehicles with a buddy and his father, a DMV janitor who paid Del ten dollars for his labors, Del eyed blank forms used for registering drivers' licenses. He stole some of the forms and converted them into phony IDs he sold to people too young to get into clubs or buy liquor. "Naturally, I had one."

Del parlayed his ID to get a cab driver's license. The legal age to drive a cab was twenty-one, at least four years beyond him then. No matter to bosses at Checker Cab, who hired Del to drive at night, when older cabbies refused to, out of justified fear. From mid-1966 to early 1968 alone, according to the Chicago Cab Drivers' Union, robbers killed five cab drivers.[1]

One murderer stood out, Del remembered, the description posted in the Checker garage. "He was a Latino, wore a Panama hat, only robbed people at night, and did not speak much." According to survivors, the man always sat right behind the driver.

A man fitting that description got into Del's cab around two o'clock one morning on East Forty-Third and South Calumet ("*really* a bad neighborhood"). With increasing certainty this was the killer, Del, speeding, nudged his mail-order .22 Röhm Saturday night special up from the floor to his hand. Animated as always when telling a good story, Del described the moment he heard a click, then spun around to shoot three times at his would-be killer's head. The gun jammed! The passenger (with another click) careened out the cab, rolling "like a tumbleweed" before running off.

Del, shaken, drove back to his apartment building. In the stairway he cursed the gun, firing again. It went off. He then raced to the Checker garage and told his fellow cabbies what had happened, how he had confronted the killer. They said, "You dumb son of a bitch. They caught him last week.'"

The mysterious clicks, Del discovered, came from the cab's seat belt. His passenger must have clicked it on during the terrifying ride, then clicked it off to escape the terrifying driver.

EMOTIONAL MOMENTS of a different kind included Del's teenage connections to civil rights icons. He worked with the Reverend Jesse Jackson, he said, and held the hand of the Reverend Dr. Martin Luther King Jr. "two separate times" during King's protests of Chicago's de facto school segregation. Del also said he made excursions to the South with CORE (the Congress of Racial Equality). In a later podcast interview, Del added he went on several "expeditions" to Alabama with SNCC, the Student Nonviolent Coordinating Committee. "We went to Selma, we went to Montgomery, we went to Birmingham when I was a young teenager. I became an activist then." He sought to apply activism to his hometown too ("because we lived in such a terrible neighborhood").

Once, with a tone suggesting "surely I've mentioned this before," Del said he had been a Freedom Rider. In an undertaking both noble and potentially fatal, civil rights activists went to the South first in 1961 to challenge segregation on buses and in later years helped with such efforts as registering Blacks to vote. But in the summer of 1961, Del would have been thirteen, an unlikely age to make such a journey, he agreed. Yet he said he did not know how old he was, only that he went with a cousin. "[We were] locked up many times. They would put us in big old vans and drive us down to the police station and put us in the backyard for a day or so."

He said when they reached Mississippi, a young white woman drove them in her car, he and his cousin ducking down whenever she spotted a car carrying white people getting close. And that they went to a restaurant, but when told he and his cousin would have to get their food at the back door, hungry as they were, Del insisted they leave, or why be there in the first place?.

He must have recognized the territorial dangers. In August 1955, when Del was a month shy of his eighth birthday, another child of South Side Chicago, fourteen-year-old Emmett Till, was murdered in Mississippi. While reverberations of grief and fury from the gruesome death exploded nationwide, reactions in Chicago were especially personal. Del's grandmother Beatrice was friends with Emmett Till's mother.

WHEN HE GOT OLDER, in Chicago, Del's work fervor led to jobs at Quaker Oats, which in turn led to a company scholarship to study accounting at Southeast Junior College. Del did so, also getting an associate degree in political science, a subject that interested him. "I couldn't *stand* accounting." Del then took engineering classes at Southern Illinois University in Carbondale "for just a few months." Why so brief? The city was too "Southern" for him.

Del said he left Southern Illinois to complete a correspondence course from DeVry University in engineering. Eager to start a career, thanks to a discrimination lawsuit and subsequent AT&T Long Lines training, he got work at AT&T in Chicago.

The physically fit, single, heterosexual former student drew the attention of Uncle Sam. The Vietnam War was ramping up.

CHAPTER 6

GRADUATION DAY

THE OCCASION, HOWEVER modest it may have seemed to passersby glancing in the street-level windows, felt monumental to those inside. This, one of Code Tenderloin's first graduations, was taking place at the headquarters of Dolby Laboratories at 1275 Market Street in San Francisco, exactly that have and have-not, tech and non-tech Market Street Del Seymour speaks of wanting his graduates to be able to cross from the Tenderloin. On a February afternoon in 2016, they had.

Dolby, an early Code Tenderloin supporter, put on a munificent lunch spread in an area off its light-filled lobby. The air resounded with upbeat voices in all ranges: the dozen or so graduates, representatives from other tech firms that supported Code Tenderloin, various friends, a local television news crew, and pastors from two churches Del attended—the San Francisco Christian Center and the ultraliberal Glide Memorial United Methodist Church.

At one point in his addiction, Del had worked as an electrician at Glide. The handsome stone church in the Tenderloin reflects on the exterior a staid past, but staid ended when Rev. Cecil Williams stepped in half a century ago. He and his wife, Janice Mirikitani, the church's formerly shy secretary, made Glide legendary in the city and beyond for its generosity toward and help to disadvantaged people.[1] "Unconditional love" and "radically inclusive" remain two Glide phrases.

Among many innovations, Glide housed a continuing education high school, targeting allegedly incorrigible children. "These were the worst kids you ever would want to meet," Del related one day. "They have robbed banks. They have sold drugs. They have burnt houses down. No school would allow them anywhere near their campus. They've shot people. Glide opened up this high school for them, and it's one of the best curriculums you could think." He said it went beyond studies for a GED and led, for example, to a certificate in construction.

"Glide had a super-formal graduation ceremony in the sanctuary." When graduation time came, Del told his boss he was going to attend. "To see the kids get their certificate and walk across that stage—" At that, he stood and walked across the Piano Fight floor, strutting in imitation. "Like they were at Stanford. I says, 'Man, of all the things we did for the kids, by giving them that formal opportunity to walk across the stage like this, that was *it*.' I modeled my graduations on that."

At Dolby, after the Reverend Theon Johnson of Glide offered a prayer, Del welcomed the assemblage and delivered thanks. They extended to a late-arriving trio he praised as "my angels from Piano Fight, [who] gave me room to run Code Tenderloin." As most there knew, the three men started the nightclub from the shell of an abandoned Italian restaurant, named Original Joe's, and donated daytime space where Del held free job-readiness classes these students had attended. Applause turned to laughter when the Piano Fight men unbuttoned their shirts and, as if playing Superman, showed off Del's signature Tenderloin Walking Tours T-shirts underneath. It was a wonderful moment.

The most moving element that day, and indeed in subsequent Code Tenderloin graduations, involved the distribution of diplomas.

Attention is called. A volunteer—today the diminutive April Trinh, a part-time pharmacist—reads out each graduate's name. Other graduates then cheer. This time, when she calls the names of two graduates who are not in attendance because, April announces, they are at *work*, the applause multiplies.

Typically, in these ceremonies, each present graduate, name called, walks or runs to the front of whatever room or space Del has persuaded a sponsor to offer. Then, beaming, the graduate may say words of thanks but often breaks down in tears, holding high the diploma. It is sometimes the first in that person's life. It features the recipient's calligraphed name, a statement noting completion of Code Tenderloin training, and, thanks to Del's powers of persuasion, is signed by the entire San Francisco Board of Supervisors.

On this day, the most exuberant graduate is Cornell Dodd, a large man who had wondered out loud at one Code Tenderloin class about his circumstances: "[Is it] because I'm Black, or is it something I'm doing wrong?" At some fifty years of age, the oldest person in the class, when he received his certificate, he exploded into testimony.

"You need a miracle!" he said, and he got it. When he met other people as marginalized as he was, he shouted, "I want to do a Code Tenderloin on 'em!" Cornell confessed that when he had begun classes, he did not want people to know he could barely afford to ride the bus. (He said Del, learning this, had taken care of such expenses.) Now Cornell announced he was even thinking of trying something new, maybe becoming an actor. "You gave me hope. I'm going to give back."

Cornell did get a role in Code Tenderloin's first promotional film, in 2016, *Crossing Market*, which shows a close-up of his big shoes stepping off the curb on the rough Tenderloin side of the street and crossing Market to the tech side. Del narrates, "The next time that you cross Market Street, notice something. There's an invisible border between those we look up to and those we look down to. Crossing it takes much more than looking left, right, and then left again. At Code Tenderloin, we're building a bridge from the less fortunate side of Market to the *more* fortunate one, by teaching people how to use technology to write a better future. And even though taking the first step may be hard, with a little work and determination, a green light to a better life will eventually turn on."

The camera then goes to earnest-looking Del, at a table. "Our students go through a curriculum that covers job education, interviews and resume reviews, mentorship, and training, and it's led by the best tech companies in the Bay Area." Del mentions a funding goal of $150,000 and ends by mentioning a "$150,000 smile" when someone gets a job. The film, shown to an audience of potential volunteers or donors, always gets cheers.

At Dolby that day, Del brought flowers, handing some to each graduate. When the time came for him to speak, he looked both energized and relaxed. He wore his typical fedora, tie, suit coat accessorized with poufy pocket square, polished shoes, fancy gold watch from a girlfriend, and three gold rings, which provided a flash of bling when he gesticulated. As usual, his unbuttoned suit coat revealed his own omnipresent T-shirt advertising Tenderloin Walking Tours, without which there might be no Code Tenderloin.

After giving an overview, he added a rare glimpse of his motive.

"We try to take people that are so marginalized. We're *all* in the Tenderloin. We're all injured. I was injured out there being stupid for eighteen years, so I kind of know injuries. A lot of people ask me, 'How did you put this together? On the internet?' No. Didn't have to go to the internet. I just knew what I needed when I was out there sick and when I was out there injured. This is kind of my give back, and I got a whole bunch of people helping me."

There it was, in an aside, an answer to what Del usually does not answer. Why, as a man his age, with considerable (usually undisclosed) health issues, does he spend virtually all day every day on this effort? "Kind of my give back."

He closed with what would be a familiar rallying cry: Everyone—he pointed to specific people by name—please help one person. "Everyone get one." He added, "You can't save everybody. Keep that in mind. God bless you all so much, and thank you for coming."

During the blast of applause that followed, Dolby executive Joan Scott, who arranged the lunch, smiled broadly. Nearby stood Caroline Barlerin, a supporter of Del's from Twitter. She whispered, "This guy should get a Nobel."

One person who missed the graduation because of being at work had a clear emotional effect on Del: Shanay (pseudonym).

Del had spoken privately about her when the subject turned to what some might call return on investment. Despite so much money, effort, affection, and help of all kinds channeled toward unsheltered people, at least in San Francisco, there remained a common plaint that "things" overall did not seem to improve. Put another way, as one person got off the street, another fell onto it. Del maintained that this summary, if true, is not discouraging.

"If you were a statistician, yeah, it could be discouraging. But if you're doing things about saving people's lives, no. If that would discourage you, you don't need to be in that business, because you're not going to last long anyway. It's one, one, one. One person and one person and one person."

To him, the same applies to people whose activities have put them outside the law. A case in point, Shanay. "This is a woman who's still in prison. She's on work release but is locked up every night." The site, just yards from Piano Fight, is a center operated by San Quentin. "She's a federal prisoner. Whatever she did, . . . I don't know. I don't ask. Legally I can. I don't want them having a guilt trip thinking I know what they did."

"I say, 'I'm dealing with *you*. I'm not dealing with that person yesterday. I probably wouldn't want to deal with that person. Because for you to be sitting in my room, you're a different person. Let's talk about the person today, tomorrow, and next week."

Shanay, free during the day, attended Del's Code Tenderloin classes. After finishing, she applied for a behind-the-scenes position at a local Equator coffee shop. Later, she called Del.

"Four words," he said. "I was tears rolling like a river. Yesterday afternoon. She said, 'I got the job.'"

Del still looked affected. "That was my treat for the day—because I took so much out of the African American female community down here. I did such devastation, personally. Ain't no way you can pay back something. If I took a chunk out of this wall," he said, gesturing to a Piano Fight wall next to him, "I could pay *that* back because I could go get some concrete and put it back. I can't repair those girls. If I was able to restore them to the dignity I took from them, yes. I can repay back to this new generation. And give them some self-sustainability where they don't . . . need a fool like me."

Because he rarely talks about that period in his addicted life, the years he pimped women to feed his own addiction, this outburst felt so emotional, the shame shimmered. It also overshadowed the more anodyne explanation of his Code Tenderloin work being a "give back." It was obvious whom Del especially felt obligated to help.

Of all Code Tenderloin graduates, however, he said Shanay was the most challenging, "the hardest one I've had to convince it's going to be okay. If you were her probation officer and you let her do nine things: 'Okay, you can paint your fingernails. You can play loud music. You can do this, and you can do this.' But when we get to the tenth thing [and she is turned down], she'll go crazy.

"I said, 'You're in a unique situation. A lot of people are still back up there in prison. Think about them. Shanay, you been in prison. There's going to be people that don't want you out here, people in your family that's going to give you resistance. Your probation officer may not want you out, may be jealous of you, because all of a sudden here you are getting a job, like he's got. Could be all kind of reasons. Ride *over* that shit.'"

A paperwork hiccup resulted in her not being let out for work one day, but Del said he would handle it, and did. "Most of the other people in the program trust me. She don't trust me yet." She does not believe anything will work out, he said. "Any minute the other shoe's going to drop." Yet she finished the course and got a legitimate job.

Because it meant her not being able to attend Code Tenderloin's graduation at Dolby, Del paid a later visit to Equator. He asked the manager, an affable fellow, to bring Shanay out front for a moment. When she appeared in her white work outfit, looking like a scared rabbit, Del handed her a Code Tenderloin graduation certificate with her name on it. They posed, holding it up for a photo. Shanay now looked merely uncertain, Del like the proudest man in the world.

CHAPTER 7

THE RELUCTANT DRAFTEE

DEL RECEIVED HIS DRAFT NOTICE IN 1967. What could that mean but Vietnam? In response, he tried to fail his physical. "Everything, I checked Yes. Do you have diabetes? Yes. Are you an amputee? Yes. Are you pregnant? Yes. I checked *every* box. I'm crazy. I piss on myself. I got leprosy. I got polio. The doctor came over, said, 'Man! You're in pretty bad shape, huh?'" End of deception.

Nineteen-year-old Private Seymour was assigned to the army's famous Eighty-Second Airborne Division and slated to become an airborne medic (a helicopter paramedic). Del said he trained at bases in Missouri, Texas, Georgia, and North Carolina. Training included parachute jumping from helicopters and planes, fifty-five times, he calculated. "I would go out on an eight-thousand-man jump and work all day. I was always the first man out the door, because I had all the medical equipment [and] had to be the first one on the ground in case anyone had a bad jump." They did. "I actually did medical work on people. I had several fatalities, a lot of fractures."

Years later, he revealed that seeing men dead at his feet from "bad jumps" was his first exposure to what would become severe PTSD.

As it turned out, Del was sent on assignments not to Vietnam but to a neighboring country he was ordered not to reveal and tries not to. Working within the military category called a TDY, or temporary duty station, his main job involved training soldiers in helicopter evacuations, that is, teaching them the most efficient methods of getting their wounded comrades from battle zones to medical ships. Being a medic, Del would not likely have experienced the trauma of standing next to a buddy whose head got blown off. But, he said, revealing his own trauma, he was the person who picked up the buddy's remains.

An especially terrifying incident involved being in a helicopter on or near the ground when someone threw in a live hand grenade. He jokes that obviously it did not go off, but joking ends when sleep comes. The incident, among others, gave Del lifelong night terrors. Someone tossing him his cell phone one night reminded him of the grenade's arc, and he exploded emotionally.

Del said he never killed anyone. "I was not a combat vet. We would come in and do what we needed to do and go right back out. I did not go to the villages. I don't know anything about their street life. I don't know anything about them. I always had compassion for people being people. I'm like Muhammad Ali." During the Vietnam War, the famous boxer famously said, in refusing the draft, that he had nothing against the Viet Cong and no Vietnamese person had ever called him the N-word.

Much of Del's time in the military he rotated among various bases in the United States, also participating in the army's "Golden Knights" parachute-jumping exhibitions.

Once, while back in Fort Bragg, North Carolina, in April 1968, word came of the assassination of Martin Luther King Jr. Reflecting on the news, Del spoke not of his emotions but of his orders. "We were mobilized within hours. We flew into Andrews Air Force Base, then moved into the city [Washington, DC]. Spent the first night sleeping on the White House lawn. The marines were already there. They stood down, we relieved them. We stayed about two or three days, then my particular unit of the Eighty-Second Airborne got assigned a brand-new Sears store." The unit was supposed to protect it from being burned down or looted. His group patrolled the area, sleeping on the roof in shifts. The store was looted, though—by its ostensible protectors. "Our duffel bags were full."

Del's account proved incomplete. Shootings and other violence around him during the riots were so frightening, he later said, they also contributed to his PTSD.

During another stay at Fort Bragg, Del became de facto leader of his unit because the first sergeant, whom he admires to this day, could not read or write. Del spurns the word "illiterate." The sergeant was "an outstanding man, got promotion upon promotion." Nonetheless, because he could not read or write, among Del's self-appointed tasks was to read the man's mail, including communiqués. One day these included a directive from President Richard Nixon for an early out for two people from every unit, the names to be submitted to a general. "I happened to be working as company clerk that day." Planning to return to college, Del submitted his own name. It worked. Within perhaps eighteen months of being drafted, Del received an early out himself and returned to college.

Thus, he became a Vietnam War veteran—an anti-war veteran. "I try not to associate myself with war at all, any kind of way, shape, fashion, form." He pointed to a baseball hat he wears occasionally, including to Veterans Day commemorations. The stitching reads "Army." It perturbs him that people wear the name of their war—Korea, Vietnam, Iraq—on their hats. "How can you celebrate death? It's like walking around saying 'Columbine' on your head, or 'Las Vegas Massacre.' Who would do that?" As for his time in Southeast Asia, he said, "I was ashamed to be there when I was there. I was ashamed to have been drafted. I was ashamed when I came home. It was something I never would have been part of, if I had anything to do with it." Yet he had been part of it. And he credits fellow veteran George Gibbs, a combat vet, for decades later shepherding him through the process of getting evaluated for a disability rating. Del Seymour is officially rated 100 percent disabled due to his service.

Back home in Chicago, Del availed himself of AT&T's obligation to reemploy him. Instead of working in familiar numbing winter weather, he chose Los Angeles. "But when I got to California, that was the most abusive, prejudiced relationship I've ever had. Nowadays we would have sued them, but that was where you just left." The problem included language. "The racist talk. The N-word when the N-word was not used at all. They used it. I was the only Black person at that facility. They let me know it too. This was their place." Del's stature as a veteran "didn't matter to these assholes."

He quit to become an armed guard for an alarm company, responding to client calls, driving in uniform to various sites as needed. He often worked in conjunction with the police, he said, and considered becoming a policeman himself. One night, that changed.

"I was going down a residential street, two o'clock in the morning, and these two police cars passed me. Zip zip! They pull up and stop. They shine their spotlights up, and there's a guy on the porch shaking the doorknob. They yelled something to him. He turns around, and they start pumping bullets into him. He's dancing from the bullets hitting his body. He hits the ground."

Del watched everything, including the man's mother, whose house it was, coming outside and screaming when she saw her dead son. The homicide unit came and interviewed the police, then Del. "I was giving them the whole description. And the guy says, 'Do you know which hand he had the gun in?'

"I says, 'What gun?'

"He said, 'The gun. You know what gun.'

"I says, 'That man didn't have a gun. He had both his hands on the doorknob. He turned around, and the officers shot him.'"

After more arguing, the homicide detective walked Del to the body, pulled back the white sheet. A gun lay next to the body.

"I said, 'These motherfuckers! Man!'"

Del was not completely surprised. "There was multiple gun plantings all over the United States. Officers always carried a plant gun." He said the commonly called "dirty gun" was standard non-issued equipment, perhaps picked up in a raid and kept in a sock or patrol car to use or plant as needed.

When police met Del at his alarm guard job and indicated that approval for the next cadet class might be affected by how he testified at an upcoming grand jury session, Del refused to change his story. His potential police career ended.

"I was through with the police department. They were through with me. I went down to my recruiter and told him. He was an understanding guy. He says, 'Well, let me put you in for the fire department.'

"I says, 'Cool. I always wanted to be a fireman anyway.'"

Del had little idea what awaited him.

CHAPTER 8

FIRST STEPS

A T A MAJOR JUNCTURE IN HIS LIFE, following two violent episodes, Del vowed to give up pimping and crack, both smoking it and dealing it. He also inadvertently gave up part-time work as a San Francisco cab driver. "I owed like five thousand dollars in red light *camera* tickets. So I couldn't get my license." And no insurance company, he said, would have covered him.

He sought new and legitimate work. "Just to do something."

A memory from a cab driving sideline came to him. The sideline was to offer passengers tours. "I would pick them up at the airport, take them downtown and give them my number. 'Here, you want to go on a tour of the city, call me.' They would." Whether they wanted to visit Haight-Ashbury or the wine country, Del was game. A feature both he and his customers liked was getting out of the cab. "I will get to the destination, then we will walk around."

In those tours, Del never took tourists to the Tenderloin, the part of San Francisco he knew best. For one thing, many tourist hotels were close by, especially the Union Square shopping area. Visitors wanted to go farther away. He did not mention another consideration: what tourist wanted to visit the infamously scary, dirty, unappealing Tenderloin?

Nonetheless, Del needed work that was legal, income-generating, and did not require a car. By process of elimination and a flash of imagination, he thought how about setting up walking tours of the Tenderloin.

Before anyone could dissuade him, he got to work on several fronts. To learn more about the area, including its history as a theater district, among other distinctions, he headed to the main San Francisco Public Library, which essentially borders the Tenderloin, and went to the archives. "It's a special room above the library. Usually only two or three people in there. You got to put on gloves, and they bring you one document at a time. These are originals." Del consulted the online catalog, then read the selected material. "I was there every day. For hours. I was one of the people they didn't even ask for my ID."

He learned how block by block the Tenderloin had evolved from a sandy Gold Rush–era residential site to a commercial area, then a place variously of vice, civic cleanup, corruption, acceptance, and, all along, varied entertainments. It took him months, he figured.

Del also faced the question of funding. Enter Dave Gomez, a director of programs and operations for Swords to Plowshares, the nonprofit supporting Bay Area veterans. "He's the one that got me going," said Del, who recalled Dave telling him he was nuts. Dave said he appreciated that Del was among only a handful of veterans who wanted to start a business and told him, he recalled saying, "Bring me a plan. And by God, he brought me a plan." And by God, he brought me a plan." It was a few pages, handwritten, but in Dave's opinion "very viable"—"and it wasn't a lot of money, a couple hundred dollars." He added, "When you don't have it, it's a lot of money."

Dave connected Del to another Swords employee, who helped create brochures. Apart from printing costs, some of Dave's investment went toward Del's plan to offer customers free T-shirts. Del's girlfriend Sheila was up for that.

"Sheila and I started out making hand-drawn T-shirts. Tenderloin Walking Tours." They came out crooked, Del recalled. "With the paint running down. Very rudimentary."

The first version featured two busty women leaning provocatively into what seems to be a lamp post but on closer inspection is a phallus. In a newer version, a less-phallic lamp post holds two street signs: Turk and Taylor.

Then Del started the tours, focusing both on archival documentation and present reality. He wanted to strike a balance. Yes, we'll see what is negative about the Tenderloin, but let's also see the positive things being done and the people doing them.

"I had an orientation at a restaurant down on 6th and Minna [south of Market Street]. About five people came." Two proceeded to take the first tour. Attendance on subsequent ones ballooned to three. "It was very challenging." Del did not charge a fee but suggested a donation of $15. The T-shirts he gave away. Marketing, he hoped.

Another challenge of the tours went beyond the financial. Local drug dealers, the "kids," Del called them, were suspicious at his leading tourists, however few, mostly white, around the neighborhood. "[This was] something new they got to worry about. What's Del *really* doing? Is he switching sides? Is he on the take? How could Del tell me legitimately people want to come to the Tenderloin? Had he fallen for a police trick or maybe become a double agent?" He tried to reassure them. "No, I'm just a tour guide."

Tenderloin Walking Tours, in sum, did not hit their stride right off. But Del kept walking and talking, talking and walking, while developing his look of panache, from fedora to pocket square. Initially, he bought most of his clothes secondhand, some emitting a distinctive consignment store whiff. Still affected by many nights outdoors, his frame consistently lean, he sometimes wore two layers of trousers when the weather was chilly.

His natural gait is loose, his lope long, but tourists may not realize the many stops along the route, where Del points out various landmarks, are also rest stops for him. Smoking crack, Del claimed, took out 90 percent of his lung function. Whatever the accurate statistic, there is no doubt he especially pauses during uphill walks.

Initially, he was also impeded by toting a heavy briefcase. The battered brown carryall, featuring an I [heart] Tenderloin sticker, held brochures and more. "I started carrying my whole office in there, stapling guns and everything."

The tours vary, depending on sites Del decides to include (best hot dog in the Tenderloin!) or to avoid (recent crime scenes). As an introduction, he often asks people where they are from, gauges the group's interests, and makes whatever connection he can from the answer. One day, before leading a tour for some fifteen mostly Mormon college students, Del launched into a short speech about San Francisco homelessness, a frequent topic.

"Right now, we have undocumented nineteen thousand homeless folks in the forty-nine square miles. They have documented seven thousand, but that's nowhere near the actual amount." Other informal estimates put San Francisco's unsheltered population at about ten thousand, while the city government estimates some twenty thousand people seek shelter at some point in a calendar year. After running down some (later outdated) statistics about city money spent fighting homelessness, he put on his fedora and said, "Let's walk through my neighborhood. This is not just about homeless. We're just a normal community that has a higher degree of homeless than a lot of communities. But I think we're unique in the way we serve and help people."

What other neighborhood, for example, had a storefront (that day's first stop) offering free storage, so people like Del in his unhoused years could safely stash their belongings?

He led the group to Boeddeker Park where he greeted people he knew "from way back." (The park, which takes up about a quarter of a city block, was named for Father Alfred E. Boeddeker, a Catholic priest who advocated for a place where people without homes or much money could relax and sleep and maybe play checkers—one of Del's innocent pursuits). Onward the group walked, to gaze up at a former United Methodist Church that had contained a dormitory for single women, then to a free tech center at the multifaceted St. Anthony Foundation. People behind the sign-in desk cheerfully welcomed Del as a familiar visitor, also from way back. He used the center's computers, he told the group, before owning his own laptop.

Across the street, the group visited St. Anthony's famous free lunch site, which according to its website serves two thousand to three thousand meals a day. Del had often eaten there too and praised the nutritionists' efforts, if irked about a recent dessert. Why offer apples to people who were often missing teeth?

Former St. Anthony's employee Karl Robillard, who worked in the education program, remembered Del as one of the regulars. "He looked like a homeless person who had come to a free dining room when I first met him, his face having that very weathered, kind of drawn-in look. It's interesting when someone discovers who they are, because now when I think of Del, I think of a very well-dressed man, very put together, immaculate."

The two men, now friends, share a humorous acknowledgment of their differences. Karl has blond hair and a gymnast's sturdy physique. "We both happen to be men. It kind of ends at that," he said. "I'm a very openly pridefully gay man who's happy to joke around. Del is extraordinarily open-minded," having overcome homophobia long ago. When Karl and his boyfriend, Bob Thornton, decided to marry in 2021, they asked Del to be the officiant. He accepted the request, plus a rainbow lei as part of his attire. Nowadays, when Karl jovially calls him "Girl!" Del just shakes his head and smiles.

Today, before leaving St. Anthony's, Del gathered his tour group to look at lobby photographs, including a 1970 dining room scene of "mostly white folks." They were Irish Americans, he said, who had lacked documentation and schooling. "No different than other cultures. Lack of African Americans [at St. Anthony's then], because in the '70s we were a prime force in San Francisco. We operated the shipyards. We had major trades. We had a lot of housing and had ten times more population than today." And, he emphasized, "African Americans culturally at that time were based on family." In short, they did not need St. Anthony's free meals.

With that, Del launched into an unusual and long riff about work culture lost to drugs and how he was trying to turn that culture around. Then he returned to tour guide mode. The Tenderloin, he announced, as he often said on his tours, had been the city's theater district. Now he indicated where some theaters used to be and showed where others still existed. A favorite stop was the Strand, a Market Street theater expensively renovated by ACT, the American Conservatory Theater. The building had been "a complete wreck," he said. Not merely a strip club, it wasn't X-rated; it was "maybe Z-rated," a "really terrible place. I was in here every night, so I *know*." ("No, I wasn't; yes, I was," he played.)

Depending on how he assesses the tour group, he might also point out a repurposed theater whose marquee reads "Power Exchange." "Couples go in together, but don't stay together," he'll say with a laugh.

At some point in the tour (up until Covid), with no advance notice, Del would take a group into the darkened side entrance of St. Boniface Catholic Church. Chatter immediately stopped. A few seconds of vestibule darkness led, on the left, to the front of the church, with its handsome domed ceiling, stained glass windows, and several rows of graceful wooden pews, in which sat a few parishioners. Del tried to arrange his visits before or after Mass, but sometimes the group entered during a service. Priests have been accommodating. Here tourists are a minor matter, for on the right, separated by a few yards of space, was the sight that caught visitors off guard: pew after pew after pew of people stretched out, sleeping.

"No photos," Del whispered to his stunned tourists. Take a picture of anything on the left if you want, the altar and so on, but not the people on the right. During this intimate trespass, it was difficult not to stare or to ignore the mingling aromas of bodies and incense. So many bodies, most adult men, most bedraggled looking, but in this sanctuary welcome and safe, presumably after having been awake much of the night outside, where both safety and sleep are elusive. (St. Boniface reportedly was the first church in the United States to offer its pews to people in need of daytime sleep.)

Del's tour group, animated, peppered him with whispered questions. One, about abusive priests, prompted his nearly inaudible answer and addendum: "I'm ex-Catholic, so I got authority to talk." And, no, he said to another question, the Catholic Church did not donate this space. It came from the fund-raising work of the Gubbio Project, named for St. Francis's hometown in Italy, for what it calls "sacred sleep."

Gubbio was run by Laura Slattery, an anti-war graduate of West Point inspired by Jesus and Gandhi. She served in the US Navy's Medical Service Corps, later receiving a master's degree in theology at the Jesuit School of Theology in Berkeley before deciding to become a doctor and enrolling in the University of California at Davis School of Medicine. Laura met Del when he introduced himself and asked her permission to bring his tour groups inside. He said he wanted to show them the situation, not exploit anyone.

"I was impressed," she said. "He's doing his due diligence."

When tourists walked out of St. Boniface, they generally seemed subdued. Laura understood. "[Del] always talks about the church being the highlight of people's tours." She finds the moment bittersweet. "On the one hand, how beautiful that that church is doing this, and, on the other hand, how tragic that that church in the United States of America has to do this."

OF ALL THE ORGANIZATIONS that opened their doors to Tenderloin Walking Tours, the most rewarding and helpful was the Piano Fight nightclub, being remodeled from the former Original Joe's, where Del had once long labored. "I would always keep an eye on the place while it was vacant," he said. "Then I started seeing these guys in the doorway, smoking cigarettes." Del and "these guys," a trio of owners, talked almost daily. Del led his tours past the place too. One day a member of the trio, the gregarious Rob Ready, offered the site as tour central. Del happily accepted, stashing his briefcase and ending the tours inside the newly burgeoning spot, symbol, after all, of a creative Tenderloin. There, Rob offered a spiel to the captive audience about Piano Fight's (often) zany programs. As both hoped, some people returned that evening. The tours had walked full circle.

Yet Del increasingly faced a major obstacle: drug dealers. Responding to them would change his life and those of many others.

CHAPTER 9

"I'M YOUR UNCLE"

A T A THEATER ROOM IN PIANO SPACE, twelve new recruits sat scattered in the bank of raised audience seats, Del onstage below them, leaning backward in a chair. He taught the first job readiness classes himself, then ceded instruction to volunteer teachers. The transition proved challenging: "letting my staff get deep into it without me hovering over them like a butterfly." Sometimes he let loose. Today was one such occasion. At ease and expansive, Del looked up at the students, people of various ages, most youngish, all Black save for a jittery white male.

"When I started Code Tenderloin," said Del, launching into a version of a familiar story, "this particular block we're on now was the heaviest crack block in the Tenderloin and was serviced by young African American women. I knew all of them, because at one time I was the biggest dope dealer on this block. I sold drugs with their moms." So out of respect for the 'hood ("'cause this is their block"), he did not take his walking tours past the dealers.

When the tours came close enough, though, dealers noticed and confronted him. In this truncated version of the story, Del concluded, "If there's anything I've done in the last few years I'm proud of . . . the number-two girl [dealer] on the block [got a straight job through Code Tenderloin]."

"That's what the original concept of Code Tenderloin was and will continue to be. To repurpose young folks [and] old folks; our oldest guy was sixty-three, so we have no exclusions at all. And we've been very successful. Of the last class of twelve people, six got jobs right away, three decided to go back to school, and three are interviewing right now."

Jobs are out there, Del emphasized. Two "great restaurants with bars" were opening on the corner of Sixth and Market. "We also have connections with the tech community. Before you say, 'I can't program' and 'I can't code,' [tech] companies have jobs like any other company. They have jobs in central receiving. They got reception. They got customer service. They got billing. They got meals. You do not have to be a technical person."

Minority representation in high-tech companies is "nowhere near" where it should be, he continued. "But that's our job to make it right. I've asked the tech companies, 'Why aren't you hiring people in community? These underprivileged people?' They say [applicants] haven't been able to pass the so-called interview. That's why we started this."

Although the job readiness course takes weeks, "If I can find you a job today, I will hire you today. We're not just going to send you to a place: 'Go on, man, good luck.' *My* job is to go to that company and find out exactly what the job is. Find out who the guy is that's going to interview you. Find out as much about him as I can." One interviewer might not like people who talk fast, because the job's for customer service. "More or less, I'm trying to find what he doesn't like." That might mean an applicant having unpolished shoes, green hair, or an opposite personality. "I went to a job [interview] once where after about five minutes I said, 'You know what, sir? This ain't going to work. Thank you for your time.'" Del said he and the potential employer had actually begun arguing.

"Most people that open up to Code Tenderloin know what we're about. We're dealing with marginalized people [who] can't generally walk in the door and get that job right off. People like myself. I got fourteen felonies. Other people in Code Tenderloin have as many or more. Some people have *never* had a job. That makes it hard to go in to do an interview."

He told the class, "Let me say this first: This is the only day we use the word 'interview.' From here, we call it a business meeting. We feel you are equal to that guy you're going to talk to. You're trying to see if your resume will fit his job needs. It's an across-the-board business meeting, that's all."

Del also elaborated on his students' need to master the meetings. "If you're still scared after weeks of classes, we've done nothing. We show you how to dress. We show you how to comb your hair. We show you how to speak. But if you're basically afraid of the concept, you're going to waffle." He called his Interview Readiness Program, as it was known, critical. "You can't get the job without the interview. Our job here is to get you acclimated. You walk in that interview with your head so high, you're up in the clouds. Not arrogant but competent, because you're not going to be afraid of anything that man asks you." When an interviewer asks why a previous job ended, do not, said Del, think the interviewer wants to trip you up. "If he had any intention of tripping you up or discriminating against you, he wouldn't even have invited you."

A person in human resources at Google, Del said to a rapt audience, is not looking to see how skilled you are ("as far as the product and training and programming"). "His job is to have no nuts come into the company. He gets paid to keep people out."

Del told another class a related story they loved, about a "Twitter lady HR person" he knew. "[She] had a guy in for an interview; she scheduled one hour. The guy talked for fifty-seven minutes about himself, nonstop, then said, 'So what does Twitter have to offer me?' And she said, 'Sorry, your time is up.'"

Del laughed. "Yeah, you're the top coder in the United States, but you're a jerk."

One aspect of Code Tenderloin preparedness is the carefully crafted resume. "We don't lie on our resumes at all. I can take the worst person out there and get a resume out of them. A resume is what have you been doing. A lot of people would love to have a person who's never had a job before, to mold the employee into someone they want." Del has bigger ideas, though. "We're trying to give you a career. So we break it down to what do you do well and what do you *like* doing? It would be nice if those things are the same, if a guy said, 'I'm a great welder and I *love* welding.' But 90 percent of the time we get, 'I'm a great welder, but I hate that shit.' We switch over. 'What do you *like* doing?' 'I like truck driving.' 'Okay, let's tear that welding resume up and start all over.'"

"It's been working well," Del said, adding that job seekers now fill out applications online. Thus, he seeks donated cell phones and computers.

Code Tenderloin job applicants, reworked resume in hand, learn what to ask and to show eagerness to learn. "We teach people how to go in and become *one* in that interview. It works so well." If job applicants are not only scared but also shaking, the person hiring has probably already decided against them.

To help marginalized applicants become more "socially able," Del tries to open their worlds by getting whatever free passes he can, whether to Giants baseball games or the Asian Art Museum. "I'm a hustler. I'll go get tickets to whatever." He wants job applicants to step up their social game, as he put it. That includes changing their lifestyle. "You can't continue to hang in front of the liquor store once you're employed. You got to start getting into the arts and live a decent life. I won't say 'normal/abnormal,' because people that go to theater might be just as crazy as we are down here but just [living] a different life. So when you're doing your job, you can discuss *Porgy and Bess*, or who won the Giants game, because as you advance in jobs, that's how they look at it: Are you socially able?" If Code Tenderloin interviewees get asked during an interview about a local event, such as a Warriors basketball game, they are expected to indicate they are familiar with the outcome but for now prefer to discuss the job opening.

Code Tenderloin training has been so successful, Del said, that at one point graduates got an almost 80 percent placement rate. But some students, he mentioned privately later, he will refuse to send to interviews. "We have one guy in here, he's nuts. Very intelligent white guy. But he'll start talking about *Star Wars* in the middle of the conversation. 'Can you give me how many years you've worked there?' 'Well, I was on Mars.' I cannot send him to a job." A woman Del hired to help run the program told Del the man had a right to a job interview. Not under the mantle of Code Tenderloin, Del insisted. "They're going to say, 'Is this the kind of person Code Tenderloin thinks is job ready? I want nothing else to do with them.' This guy will *never* be ready for a job. He's mentally ill." Del added, "He needs to be in a program that offers employment to the mentally ill. Until I get a pipeline there, I can't help him."

People with other unacknowledged problems show up as well. "We had a guy come not too long ago. Irish guy. Real sharp-looking, suit and all. He came with this great resume and says, 'Look man, I don't need to go to class or anything, I just need you to put me to work.'

"I said, 'As articulate as you are and as good as you look, you shouldn't *need* us. There must be a reason you came in here.'" Del insisted they sit down and talk. Did the man drink? Well, "a couple of beers" when he got up, a couple more toward noon, and by the end of the day twelve. Del asked if the man thought drinking was an issue. No, he didn't. Del asked about the man's relationship with his boss. The man responded that no "stupid person" could tell him what to do. Del summed up, "We have a drinking problem and an anger problem. We had to address those first."

Anyone Del considers unemployable is not accepted into Code Tenderloin in the first place. "It's wrong to *you*, and it's wrong to us." If someone uses hard drugs, for example, they are out. "We can't deal with you, because that's not fair to the rest of the students. If you're using weed, we kind of overlook that." The main point, he has said repeatedly, is by taking classes at Code Tenderloin, your whole life could change. Do you want to change it?

Most people who arrive at Code Tenderloin wanting a job are the very people with whom Del especially identifies: people without homes.

"You cannot go to work homeless." That is, he clarified, unsheltered. "I could go to work living on your couch. I can't go to work living in a tent. My eyes are bloodshot because I've been up all night, people walking by my tent." Surviving homelessness is itself a job, he said. "You may have to stand in line to try to get a bed for the next night, or you may not have slept at all. You don't have any idea what time it is, or you try to find a place to do some things you need to do, bathroom duties. If you're homeless and you need to take a BM, it may take you an hour before you can find a bathroom. That adds to the dilemma a housed person does not have."

Del and others were trying to convince San Francisco officials to offer a shelter solely for people looking for work. "Especially the night before your interview, you *have* to have eight hours sleep in a decent place, and where you get up and wash your butt. Can't go on an interview smelling funky. That's very important to us, to convince the mayor at *least* for that interview process, have a place where our people can go and shower and shave and take time to look decent."

If Del's students land a job prospect, he continued in the theater classroom, they need to be prepared. "I may send you on a job for a desk clerk. Then you find out what a lot of people don't know. If you get the graveyard shift, you got to bring the garbage up from downstairs. That's a typical job of a nighttime desk clerk. There's no janitor on duty." Be ready to say, "'I got to take the garbage out? I'm cool with it.'"

Whatever a job applicant's situation, Del also advised, they should not act desperate. As he once told a group at the end of a walking tour, some people are so afraid to miss out on a job, they say they'll do anything. He now told the Code Tenderloin students, "You can't go on a job saying, 'If I don't get this job, I don't know what I'm going to do.'. . . I want you to go in there saying, 'I may get this job, and I may not.'"

Still, Del ended this part of his talk by urging recruits to approach a potential employer seriously: "This is one of the most important days of your life. For you, your kids, and your grandkids. This could change all those people's lives. This is the day your life could either be spent in the Tenderloin or Orinda [a wealthy San Francisco suburb]. That's what a decent job could do, even a BS job. It's a start. And it beats what you might be doing now."

Del then had the students say something about themselves. Most said they hoped to find interesting work.

He urged them to be early for Code Tenderloin classes, as training for employment. If a class is supposed to start at nine, be there at eight thirty, not one minute to nine. Do the same for prospective employers, he said. If asked why you showed up so early, say you're going over your questions. If the employer is told his nine o'clock is there early, "that's going to impress him."

On another occasion, however, Del steamed about a Code Tenderloin staff member's "bureaucratic bullshit." So what, he asked, if someone is a few minutes late to a class? "We deal with the person." If the president, the pope, the head of Apple is late, nobody would say a thing, he said, getting hotter. "Come on, don't have that double-standard bullshit. Now, if I don't show up that day, *then* maybe we need to have a conversation. But if a guy is struggling, you see him running through the door, 'Oh, man, I'm sorry I'm late.' Why beat him down? He's trying to be here, fool."

Del acknowledged Code Tenderloin's limits in making systemic changes. "I'm a very, very honest person. I couldn't care less about PC correct. I have no problem telling you, 'Man, that company don't hire brothers.' I'm not going to waste your time or my time. Messed up as it is, they don't. Some companies don't hire people over sixty."

When Del was nearly finished talking, saying he should have left five minutes earlier (to chair the monthly meeting of San Francisco's Local Homeless Coordinating Board), he told the students they could call him as early as five in the morning, because he gets up before then, but only text him after eight in the evening, when he goes to bed.

Before leaving the stage, Del said Code Tenderloin is not unique. "People been doing this for years! This is nothing new I thought up. Unfortunately, in our community, we generally don't have an uncle or auntie or cousin working across the street, because before, in traditional jobs employeeing"—one of Del's invented words—"these people got uncles or cousins. They'd say, 'Hey, got a guy in HR?' But I'm your uncle."

He then turned the class over to volunteer April Trinh, who outlined the next days, including upcoming guest speakers, and requested that, as part of preparation for getting job-ready, everyone wear interview-type clothes to class the next day. Finally, she told everyone to help themselves to the refreshments, at the time bottled water and doughnuts.

CHAPTER 10

WELCOME (NOT) TO THE LAFD

DEL'S PARAMEDIC EXPERIENCE during the Vietnam War led to his be-
ing hired in Los Angeles as an ambulance driver for the LA County
Hospital. After a year's training at the Los Angeles Fire Department
(LAFD) paramedic school, in 1971 he became a firefighter/paramedic.
Del spoke with nostalgia . . . briefly. "Can you imagine wanting to be
something and actually be it? You couldn't get no better than that."

Actually, it could have been much better. The LAFD station to which
Del was assigned welcomed him with closed arms. He learned that the
department, having been forced to integrate only a few years earlier,
retaliated with insults such as assigning the new Black firefighters to
one station, Fire Station 33 on Central Avenue (a "hub of the Black
neighborhood"). Then the department took away the hoses and rescue equipment, reducing Black firefighters to mop-up operations, not
heroically putting out fires. The federal government, said Del, called
that approach "bullshit" and demanded a Black firefighter be assigned
to each station.

"Man! The fire department went crazy because they didn't want
any Black people. . . . This was *their* job. This was the Irish American
tradition. 'You're not going to get those jungle bunnies in our house.
We're not sleeping with no Black people.'" In response to the edict,
Del learned, the LAFD devised "station security." One hour a day, the
token Black firefighter had to walk around the perimeter of the station:
during breakfast, lunch, and dinner. "Because they would refuse to eat
with a Black man."[1]

Del's fellow firefighters, if "legally subdued," seemed equally prejudiced. The captain himself set the tone nastily, making Del take hours to write up a minor accident he had not witnessed, while the rig's driver, who caused the accident, went to bed. The captain also got after Del for his hair length. "I always kept my hair military." The captain told him to cut it even shorter. Del pointed out firefighters whose hair covered their ears. The captain replied, "I'm talking about you."

While seething, Del got advice from someone in the fire department personnel office whose name he never forgot: Tessie Cleveland, "a Black woman, which was very unusual to have any Black people in city jobs at that time. She says, 'Let me tell you something, Seymour. They're going to fight you and fight you. But don't let them see you sweat. Probation is a year. Do what they tell you to do. Bite your tongue. The day you make probation, call everyone and say 'Fuck you.' Even the captain. But make probation.'"

Following her counsel, Del became a protected civil service employee. Assigned to Fire Station 34, serving a neighborhood then part Japanese and part gentrifying Black, he worked for the LAFD for seven years. "I was the third Black paramedic in the city of Los Angeles. Saved a lot of lives. A *lot* of lives." Some he could not save, such as a boy killed when a forklift, which the boy and his buddies had commandeered as a prank, fell on him. Del still remembers the screams of "a Black woman running like Jesse Owens" toward the child. Another wrenching assignment led to a woman decapitated in a car accident. Del had to pick up her head.

He also witnessed the violent death of the Symbionese Liberation Army (SLA). In 1974, members of the militant group had kidnapped newspaper heiress Patty Hearst in Berkeley. The ensuing dragnet, amid many turns in the story, including Hearst's alleged conversion to the SLA cause, led on May 17 to a house in Compton, where the SLA was believed to be hiding, along with Hearst. Los Angeles police, learning of the situation, got ready to pounce.

That day, Del neared the end of his twenty-four-hour shift, having swapped his night shift with someone else to attend a much-anticipated Marvin Gaye concert. While waiting for his relief, an emergency call came into the firehouse. Del was ordered to Compton Avenue, far from his station, and told not to use his siren or flashing lights. This was clearly a secretive situation. But with his Marvin Gaye evening disappearing, Del was so annoyed he used his siren and lights anyway, to the greater annoyance of officials where he pulled up, near countless police vehicles.

"They think they've located Patty Hearst in the house back there, and they're about to raid it. Biggest news story of the year." Recounting the tale early one morning on the bandstand of the Piano Fight nightclub, Del went into intense storytelling mode as Tenderloin street life transpired outside. "Police and others surround house, on rooftops too. Shooting starts. Everyone is firing into the house, people inside shooting out. Bam! Bam! Bam!"

The gunfire, in Del's mind, lasted twenty or thirty minutes. At one point, police pulled a woman and child out of a house window, dragging them to Del's rig. "They'd been shot in the back." While he readied IVs, his chief interviewed the two and showed them pictures of Patty Hearst and fellow SLA member Wendy Yoshimura. Were they in the house? The two said no, but Cinque, the SLA leader, was still there.

Then came word a police officer had been hit. Del saw, however, that the officer had accidentally rolled off a low roof while reloading. But the rumor, coupled with the report Patty Hearst was not in the house, launched what happened next, he said: police shooting incendiary devices into the house. One hit a gigantic palm tree, which exploded onto the house, said Del, his arms waving in imitation of the falling fronds. The house burned fiercely.

Del remembered fire trucks parked a block and a half away, but not a drop of water was used to douse the flames. Retribution, he said. The police thought a cop had been shot and that the only people in the house were Black. "That's how LAPD rolls."

In the house debris, six bodies were found. As the LAPD knew, Cinque's was among them. Patty's was not.

The inferno at an end, Del headed to a hospital emergency room, unloaded his two wounded passengers and went to the bathroom to recover from effects of tear gas. A charming blue-eyed, brown-haired reporter followed him in, tenderly helped clean him up, and, despite strict LAFD rules, got him to tell her everything he knew and had witnessed, solely for her "own personal knowledge," she claimed. "I was bamboozled." After the interview, Del headed back to his fire station and congratulations from his colleagues. Ice cream was set out. The whole crew gathered to watch the news, including heroes such as Del. The chief even invited Del to sit with him. Del gladly did, in one of the comfy chairs (repurposed first-class seats from an airliner, he said). At the post-fire part of the news, firefighters cheered watching Del drive up to the hospital.

Then the camera switched to the brown-haired woman reporter in the studio. Del recalled, "'Paramedic Seymour told me . . . ,' and she tells the *whole* story. The chief roars, 'Upstairs!' I went from hero to asshole in ten minutes."

DEL ALSO INSTIGATED FIRE STATION DIVERSIONS that may have gone over better with the firefighters than the brass. His partner on a rescue rig had two sisters who were both *Playboy* centerfolds. "I would bring Playboy bunnies in to cook us lunch and dinner a lot of times. Or for a firefighter's birthday, I'd have the girls from the club come down." And "one of my other lady friends was a stripper," who brought her coworkers to visit.

The captain was not won over. During an LA mayoral race, after firefighters supporting incumbent Mayor Sam Yorty ("a racist," in Del's opinion) put Yorty bumper stickers on their pickup trucks, Del drove to work with a bumper sticker for Yorty's Black opponent, Tom Bradley, on his car. The captain said Yorty supporters could park in the station lot. Del could not. Perhaps part of the reason? "While they drove older pickup trucks, I drove a brand-new Mercedes Benz. I was fairly well off financially." That was putting it mildly.

At the fire department, Del's typical schedule was twenty-four hours on, seventy-two hours off. What to do with the off days? Already no stranger to entrepreneurism, Del started a construction company. Along with friendly competitors, he made huge profits from the foreclosure epidemic of the early 1970s.

Seymour Building Systems boarded up, secured, and sometimes renovated foreclosed houses on behalf of the federal Department of Housing and Urban Development (HUD). Del was termed an area manager broker. "Local HUD representatives were middlemen"—real estate professionals taking kickbacks, he said—"to give the contract from HUD to me or whatever repair contractor this guy wanted to give to." It depended on the kickback. "All these guys were on the take. Every one of them were crooks, all the property managers."

Business boomed. "I had five trucks working and couldn't keep up. People were losing their homes by the hundreds." Del said every morning HUD sent him a list of twenty-five houses to board up. "The lumber company would come with an eighteen-wheeler and unload plywood once a week. I had just as many two-by-fours, because when you board up a window or a door, you put the plywood on that side, then you put two-by-fours across and run rods through it to seal it together."

The renovations he termed minor. "If the government wanted to get the property ready for sale, they would contract us to [replace] roofs, fences, water heaters, sinks. At any given day there was *hundreds* of these needs in the community."

Del's local HUD intermediary and real estate professional wanted to get his kickback as quickly as possible. "He knew we *all* gave kickbacks because that was the only way to stay competitive. I had just regular guys working for me." Thirty, he said. "I had so much work, no way in the world could I be out at all those properties. I didn't have time to be a micromanager." Instead, he relied on his "hard-core foreman," one Bobby Dugan.

The crooked middlemen not only took kickbacks from people such as Del; they might also take three kickbacks for the same job. "All to put a water heater in this house. It more or less came down to whoever gets there first. My guy Bobby would get to the house. I gave him a whole stack of jobs for the day. He would get out to the first job to put a water heater in. He opened the door, brand-new water heater Bill put in yesterday. Normal human being, what's he going to do? Well, 'Complete.' Then they would go to the bar for a couple hours because they said, 'Del screwed up.' All the water heaters everyone bought from the same place, so you couldn't tell if it was mine or whoever. . . . At the end of the week, I would see Bobby's invoice 'complete' and signed my name and put it in for payment to HUD. I was paying someone else, had a pipeline, and got my money almost immediately. This went on for two or three years. I was getting probably twenty checks a day. The federal government, they paid you per invoice."

Del housed Seymour Building Systems in "a big, old, corrugated tin seven-thousand-square foot warehouse" where he kept his tools and materials and parked some of the trucks. The warehouse lay in a rough neighborhood, on Normandie and Gage in South Central Los Angeles, only a few blocks from where the 1992 Rodney King riots later broke out.

Two secretaries, including one of his girlfriends, Joanne, worked in the warehouse's front office. In the rear of the building, Del set up a private office, outfitted with whatever refreshments visiting police and firefighters might enjoy. He described it as "very plush: gigantic, with all those Day-Glo pictures and chaise lounges. The big captain's chair, a bar. Shag carpet this thick," he said, holding his thumb and forefinger an inch apart.

Del referred to his business rivals as friends. "We drank together at night. We were making so much money, it was unbelievable. We'd go to Hawaii on the weekend. I had a Mercedes 450SEL and a brand-new Corvette. One of my girlfriends, I bought her a Camaro." That girl-friend was Bonita, he later figured. He gave his girlfriend Joanne a Corvette, but which one he could not recall. "Larry [a friendly competitor] had a Rolls Royce. Brand new. We were youngsters, but we had plenty of money. I was probably making ten thousand a day. Easily! And we charged the highest rate." All billed to HUD, all due to foreclosures. "It was terrible times."

It was not terrible times for Del. Earlier, in Los Angeles, he had met a woman, Elaine (a pseudonym), with whom he had two daughters: Deleana, born in 1973, and Regina, born in 1974. He and Elaine lived with the girls in a Palos Verdes house he called a mansion. How much Elaine knew of Del's various girlfriends remains unclear, but when she learned about Joanne, or perhaps something about Joanne, she picked up a gun and drove to the warehouse.

CHAPTER 11

TWEETING HIGH

CONTROVERSY IN SAN FRANCISCO about the techie influx did not abate. In April 2014, Caroline Barlerin stepped into the fray, hired to become Twitter's—she consulted an old resume to get the title correct—"global head of community outreach and philanthropy." A woman recognizable from a distance for her long brown hair, Caroline had lived in San Francisco some twenty years, working in "a jigsaw puzzle background" of profits, nonprofits, startups, and foundations. Now, protests or not, she wanted to "harness the power of Twitter for good in the community." She had also heard Del proclaim, in one of his two TEDx talks, that when people have a problem in the Tenderloin, "Don't call the police, call HR [human resources]." His words stuck.

Speaking in Twitter's vast free lunchroom (years before Elon Musk bought the company and obliterated such perks, among other more substantial changes), Caroline joked that to her the catchphrase "Facebook fifteen" means not being famous on Facebook for fifteen minutes but for the fifteen pounds tech workers typically gain from lunchroom largesse. Free tech lunchrooms, if popular with employees, angered others. Why weren't tech firms, recipients of local tax breaks, supporting local restaurants?

Caroline's initial self-assignment included a listening tour. "I met with sixty-five nonprofits in my first six weeks, trying to understand the neighborhood and community." In that time, she heard about Del's walking tours and contacted him. They met near Boeddeker Park, then walked to a coffee shop and talked. "I wanted to understand who he is and what the neighborhood is and which organizations he supports."

Her first impressions were that Del was "a lover of history" and someone "trusted by the community. He was very thoughtful and very strong, intentional in design, and very entrepreneurial, trying to figure out a way of helping all sides." Afterward, as she and Del walked around the Tenderloin, many people stopped him to talk or called him. "Already that day I was, like, 'Who is this guy?'"

She continued, "Del and I connected on a real human level rather than . . . a transactional level of how we get stuff done." The match worked for both. Caroline needed a guide to the community. Del, for nascent Code Tenderloin, needed more access to the tech world. The relationship grew into a friendship.

Caroline may or may not have been the person who first called Del "the unofficial mayor of the Tenderloin," but she sticks by the label and more. "He is a very thoughtful, generous person, in spirit and in knowledge. And in meeting people where they are, which I think is an extraordinary thing. Two years ago, there was a lot of vitriol about the new [tech] people coming in, people protesting outside Twitter. It was a very hostile time." Del's feeling, she said, was: "The neighborhood's been abandoned for a long time, and you guys are coming in, and how can we make the most of it?"

In the Twitter lunchroom where Caroline hosted Del, at one point twice a week, she brought up his work ethic. "He does more in a day than most people do in a week." After he arrives in the Tenderloin about 5:45 each morning, she said, "He'll be at the hearing or the event or the fund-raiser until nine o'clock at night." Then he would return to Fairfield, in Solano County, where he was living, well over two hours via public transportation. Or, she continued, if he had an evening event in San Francisco, he might sleep in the office or basement of a nonprofit. Recalling the sight of one basement accommodation she exclaimed, "For goodness sakes! We need to give this man a room here in town." Del professed not to mind, though, and, for a small audience of friends, demonstrated how he squeezed onto a narrow settee, using a stool to prop up his legs. The bathroom down a dark cellar hallway may have unnerved others but not the man who had slept on the streets. A private bathroom!

Caroline especially admired Del's comfort with a spectrum of people, from "probably the most drugged-out homeless disenfranchised people" to "the San Francisco power elite," including tech CEOs and mayors. "Somebody who can navigate both of those worlds and work in both is quite remarkable. It takes different traits for both. And, oh, by the way, he's not just doing it here." She cited his efforts on behalf of unsheltered people in Fairfield and in Los Angeles. "And oh, by the way, he's not just doing Code Tenderloin, he's doing the Tenderloin Walking Tour and [is involved with] Swords to Plowshares. I think he wants to do a lot on the planet as long as he can."

Of professional interest to her was simply that Del welcomed tech firms. Soon he led their often wide-eyed employees, some from other towns or countries, on his tours. "A lot of the employees don't know much about this area, so for him to be a guide and to help and explore and not be upset about X, Y, or Z is also pretty extraordinary." Of course, connections to grateful tech leaders were a wise investment.

Del, asked during an early walking tour whether he hoped that tech companies would provide jobs for Tenderloin people, answered, "I don't *hope* so. They *have* to." He added, regarding promised tech investment in the Tenderloin, "They're not as good as they need to be yet, but who's to judge? They're out doing something." At least they patronized some local businesses. "We appreciate the things they *do*, because, if they didn't get the tax break, they wouldn't be here at all."

At a panel discussion in early 2020 about San Francisco homelessness, he told the audience, "Don't blame tech. Homelessness was here before tech." And don't blame tech workers for skyrocketing rents, amid other price increases. Tech people are the tightest people he knows, he said to laughter. Del raised his voice. "Blame developers, blame landlords." His usual phrase is "greedy-ass landlords," but this time he was more circumspect.

CHAPTER 12

A DOUBLE END

ROUND 1976, DEL LEARNED the federal government had gotten wind of the widespread deception involving foreclosed homes. "The FBI started sending undercover contractors out. At the time, because [an] indictment was in the works, they started freezing the money coming out of DC but not telling anyone why they weren't writing checks. 'Paperwork back up' or something."

At the same time, a bizarrely interrelated act of violence played out.

"My kids' mother shot my secretary."

Joanne, Del's girlfriend-secretary, was at her desk, on a conference call by speaker phone with HUD personnel back in Washington, trying to learn where the checks were.

"I was having breakfast with my friend, not too far away," Del said. This friend was Rolls Royce–owning Larry. "We would have breakfast the same time every morning, because we were competing on contracts, where we really weren't. We just did our catch-up to see what contracts are coming out and how we can leverage each other's businesses."

After breakfast, Del planned to inspect some of the three hundred properties he said he had under contract, then send in more invoices. He drove by the office on the way. "I see my front door open. It was the middle of the summer." Del had air-conditioning units in both the front office and his own, in the back, and was pissed off, he said; someone had left the door open.

He saw a man at the entrance, "one of the street guys, not home-less, because we didn't use those words at that time. He used to stop on the block, one of the OGs, old guys on the block. He was leaning inside of my door. I'm thinking he's in there flirting and messing with my girls. I said, 'Get the hell away from my door'—in a joking way, because I knew him. He said, 'Man, you better come in. Your girl been shot.' That's how I found out."

Joanne was bleeding badly—whether conscious or not, Del did not remember. His other secretary, Sheryl, Joanne's sister-in-law, stood with her hands over her mouth. "I said, 'Have you called anybody?' She couldn't talk. I picked the phone up and called my dispatch. 'This is Seymour. I need everything you got to my office.'" The connection was well established. "I would talk to them every day. Within seconds you could hear the sirens coming from everywhere."

Twenty-five police cars and three ambulances pulled up, he said. "Everyone that walked in that room I knew. All six paramedics were people I went to school with or worked with. On my day off and they were working, they would stop by my shop. I always have a fire engine or a couple police cars in front of my office. They come here, give them some coffee. When they heard that address, they came running. When the first paramedic walked in, he says, 'Get back, Seymour. We got this.' Because I was holding pressure on her wounds."

Del went to his office "to try to get my mind together." He knew it was a rough neighborhood, so had made a point of hiring only from the local community. "I was doing the same thing I do now. Why would someone come in and rob me? What's going on, what do I need to do? After the initial trauma, I got to start thinking financial damage control. Then one cop I know comes in and asks me for the license plate of my Thunderbird, which I kept at home. I never drove it, but the keys were there. I'm saying, 'What the fuck does this have to do with it?' I'm thinking he's some real bureaucratic guy that wants to know my Social Security number and place of birth and all of that.

"He says, 'Your wife is driving the Thunderbird.' 'What do you mean?' Then I put it together, boom-boom-boom-boom-boom. 'Oh, my God.' My first question, 'Where are my kids?' He says, 'They're with her.' I say, 'Stop her, stop that car!' He says, 'We're doing it, but we need the license plate number.'

"Now I got two tragedies going on. One, this girl is laying there, shot, and now this shooter's got my kids. What's she going to do next?"

The police told Del an Air 1 helicopter was on its way. It followed the Thunderbird to wide Vermont Street, landed, and stopped it. "She had the girls in the back of the car."

Elaine was arrested and booked at the Sybil Brand Institute, a women's prison in Los Angeles.[1]

Joanne, hospitalized in critical condition, was paralyzed, at least temporarily.

As for Del's little girls, whom Joanne loved, he said, Joanne's mother took them into her home nearby.

"That night, I'm at my office with my partner, Walter. He and I were inseparable. We're sitting here trying to go over this whole day. I had already been to the hospital. We still got a million-dollar operation. We got places to do, places to board up. I mean, we got contracts. I'm trying to figure out financial liability, everything. I've got two different dilemmas here. I've got a girl laying in hospital, shot, and then I've got my kids' mother in jail. I mean, my life is a little splintered right now. Elaine's family calls me and said they need to talk. I said, 'About *what*?' I'm not feeling her family at all." They insisted. Del said okay, come to his office. It was about 10 p.m. Soon about twelve members of Elaine's family showed up. They brought up the subject of Elaine's bail.

"I'm saying, 'Why would you come to me with some shit like this?' They kept talking and talking, mainly her brother, Steven, because he and I were in the service together. He kept ranting and raving, going on and on and on, at this end of a very tragic day. I can't listen to this shit no more. I said, 'How much you need?'"

The answer was $5,000. Del got it from a hidden stash he kept in a shoebox and handed it to him. "Here. Bye."

"He says, 'Okay, well, we're going to get her, and we should have her back home . . .'

"Wait, wait! What the hell are you talking about 'back home'? Are you crazy? They actually thought they were going to bring her back to my house. I said, 'This ain't part of the deal. Before you touch that money, this is not part of the deal. Here's the $5,000. You go. Don't even *think* she's coming back to my house.'"

———————

DEL SAID THAT AT HIS LAWYER'S ADVICE, he did not attend Elaine's trial. Nor, he said, did he want to. He later learned Elaine's defense was mental instability. "Her plea," said Del, "[was that] she was a victim of a relationship affair. The presumption that she was the mother of my kids gave her credence back then that this is like a common law marriage."

As far as Del knew, Elaine served some time but was released and went to live with relatives. Joanne recovered only partially. She required a wheelchair for a while and eventually was able to walk with crutches. Del lost connection to her, but later tried to find word of her through internet searches. Then, through her sister, he learned she had died.

When Joanne was shot, the HUD people she had been on the phone with became audio witnesses. "Everyone in Washington heard it on speakerphone," said Del. "They immediately say, covering their ass, [what] about their liability by being sued for what was common law? They immediately distanced themselves from us by canceling our contracts."

Then came an FBI investigation, Del uncertain however about the timing of events. At one point, FBI agents "dressed like moving men in coveralls, with guns," came into Del's office and removed his file cabinets. Quickly, the HUD program ended. "This was government money. FBI started indicting *everybody*. They indicted me. Indictment really don't mean nothing until they actually charge you. It was over a hundred people in the indictment."

Del went to trial with his attorney. "Now they [at HUD] owe me $27,000, which was a *lot* of money then"—if only three days' worth, he acknowledged. Charges focused on whether work was completed or not. The prosecutor, Del recalled, placed a pile of yellow invoices in front of him. If they represented an "accurate truthful request for money," Del was to sign each, stating Seymour Building Systems had done the job. "He says, 'Wait. If I find *one* in there you didn't do, I'm putting you in prison for ten years.'" He indicated a nearby paper shredder.

"I turned to my attorney. My attorney gave me a look like, 'Can you do that?' I looked at him like, 'No, I can't verify I did every one of those.' He says, 'Shred it.'"

The "gleeful" prosecutor, Del recalled, "looked at me and smiled" at every shredded invoice. After the last one, "he said, 'Have a good day, Mr. Seymour.'"

Outside, Del saw Larry, the Rolls Royce owner. "He was a little flamboyant guy, reminds you of Redd Foxx." Del affected a stage whisper. "'Seymour! What happened in there?' I said, 'Larry, the federal prosecutor's not playing. Don't go for it because he will put you in jail.' 'Man, fuck them people. I'm getting my money.' I said, 'Larry, this ain't LAPD. This FBI.'"

Del paused. "Larry might still be in prison."

The end of Seymour Building Systems signaled a concomitant end to fast cash. "I figured this ain't never going to end. Why save money? I was buying cars and going on vacation, buying houses. Buying diamonds. And I was using then but was not an addict. It was recreational cocaine. Like all the movie stars did." Del said he also sold cocaine to colleagues in the fire department. That's how it is always done in fire and police departments, he added. If one person goes down, all go down. In his case, nobody went down.

Del did have a stash of some $40,000 but also a house mortgage and payments for five trucks and his cars. The stash would not last long. He needed to find other work quickly. And there was Joanne, in the hospital. And there were his little daughters—babies, he called them. He felt he could not properly care for them. "Maybe, had they been boys . . . ," he said at one point. Maybe. And he figured Joanne's mother, no matter how kind, would not want to continue caring for the children of the woman who shot her own daughter. Steve, Elaine's brother, stepped back in.

CHAPTER 13

BAD NEWS

THE TIMING MUST HAVE FELT SHAKESPEARIAN. In 2013, Swords and Plowshares honored Del at a gala with a Profiles in Courage award. His acceptance speech, both self-deprecatingly humorous and pathos-filled thankful, Deleana recorded on her cell phone, panning to show her sister Regina, as well as Del's sister Ethelear, here in San Francisco all the way from Chicago. Aware of Del's earlier setbacks, Deleana said she recalled thinking, "He wouldn't mess *this* up."

Then in 2014 came two hammer blows of news. First, Del was diagnosed with prostate cancer. As someone preternaturally opposed to self-pity, his various health problems (including getting stents for a heart condition) are not subjects he discusses easily. No pity party for Del Seymour. "I'm good, I'm good," he will say when asked how he is—even when he does not seem good. A dismissive wave of the hand typically stops any expression of concern.

Regina was more candid. While driving along the streets of Fairfield, near where she then lived, she spoke about the scare. "At some point we didn't think he was going to make it. They were finding more stuff and more stuff. Being a very stubborn man, he didn't like taking that medication. It made him sick. I thought he was just going to say, 'Screw this medication. I'm going to go do me some drugs and go out with a bang.' But he kept fighting. He kept working with the doctors and demanding certain types of treatment more comfortable to him. And he did research on certain treatments to say, 'Hey! I know you guys can do this. Don't treat me like this because I'm a VA veteran. Why would you have me uncomfortable when you could make me comfortable?' He fought for his own medical care," she said. And he got it.

"That's why he survived. That's where that intelligence comes in. He *knows* how to do research." She paused. "I think he knows what he has to offer to other people who can't figure it out. He knows that, if given the chance, a lot of people *will* make it. I think his whole idea is, 'Some people don't have the brain or the thinking power or the knowledge that I have, so why don't I use it and help other people make it?'"

She continued, "It is, to me, overwhelming. At some point aren't you going to get tired of not having your own life? But that *is* his life." Del's prostate cancer upped the ante, in Regina's opinion. "That's why he does so much and he's *so* busy, because he's trying to jam-pack it all into the years he has left."

Del was treated in San Francisco, at a University of California, San Francisco (UCSF) facility. When released, a photo of smiles recorded the occasion, Del in a wheelchair, Deleana, on one side, Laura Slattery of the Gubbio Project on the other. Del had insisted Laura not come—he opposes hospital visits—but she defied him and brought a bouquet of flowers.

By all indications, Del got back to work as soon as possible, building Code Tenderloin.

The other hammer blow may have hurt more. A young man (unnamed here) in Del's family and four other young men were arrested in Oakland for sex trafficking and assaulting teenaged women. As Del put it somberly, "Unfortunately, [he] took up the same thing that I did." Del's family knew that years earlier the young man had lived for a time with Del and Del's prostitute girlfriend. "Everyone—his mother, his aunt, his brothers, the whole family—are sensitive right now that he wouldn't be in prison if it wasn't for me, that he emulated what I did." To the accusations, Del said somberly, "It's very possible."

At trial, the young men pleaded no contest and were sent to prison. Especially upsetting to Del was that "the ringleader" was reported to be Del's relative. He received a sentence of twenty-four years, a length of time reflecting that the victims were underaged.

According to one news report, the Oakland prosecutor said, "The four defendants preyed on the girls because of their young ages and because some of them were vulnerable because they didn't really have homes."

In other words, they were quasi-homeless—precisely the kind of girls Del was trying to help. Del has visited his relative in prison, efforts a friend indicated are beyond painful.

CHAPTER 14

PIMPING

DEL FIGURED HE "probably" started pimping in 1992. That sounds late, considering he became addicted to crack around 1986 or 1987 and supported his habit in part by pimping. Yet he pursued other money-making activities too, including dealing crack himself and taking on electrical and plumbing work.

If the date is a guess, there is no doubt the subject affects him emotionally. One might not know it during his familiar beat, walking the Tenderloin, interrupted as those forays are with virtually nonstop greetings to and from people, some in wheelchairs, some sitting on the ground, most standing. Then Del seems at his most relaxed, the subject of prostitution coming across as almost casual. He might greet various women with a friendly handshake or hug, then later say she was "one of my girls." One day he mentioned seeing five of his former prostitutes that morning, and they'd gotten off drugs. Another time, a very thin woman, who clearly had not, stopped Del on the sidewalk for counsel and comforting. She was with a man who had PTSD and yelled at her a lot, she said. Del leaned down, listened, and advised she try not to match the man emotion for emotion. At the end of the conversation, she hugged Del and staggered on.

On such occasions, one might get the impression he had come to terms with his trafficking past. That was not the impression when he sat down privately to talk about it. Gone was the meet-and-greet Del of the streets or the Del who exploded about such situations as police handing out citations for "quality of life" infractions to poor people, whose poverty led to the infractions in the first place. In fact, he was so often in a lather on the subject of distressed human beings in whatever situation, it was highly unusual that he all but fell into silence, seeming like a pinned butterfly rather than the alpha male he often projected.

He had agreed to talk about pimping only on the premise that the subject is part of his larger life story and, more importantly, informs his work helping young women from similar circumstances as those of "the girls I ran."

The chosen site for the talk was not the Tenderloin, where interruptions were frequent, but instead his home at the time, a duplex apartment in Fairfield, on a street where the few parked vehicles looked larger and sturdier than the houses.

Del rented the apartment, with help from the Veterans Administration, at the suggestion of Regina, who lived nearby and heard about a vacancy. Fairfield, the rural seat of Solano County, lies midway between San Francisco and Sacramento. Sometimes Del expended three hours (by bus, BART, and/or carpool) commuting to or from San Francisco, some fifty miles away.

Although he treasured having a home, Del was no homebody. He furnished his place quickly, with items from a thrift store that benefits a homeless shelter. A brown sofa took up most of the living room and faced a large screen television. On a crowded coffee table sat plastic flowers and a silver tureen, from the same thrift store. Del figured silver might be a good investment. The kitchen, just off the living room, looked all but unused. Del did not cook much but learned when he did that the plastic fan over the stove was meant for a bathroom. It caught fire. A metal fan was later installed.

Upstairs contained the bathroom and two bedrooms, Del's with a big bed, a television almost as large as the one downstairs, and a computer. The other bedroom, its door closed, was home to whomever needed a place to stay that night, week, or month. Del professed to being bad company, but his spare bed was never empty long.

As a measure of how difficult the subject of prostitution was, despite the heat of the day, Del closed the living room window on the "American side" that faced entrances of nearby apartments, saying, "We're real tight here, far as conversation." He then opened the kitchen window. "My Latino side. All these people here, they don't speak English. I don't care."

Clearly, he did. Hunched forward on the sofa, his body almost motionless, his voice muted, his answers were often uncharacteristically short, including about the beginning. "I don't know how it started. Undoubtedly, I had a lot of young promiscuous women around me and . . . I needed money, and that was a way to get it." He was sure he did not come up with the idea: "The girl probably suggested it to me."

No, he did not remember the first women by name.

"*All* of them" were using drugs by the time he began pimping them. "In most cases, yes," they were already prostitutes. Although he "snagged" one woman whose girlfriend was his prostitute, he objected to the word "recruited." "It wasn't recruitment, as . . . this girl knew this girl and knew how much she enjoyed her life with me, so she wanted to get on the bandwagon. They came to me." Del's street nickname was Pimpin', which he said was like a term of endearment. "You didn't have to be involved in pimping to be called that name." It did imply, he added, you were a man who "had a way with women."

The women Del pimped had several commonalities. One was youth. He estimated they ranged in age from eighteen to thirty at the most. (In 1992, Del turned forty-five.) The women all were Black. "I would say generally: Didn't finish school. Victims of abuse. They all had children somewhere and someone else is taking care of these children. Some from good neighborhoods, some from bad neighborhoods."

He added later, they were all "crazy"—"every one of them. They were completely disorientated with the world, with life. I bet if I got all my girls together, not one of them would even know who the president of the United States was." He added—the year being 2016—"They'd probably know because Obama is Black. But if Obama wasn't Black, they wouldn't know who the president was."

One pimping cliché holds that a pimp offers a type of safety net to women prostituting themselves. Del essentially confirmed this. "*Nobody* messed with me in the Tenderloin. That was just the way the hierarchy at the Tenderloin went at the time. And they knew not to mess with any of my girls." That statement later proved untrue.

He and the prostitutes lived together, often in an SRO. Whenever he got evicted, for whatever reason, "I took all my girls with me.

Average would be three. Three of us or four in a place this size. Size of this room," he indicated with an arm sweep—a small living room in Fairfield.

Del was intimate with all of them. "Sometimes. Sometimes not. Depending on mood."

The way pimping worked, he said, "I would send them to people I knew that wanted girls." Transactions were generally by phone, to or from Del, or followed a conversation on the street. "'You got any girls over there?' And that would be it."

Virtually all "dates" were in the Tenderloin with Tenderloin men. Del gave the women instructions first. "I would just tell them what I wanted them to do. That was it." The "what" he would not answer. They would be gone for "an hour. A day. Two days."

With one exception, Del got the money from the trick first. "I had to go get my money." Yes, he meant *his* money. "I got all of it." He collected "wherever the act went down, at someone else's SRO or in one of the hotels around. The Hilton. Wherever."

One woman, "my most profitable girl," he trusted to do her own collecting. Upon her return from an assignment, she would throw thousands of dollars on the bed in $100 bills. Del said the amount made him nervous; he figured the police would be knocking at the door next.

In general, though, the women kept none of the money?

"No. I gave them whatever money they needed. There wasn't anything to spend on. I got them clothes, we brought food in. All kinds of drugs. You didn't need money."

The women were always on call. "I wanted them acceptable and pleasant around me all the time, so I kept them ready at a moment's notice. . . . I always had multiple girls, so I had one girl that dressed the other girls. One girl would go shoplift and get all the outfits. That's how we did it." As to whether he paid attention to the outfits, he said in an equally uncomfortable later interview, "Of course I did. I was their pimp. They would ask me, 'What do you think?'"

No, he said, the women did not fit the stereotype of how prostitutes dressed, with high heels and short skirts. "That's TV." They wore regular clothes, he said. And "when they went out working, I made sure they all had condoms." Someone would shoplift them or buy them on the street. "They came from all different kind of ways."

Nonetheless, he said, "There were some pregnancies involved. Every one of them that I know lost their babies, through the government, because you have any trace of narcotics in you, the hospital would take the baby. It's the law." None of the women he knew of, he said, had an abortion.

Two got AIDS. "They're both dead. One girl, she was so beautiful. I can't remember her name right now. She was a beautiful, *beautiful* girl. She just kept getting smaller and smaller," he said, his hands describing decreasing circumferences. (By whatever fate, Del has avoided AIDS. When he finally underwent testing for HIV in his sixties, he was so surprised he was negative, he said, that he told the doctor to test him again.)

Del set the prices, which he said the women agreed to. "They wanted to make sure I was okay. Whatever was comfortable with me, that's all they were concerned about."

One of Del's own concerns was corrupt police. He said members of the San Francisco police vice squad arrested him twice for pimping. "The vice squad was on the take, and you had to pay them constantly."

He cited a well-publicized scandal (not involving prostitution) reported in the *San Francisco Chronicle* in February 2014. The article stated, "Five veteran San Francisco police officers and a former officer faced federal corruption charges Thursday after a three-year investigation that began when the city's public defender released surveillance videos appearing to show officers abusing and stealing from residential hotel dwellers."

Said Del, "They used to take my money all the time. Same guys. Whatever they could get from you. Whatever they could scare you out of. Hundreds."

In one arrest, "I didn't have the money, or I dodged them, or 'Hey, I ain't got no money today. I'll hook up with you tomorrow.' Then you avoided them for two or three weeks, and when they saw you, they were really pissed."

In another arrest, "I was in dispute with my landlord, and he couldn't put me out. He had deals with them also, because he would let them have rooms so they could do surveillance on the street by taking pictures from inside. He called them as a special favor, to have me arrested, because I wasn't leaving." It worked.

Del was also arrested, he said, by undercover police posing as tricks. The arrest would happen when Del went to collect money for an about-to-take-place sex act. "Once the girl would have an encounter with the guy, I would go pick up my money." If the trick was really a police officer, Del said, "they would book me and take me down to the pimp place [a holding facility on O'Farrell Street]. It's where they used to take all the pimps. Pimps *and* tricks, when they did the reverse thing." The other pimps "were just guys like me," Del said. "Most of them were a little younger than I was. I was always the OG pimp. Not really, because there was a generation over me."

Arrests, financial shakedowns, and landlord disputes were not Del's only prostitution-related problems with the police, he said. "At one time I was running a competition with the cops because the cops had their own prostitutes in the Tenderloin. We worked together sometimes. When my girls got in trouble, they would call me and say, 'Del, we got one of your girls down here. You going to come down and get her or what?' Or they got jumped on. Couple times, they came and picked me up in the vice car and took me to the hospital to see one of my girls." He remembered one woman who "got cut up, beat up real bad by an ex-con" who had just gotten out of jail. "Undercovers came and took me out to the hospital."

"One died. I don't want to talk about her." He did later, a little. Her trick killed her.

Another time, Del indicated he was not concerned about his prostitutes' safety. "My girls could handle themselves. They were from the 'hood. These weren't girls from the suburbs."

The woman who got badly beaten by the ex-con recovered, he said, quit prostitution, and became a registered nurse, working in Contra Costa County. A lot of others left prostitution, Del said. "I didn't try to keep them in if they didn't want to be in. I didn't need negative vibes around me. [One woman] cleaned herself up, and she's living near or with her daughter down in Beverly Hills." The daughter became "a very famous singer." Online mention of the mother's nickname matches the same name Del used.

What about the stereotype of the abusive pimp? That depends, he said. "If you were a physical abuser and you became a pimp, you extended that into your pimping. If you were a humble, God-fearing, loving guy and you became a pimp, you extended *that*." Del claimed initially to be "the humble guy."

If a woman came back from a sex assignment in an unhappy mood? Del gave two answers. One was, "I didn't care. I'm not an emotional person, which is hard in a relationship because you got to have emotion." Another answer, expressed emotionally, was, "I would have to handle that and bring that energy level down. '[I] don't want to *hear* that shit! Take that shit outside. You messed up the whole mood of everyone else.' I would physically push them through that door. Maybe that *would* be abuse."

Yet the woman could have been roughed up, treated badly, right? Del now responded as he may have responded to them: "You know what job you're taking! You know you're not going out to the knitting club! You're going on a date. So I don't want to hear that. Part of the job."

Obviously, the clutch of memories made him uncomfortable. "Of course it does. What sane person wouldn't [be]? I was a little insane then. I'm not insane anymore."

"Every once in a while," he added, one of the women challenged him. "You're not going to keep jealousy out of it when you've got a group of girls. That was always an issue I had to deal with constantly."

Five months after those statements, Del offered a rougher version of the relationships. "I was in fights a lot with my girls. It was constant fighting." The fights were "about other girls" and involved "punching," he said. "I fought those girls like I would fight a man—because they fought *me* like they *were* men. I've had hundreds of fights with girls. They ended all different kind of ways. Sometimes the police come or whatever."

As to developing emotional relationships with the women, "Nope. It was all business. Business entertainment. I wouldn't even call it business. Entertainment."

This proved not the case in at least two relationships. One ended in a fight in which he almost died. But that was years later.

Months after the exceedingly uncomfortable talk at Del's home in Fairfield, he spoke on the same subject at an office in Glide Church, the institution that had helped him in countless ways—including employment, shelter, food, and compassion. This was a debt repaid, a request from two Glide interns, women graduate students, who were studying human trafficking in the Tenderloin. According to a third woman in the room, Emma Slaats, a visiting Dutch volunteer helping Del with Code Tenderloin, the focus was on the triangle of prostitution: consumer, pimp, and prostitute. In her notes, she recalled Del said "fifteen girls" worked for him, that they grew up without fathers, and a pimp provided a kind of paternal love.

One of the graduate students, Neha Jain, wrote later in her notes, "He clearly did not like talking about his pimping days." He also asserted there was "currently no organized street prostitution in the Tenderloin," contrary to her research. She wrote that she wondered if Del felt "a need to protect the TL from negative truths," because of his current status.

Neha's notes continued: "He treated all of them with no/little regard, and the women would compete for his attention. All treated Del as if he was their boyfriend. When I asked him what the best solution is to ending human trafficking/pimping of women . . . he said women need to start feeling worthy. The women that came to him to fight for his attention would do anything for him. He told me about a time when he woke up next to a woman who was bruised/hurt and Del asked her what had happened. She replied, 'Don't you remember? You did this to me.' Del told me he didn't remember hurting her."

He also told the graduate students that two prostitutes had attacked him, one shooting him in the leg. However, he did not tell them the bullet is still in his leg. Recalling the incident later, he pointed to his left thigh, just above his knee. Because the shot caused much bleeding, he did visit a doctor, he acknowledged. "I didn't want him to say, 'Take it out,' because it would have been too much surgery. And I would have had to have her arrested." That is, he let the bullet stay in his body rather than allow it to be evidence against the woman who shot him.

Del's emotions about his years as a pimp remained painful. He compared himself to a former serial killer who cut up a lot of people, "because I did cut up a lot of people spiritually and emotionally." He vehemently declined to read Emma's and Neja's notes for accuracy. The only reason he talked with the women at Glide, he said, was because they were trying to help other women avoid trafficking. If his testimony "would help just one girl, what could I say but 'Sure'"?

CHAPTER 15

THE DAUGHTERS AND THE AUNT

WITH ELAINE IN JAIL, her brother Steve came back in the picture. He suggested Del's daughters Deleana and Regina live in Oakland with him and his wife, Lovenia. Their marriage was not going well, and Lovenia was already raising her three young sons in the couple's two-bedroom house. But she said yes. Del drove the girls to their new home around 1977.

Some forty years later, the sisters reminisced over lunch around an outdoor patio table at a restaurant in Fairfield, where both then lived, as did Del. On a broiling June day, the sisters favored loose summer outfits. In contrast to their slender father, Deleana (pronounced De-LAY-na), the "unofficial junior," she said with a raised eyebrow, and Regina, often known as Gina, are large women who, according to their aunt Lovenia, take after their mother, whose inheritance is thought to include German and English ancestry. Or as Lovenia put it in one of several sharp-tongued moments about Elaine, "We always said, 'As long as she doesn't open her mouth, you would think she's a white lady.' That's awful to say, but it's the truth."

Deleana worked as a manager for Kaiser Permanente, where she oversaw people who coordinated medical appointments, while Regina's professional work included a decade in "banking/collections/repo" and another decade in workers' compensation insurance, until later finding more satisfying work with special needs children. The sisters seemed close emotionally, Deleana the more assertive. Regina professed to being tired, having been up much of the night getting extensions braided into her hair. Deleana kept her hair short and dyed, one striking color after the next.

That day, Regina brought along her amiable teenage daughter, Tyra, whom she called a special needs child, who mostly nodded to music on her earbuds.

Although the sisters were little older than toddlers at the time of the shooting, they had heard about it enough that they may as well have remembered each moment. Their interpretation was that when their mother found out about an affair between Del and his secretary, she "kind of went on her haywire situation," in Regina's words. "She's schizophrenic, bipolar. She had a criminal situation. Would he want us to say that?" she asked Deleana.

"Well, we're going to say it," Deleana answered.

"I guess he was a bit of a philanderer," Regina said with a laugh, "and she's like ten years younger than him. He had a lot of money back then and was living flashy and having a good time. She already had mental issues. I like to say he kind of drove her crazy, but she was already a little chemically imbalanced," if possessing at times a "charming aura," she added. "The basic part of the story I know is she went into his office and shot his secretary. She was permanently disabled, but she didn't die."

Deleana put in, "I think it was an insanity thing or something" that led to her early release. "She said the lady was harassing her and making her feel insecure."

"Paranoia as well," added Regina.

"Paranoia. She probably was easily upset," being "crazily infatuated" with Del.

"And two new babies," said Regina. "That's when my uncle came and was like, 'I got to get y'all from down there.'"

The daughters said they understood why Del did not intervene to keep them with him. "I don't think he could have handled it at the time," Regina remarked.

"He had to deal with all that criminal stuff afterwards," added Deleana.

"The way he's explained it to me," said Regina, "he couldn't deal with too much of anything at that time. And his life was wild back then. I always say, where we ended up is probably where we were supposed to end up, because we could have been in a way worse situation with either one of them."

LOVENIA, A STURDY-LOOKING WOMAN despite physical ailments, recollected the years while sitting in her tidily jam-packed house in another part of Oakland, which to her disgust and concern was becoming drug-ridden and trashed. She would soon move to New Orleans, where she had once lived.

It was clear from almost her first words, Lovenia had been all for helping Del. "Regina and Deleana's mom kind of messed things up for him," she said placidly. "She was so jealous of him and all the women that were after Del." Although Lovenia's husband Steve stepped in to help, "We had our issues too. At the same time, I wanted to make sure the girls were okay. Then *we* broke up. But I kept the girls. Not thinking it might be permanent. It's just that they needed a home and someone to take care of them."

One boon to caring for them seemed the connection to their father. "I love Del. At the time, he was in Los Angeles—and he would always come up north here and visit me. He was doing quite well. He was making money hand over fist, and he would spread it around to us," she said with a laugh. It was unclear whether Del still was getting income from the last throes of Seymour Building Systems or had begun his next career. "He was always so appreciative that I took care of the girls, because the mom was a little more than desired." She added, "Not to put her down too much, but . . ."

"When the sisters arrived, she remembered, "Regina was starting in kindergarten along with my son Steven." Lovenia's older son was entering middle school, she said, "while my baby was still at home." She hired a babysitter to watch the children in her absence and commuted to her full-time job writing public service announcements for a television station across the bay in San Francisco.

"We didn't have much money," Regina recalled, "but we wouldn't know that until we were grown. We were happy, played outside every day." The little girls and their three cousins "had a good time."

Del visited often, according to all parties. Every weekend, he said. But his financial impulses sometimes flummoxed his daughters. Said

Regina, "When we were little he used to come and take us to the doughnut shop. Remember?" she asked her sister. "He'd give us a hundred-dollar bill to pay for a doughnut and a milk. *What?*"

During one of Del's visits, he got very angry at the girls. They remembered the situation in detail because it was so rare and humorous.

"That's one thing," said Deleana. "He's not violent."

"The most peaceful man ever," put in Regina. "I remember the one time we got a spanking. I so deserved that spanking."

Deleana started to laugh. "He didn't even know how to do it."

Regina picked up the story. "Because my dad was a paramedic, and I was playing with matches. I was lighting matches and throwing them in the toilet, just to hear it sizzle. I must have lit a lot of matches because as soon as he walked in, he smelled matches."

Deleana had told Regina and a boy lighting matches with her to stop, but "I didn't *tell* tell." She got in trouble too. "Because I was the oldest."

Regina's laughter joined her sister's. "The spanking. We'll never forget it because it was the only one. And you could tell he didn't want to do it."

"Remember back when wristwatches had a clamp?" Deleana asked. "He kept stopping to fix his watch because it unclamped every time he tried to spank us. He was like, 'Ohh, hold on for a minute, hold on for a minute.' We were trying to hold in laughter."

Regina shook her head. "The only time he ever put his hands on us."

Deleana remembered, "He made us write we couldn't play with fire."

The sisters laughed again. Part of what Regina found funny was that her father had no idea what else she had been up to. "You don't even realize I've been drinking the end of your beer cans forever!" Playing with fire, though, was another matter.

Throughout their time at their aunt's, Lovenia counted on Del's largesse. "He provided income, child support you would say. I would buy their clothes and food and everything and took care of them like a mom would, because the mom [did] not have it together. But when she thought she *did* have it together, she tried to take the girls away from me. She comes up to my house, then goes and got the policeman. At the time, I was combing the girls' hair to get them dressed." After the police office saw the children's environment, his view, said Lovenia, "was that the kids seem to be doing well." The daughters said their mother resumed visiting but did not try again to get them back.

FACING THE FINANCIAL FALLOUT from the end of Seymour Building Systems, Del scrambled to get freelance electrical jobs. He also hired headhunters "to get from A to B." The jobs he sought were in engineering—perhaps Del's longest-lasting love.

Like his childhood interest in firefighting, Del's interest in engineering started early, too, and never abated. He relishes knowing how things work and explaining them. Riding a San Francisco bus, he'll point out how much voltage overhead transit wires carry and why they cannot be insulated. During one interview in the Tenderloin, he stood to demonstrate, with sound effects, how a blade on a manufacturing table was programmed by computer input to make specific cuts, then went on to talk of working with benders and brakes, of laser cutters. "CNC machine tools. That's computerized numerical control machine tools." He sometimes took walking tour groups into a department store to point out the spiral escalator as an engineering marvel. He's so enthusiastic about nuclear submarine engineering ("I'm a Trident fanatic.") that when he learned Trident commanders were on his walking tour, he refused their money.

The headhunters' leads landed Del impressive stints, starting (as far as he recalled) at Astrophysics Research Corporation based in Harbor City, Los Angeles. Among its many operations, Del's work involved installing secure mail systems around the country, including, he said, for the federal government in Washington, DC. He cited engineering work at Di-Acro Machine Tool Company in Lake City, Minnesota, and with French-based MEG (Materiels Equipements Graphiques). "We were building block-long newspaper presses." He stood, arms akimbo, to demonstrate MEG's newspaper printing system that glued together enormous rolls of paper at high speed—the flying paster. MEG, he said, involved many overseas trips. "I went to Bangkok. I went to Uruguay. I went to Colombia, to Peru, to Brazil. I went to Ecuador. I've been all over Canada. Where else did I go? Went to Costa Rica, Mexico City, Belize." Once, changing planes at the Denver airport, he happened to cross paths with his brother. Neither acknowledged the other.

As a well-paid field engineer, Del made certain of entertainment perks too. Was it in Montevideo where he said one could safely leave a gold cigarette lighter on a nightclub table while getting up to dance? There where he won a dance contest?

An assignment closer to home in California arguably changed his life. He was working for New Jersey–based Sun Chemical company, whose products included ink for printing presses. At some point, Sun had him oversee installation of a press for the *Sacramento Bee*.

"We're working like eighteen hours a day because we were so behind on this project. I haven't taken a day off in a month. I'm the primary engineer. I've got a crew of about twenty-five local people, electricians and plumbers, working under my supervision, that I hired." One evening, either Christmas Eve or New Year's Eve, he told fellow engineer Ed Buck he was going out but would be back to work as planned at 6 a.m.

"I go to this club in Sacramento and party down, drinking something I never drank before, Grand Marnier, some old weird shit. The bar closes at two. The rumor going around, there was an after party somewhere." Del, immediately interested, accepted another customer's offer to follow him. Soon the highway patrol pulled the customer over. "Undoubtedly I'm drunk," Del remembered, "because I pulled behind the highway patrol." The officer told him, "You get the award for dumber than dumb tonight."

From jail, about three-thirty in the morning, Del called Ed and asked for help with his $5,000 bail. But between them, they were $4,000 short. Del asked Ed to go to the *Bee*—the middle of the night being when newspapers are printed—and see if anyone would lend them the money. Ed agreed to try.

"About five thirty, the jailer comes in and says, 'Seymour, roll up. You've been bailed out.' I said, 'Oh, thank God.'"

"I go out . . ." Del's voice broke. "This is one of these hard-to-tell stories. I go out in the lobby. It's Ed and this white older guy. He says, 'Del, this is John. He lent us $4,000.' I don't even know him. I said, 'John, thank you so much. I'll have your money back before the day is over. I sure appreciate you coming out here.'" John told him he was not worried about the money.

"We go out to the job. In the meantime, Ed had asked everyone out there to borrow money, so they all know I went to jail for drunk driving. These are contractors, working-class guys like me." They started razzing Del. "'You couldn't handle your liquor, ha ha.' Everyone's having a great time with me. It goes on all morning. I'm not tripping, because they had a right to do it."

Del paused. "We're sitting in the lunch room. Everyone's still yelling about my escapades. When one man yelled what was his bail, and Del told him $5,000, "He said, 'You had $5,000 on you?' I said, 'No. Ed came out last night and borrowed $4,000 from John, the maintenance engineer.' The room went dead.

"He says, 'No, he would not have given you $4,000.' I'm thinking they were trying to pull up some racial thing, like John was a racist." Another man insisted John would not have put up the money. Del insisted he did, clarifying by description John was an older short white guy with the van.

"I finally get down to it. 'Why wouldn't John have given me any money?' He says, 'His daughter'—Del, crying, barely continued—'got killed by a drunk driver last night at nine o'clock.'"

The news wrecked Del. Half an hour later, he happened upon John in a hallway, "where I had no exit." He managed to say he learned what had happened, then asked one question. "How could you have done this for me?"

"He said, 'I'm a Christian, brother. I'm a Christian.' And he walked away."

John's simple declaration made Del feel even worse. He said he felt he would have committed suicide if he saw John again and pleaded for an immediate transfer. It was granted.

In the years since, Del said he knew he would not be able to replicate what John did but tried to model his "forgiveness behavior" on him.

AT LOVENIA'S URGING, Del eventually moved to Oakland from Los Angeles, to be closer to his daughters. Before he even unpacked his U-Haul, he asked Lovenia where he could get a drink, drove to a bar, and met a local woman who suggested he live with her, immediately. He did. He still visited his daughters every day, he said.

Lovenia continued to take care of them, although there had been interruptions in their seven years with her. Once they lived with a woman Lovenia called "a play mom," another time Del rented a house near Lovenia, and the girls lived with him, but she was their safe harbor. Then her new fiancé announced Deleana and Regina had to go. Lovenia complied.

The girls were about ten and eleven, Deleana thought. Where could they go? Their mother reportedly was unstable. Del, for whatever reasons, including out-of-town engineering assignments, was unable to be a full-time father. Only one option remained. Deleana took up the story. "He ended up contacting his brother who he *hated* and still is a mortal enemy to. It was a lot for him to do that because he hadn't spoken to him in decades." She half laughed.

"That was probably the only bad part of our childhood, because he has a reason to hate his brother. He's a pretty evil person."

The brother had moved from Denver to Chicago, where he lived with his wife and became successful in the computer business. The girls believed he was "some type of head honcho at IBM."

To Chicago the girls went. Were they okay? Lovenia said her attempts to reach them by phone went nowhere. "Whenever I would be trying to contact them, [the brother] would intercept calls and wouldn't let me talk to them." They stayed with their Chicago uncle and aunt three years. During that time, apparently nobody outside the home knew what was happening to them, least of all Del.

Back in California, unaware of anything amiss, Del fell for the only woman—as of this writing—he would marry: Lachelle. From his description, she exuded competency and competitiveness. Her father, a farmer in the Central Valley city of Fresno, made sure his daughters could accomplish such tasks as fixing a lawnmower.

Because Lachelle was "very sharp," said Del, he took her as his assistant on his new enterprise, being an independent electrician. After about the third day on the job, he said, Lachelle figured she knew as much as Del did, even questioning safety codes. "It was impossible to tell her, 'I know what I'm doing. I've been dealing with these inspectors twenty-two years.'" Nonetheless, the relationship continued, Lachelle became pregnant, and she and Del married. He rarely tells the story without laughing.

"We fought *in the church*."

The issue was Lachelle's insistence that "raggedy, beat-up-pickup-driving" Del pay the Mercedes-driving pastor a hundred dollars for the brief ceremony. "Hell, no!" said the groom.

Del moved back to his own place and did not see his bride until six months later, when their daughter, Carmaila, was born.

What Del calls his "fifteen-minute Hollywood marriage" (which lasted, officially, much longer) had no Hollywood ending. Years later, Carmaila—who studied law, passed the bar, and then became a DJ—described herself in an online site as the daughter of a single mother.

Over time, her responses to Del's various attempts at conciliation might best be described as uneven.

CHAPTER 16

PROSPECTS OF MURDER

IN THE EARLY YEARS of Del's addiction and homelessness, he lived mostly in the Bay Area, as far as he could remember, but moved around too. A web search states that in 1994, for example, his addresses included San Francisco, Oakland, Fresno, and Sacramento.

Scenes Del remembered or cared to relate from that time reveal various moods—of ebullience, despair, entrepreneurship, pique, hope—as well as comedy and tragedy masquerading as each other.

One such episode took place in Fresno, a city known for its sprawl, heat, agriculture-based economy, and, according to Del, lawlessness.

From whatever straight job, he had been getting unemployment benefits. But in a bureaucratic snafu, his account closed. "I'm not broke, I'm *super* broke. But I'm using drugs. My drug dealer, who I've known for a while, he's giving me credit. My credit is blossoming up to couple thousand dollars. My drug dealer's also a straight gangster. He'll shoot you in the head in a minute without any cause."

After calling the Fresno office of the state Employment Development Department several times a day, "fighting and arguing," Del learned the problem had been solved. A check for $7,000 would be delivered by mail the next day. Del called his dealer with the news.

"He said, 'I'm so glad you made this call because I was making arrangements to have you killed.' *Oh yeah*. I would have wound up in one of the vineyards, because they do it all the time. Fresno don't play. He says, 'Well, you want some dope? Let me bring you some, so you can have a little something for tonight.'"

Del looked relieved even decades later. "My whole life was—*whew*! The elephant is off my shoulder. This man ain't going to kill me, and I got some money. I'm already on the phone, calling girls. 'Party's at my house tonight. As skimpy as you can. Come on over.'"

The next morning, the dealer picked up Del in the countryside, where he lived in the home of a retired drug dealer, and parked near Fresno's Chandler Airport to intercept Del's usual mailman on his route. When they spotted him, he said he would be right back, to get Del a certain piece of mail from his truck. Then, "I hear this UHHH-hhhh!" Del imitating with voice and arm movements a plane coming down fast. The plane crashed onto the mail truck, which exploded.

"It took me a while to realize what happened. I *run* over and start pulling boxes out of the truck. Fresno police pulled up, grab me, yank me out of the truck, and handcuff me. I'm arguing, 'I got to get that mail.' They told me it's a crime scene, I could not touch anything."[1]

The bizarre account had a silver lining: Del's dealer witnessed everything. "He said, 'If you told me this, I never would have believed you.' He gave me something to calm my nerves, because he felt bad for *me*."

Del returned to the house in the countryside. There he inadvertently changed roles from potential murder victim to potential murderer.

HE DESCRIBED THE HOUSE as a "villa" built by a "big-time" heroin dealer named Dave, last name forgotten. Dave, some thirty years Del's senior, lived there too. "When I met him, he was at the end of his career. Just come out of prison."

Paid for with heroin money, the enormous single-story house sat on some fifteen acres and included two swimming pools, Del recalled. "It was an amazing place. Run-down, because he was an *ex*–drug dealer."

Years earlier, concerned the property might be seized in a drug arrest, Dave had put it in the name of his son, Dave Jr., then age five. Decades later, according to Del, "They weren't on bad terms. They weren't on *any* terms." Dave Jr. was "one of these young elite Blacks" who refused to have anything to do with a drug-dealing father.

At the villa, Del managed various illegal activities of his own, including drug dealing and prostitution. He also kept track of Dave's mail, Dave being, like many intelligent men Del knew from the US

South, such as his former army commander, unable to read or write. One day a legal form arrived. Del read it to Dave. It was a thirty-day eviction notice.

"He says, 'What are you talking about? This is my house.'"

Not according to Dave Jr. In Del's words, Dave Jr. had a new wife, "some little, young, sharp white girl, who found out this villa [was] in her new husband's name."

Dave Sr.'s verdict: "He needs to die."

"I says, 'I agree.' I was living the code of the neighborhood."

"He says, 'D, why don't you do it?' I said, 'Hell, yeah, I would be glad to do it.'"

Del was so angry on Dave's behalf, he says he would have taken the job for nothing, but Dave offered $5,000, which was fine too. "I guess that's the reason people commit murder for hire."

Dave went to his bank and returned with cash stuffed into a sock. He handed Del $2,000, promising the rest when Dave Jr. was "no longer here." That was fine with Del. "I went and bought a throwaway car. And got a gun from the streets, which was basically a throwaway gun." At a Fresno homeless shelter, he hired two Mexican men who spoke little English. In that part of the Central Valley, Del added, live *"real* illegal aliens" ("that have no connection to nobody, no ID, no nothing"). One of them Del assigned as his getaway driver. The other was to help with backup. "They were throwaway people too, because they didn't know me, I didn't know them. Once we did the deed, they would take the car. It would be over."

That Monday Del picked up his accomplices to surveil Dave Jr.'s daily routine. "We followed him and found he was a schoolteacher at Fresno Unified School District." They drove to his house, parked a distance away, and waited. "He came home like 4:17. We watched him get out of the car." It was a new Chrysler. "He got his briefcase out of the trunk and walked in the house. Tuesday. He came home like 4:19. Got his stuff out, walked around the car. I'm watching his pattern. Wednesday, same thing. Thursday's the hit."

"Thursday I'm so nervous, my whole body is shaking, because I'm getting ready to kill a man." Del arrived at three o'clock to wait. "Four o'clock and I'm shaking. I'm getting ready to throw up: 4:05. 4:10. 4:15. Now I'm really trembling, because it's within two minutes: 4:16.

4:17." He counted off the minutes to 5:15. Still no Dave Jr. Del decided, "*That's it.* Can't do this. I am so stressed and nervous. If he rolled up right now, I won't do it, because I'm shaking too much."

Del aborted the hit. "Get rid of the gun. Get rid of the car. Get rid of my compadres. I'm done."

Returning to the villa, he confessed to Dave Sr. that he had not killed Dave Jr. after all and would repay the $2,000. Oddly, Dave Senior acted unruffled, said he understood. The matter seemed to end there. Two days later, however, a man who lived in a guest house on the property told Del the police had come by that morning looking for him. Del assumed the visit involved one of his activities. Maybe a prostitute he had "put out" the day before had snitched. Figuring the police would return, he hid incriminating evidence, such as crack. About an hour later, a knock on the door, then: "Fresno police!"

A man who identified himself as being with the homicide department warned Del in a rough voice that if anything happened to a certain unnamed person, Del would go to prison for life. Then he left.

When Dave returned to the villa, Del related the visit, puzzled. "These two Mexicans didn't have any idea who I was, where I lived, anything. No one knew." Yet the police knew about the murder plan. "I said, 'Man, did you say anything to anyone?'"

"Well, uh, I told Dave's mama."

"You told his *mama*?'" Del yelled.

She—Dave Jr.'s mother—called the police, who in turn warned her son not to go home that day.

At whatever point Dave Sr. changed his mind about the hit, Del reasoned, "All he had to do was tell me. It wasn't a big machine getting ready to do it. It was *me*. I'm sitting there thinking, man, if Dave [Jr.] wouldn't have *not* come home, I'd be in prison right now. I don't know if senility got him. Why would you tell the boy's mama we're going to kill her son?"

Del, incensed if relieved, was finished with Dave. "I moved out right then."

CHAPTER 17

AN ADMIRER

ONE OF DEL'S ALLIES working to change the misery of the Tenderloin is soft-spoken, megawatt-smiling Sam Dodge. As a city employee, primarily with San Francisco's Department of Public Works, Sam has undertaken decades of efforts: Tenderloin tenant organizing, helping direct the Tenderloin Housing Clinic, putting together a Latino family project, later overseeing the enormous Navigation Centers erected to shelter the unsheltered. "I worked with literally thousands of tenants in their residential hotels. Many campaigns, many issues, from individual assistance to organizing meetings," he said. One such individual was Del, whose memory of Sam helping him remains stronger than Sam's memory of doing the help.

After Sam went to New York City to run outreach programs, then returned to San Francisco, he said Del "was in full bloom." He added, smiling, "He's so dapper, right?"

The two got "fastly re-acquainted," Sam said. "He's been active everywhere and taken all these great leadership roles around homelessness particularly. To re-meet each other in this setting has been really powerful. Part of my role now is talking at various places about homelessness and solutions of homelessness and what's going on in San Francisco, why [it is] so horrible on the streets." One night after both men were on the same panel, they decided to hang out. Del showed Sam the Code Tenderloin operation at Piano Fight and also described his commute from Fairfield and mentioned sleeping in makeshift offices. Sam became concerned. He knew Del's history. "He dealt drugs.

He did horrible things. The way he talks about it is so relatable." Yet Del held personal matters close. Sam's concern focused more on Del's expanding workload, from Tenderloin Walking Tours, to helping some people get jobs, then "all of a sudden it was Code Tenderloin."

"What is it about Del?" Sam mused, in his City Hall office. "He's kind of electric, he's fun to be around, he's whip smart. And his politics are really good, which is something that attracts *me*," he added. "He's carrying around a lot of grudges and some deep scars, and maybe some past habits around hustling are repurposed in his current form. That can be good and bad." Sam wondered about "some guilt or shame or other kinds of things."

He is impressed by Code Tenderloin's "legitimacy," as he put it. "Where I sit [in City Hall], I get a lot of people saying, 'I've got an idea, and give me money, and I'm going to do this and that.' You have to be a little bit cynical. But Del has shown up. I don't know where the top is for Del. When he's going to be full."

In a way, the two have traded roles. Once, Sam managed Del's care. Later, Del, appointed cochair of the Local Homeless Coordinating Board, oversaw San Francisco's Healthy Streets Operation Center, which Sam directed.

Del's publicly told story, Sam implied, features the complexity of life. "He's both a victim of circumstance and addiction and an agent in that addiction and circumstance. When we look at people in that more complex lens, we get much closer to the truth. And when we look at complex social problems like homelessness and you can hold contradictions, you get much more effective programs and results."

"I often have a problem with people thinking of homeless people as somehow subjects of charity, somehow less than human. He knows that people aren't good or bad, that we're all complex and that life is long and we have many phases and stages. That can develop more empathy and more accountability in a certain way. It's different from a lot of service providers and medical providers [who] often try to see people as clients or subjects." As Sam put it later in an email, such providers are not the only people who hold such views. "Even newspaper columnists and elected leaders and businesspeople [include] these sorts who often thought of homelessness as a problem of homeless people rather than a systemic flaw."

Sam's work got interrupted in 2019 when he took a sabbatical to Norway, where his wife received a Fulbright. Having a year to think about homelessness from another perspective, the verdict about the United States was not favorable. "I have always felt this country is bizarre, but now I truly know this is the outlier . . . much of the rest of the world is doing much better."

MONTHLY MEETINGS of the Local Homeless Coordinating Board, at which Sam often testifies, follow a pattern. At least several dozen people usually show up, most representing organizations trying to confront the city's vexing homelessness issues. Anyone attending might be overwhelmed not only by the problems addressed but also by the bureaucratic minutiae referenced: various requirements for continued HUD funding, statistics, reports from numerous city agencies, and more. One handout referencing "community-based nonprofits serving homeless populations" included the Council of Community Housing Organizations (CCHO), Homeless Emergency Service Providers Association (HESPA), Homeless Employment Collaborative (HEC), San Francisco HIV-AIDS Provider Network (HAPN), San Francisco Human Services Network (HSN), and Supportive Housing Providers Network (SHPN).

Members and speakers alike seem focused on providing whatever help they can, while coordinating efforts on behalf of unhoused people themselves. How about, for example, people not having to go all over San Francisco filling out form after form to search for one night's bed? Among the audience are apparently homeless regulars—such as an elderly white woman with a walker and a younger Black man in a conical straw hat—who speak their piece, usually with displeasure. Example: a shelter staffer was rude.

At one meeting, the famously corny Mayor Ed Lee addressed the board, opening his remarks by saying, "Happy Year of the Monkey" and adding he hoped no monkey business was going on. The joke got little obvious reaction. Del, whose knee had been jiggling up and down as his time approached to question the mayor, was respectful, steering clear of in-your-face questions. Mayor Lee, after all, controlled grants to such organizations as Code Tenderloin.

Del showed professional courtesy to all, thanking them for their comments, but offstage he could be blunt. He has long criticized, privately, individuals he and others call the "homeless Mafia": people who started organizations to help the homeless, got grant money, and helped themselves. "They pay themselves well. They don't eliminate homelessness. It's *them*. Money don't trickle down. And they're not changing any lives, changing anything." A term he uses with equal derision to "homeless Mafia" is "poverty pimps."

He also got upset about issues discussed by the coordinating board, such as the proliferation of tents. Later, during a walking tour, a young man in a group of wide-eyed students asked Del what he thought about the tents, people living in countless rows of them along various San Francisco sidewalks.

Del replied, "This ain't Yosemite."

As he revealed during one of several Sunday talks at Glide Memorial Church, however, when he himself was homeless, he used a tent. "During the Vietnam War, I served our country, living in a green tent. When I got back to the Tenderloin, I traded that green tent for a blue one right across the street."

When a long-time local and progressive enterprise, Rainbow Grocery, complained that tent encampments near it on Division Street in the South of Market area had become more than they and their customers could cope with, Del was sympathetic. The liberals who run the grocery, he said, are responsible people. "They've been responsible to the earth, the environment. Everything the [tent-dwelling] people on Division do is anti-environment. *Everything*. And it's anti–civil rights for the people that need to walk down that street or want to live cleanly in that neighborhood. It's against all normal human behavior. Division Street is just a big drug den. The police cannot go in their tent, just like the police can't go in your house. They know that. They sit there and do whatever they want."

"I understand their point of view, but if you want to do that, get all your Social Security checks together and go rent some property out in Marin County or San Mateo County." He mocked the tent dwellers' defenders. A "band of Nazis," Del called them. "'Oh God, save the homeless people, don't take these tents away.'" Meanwhile, he said, San Francisco is in a crisis. "This city has turned into a zoo."

A couple years later, Del put the situation another way. Although he did not consider tents a solution for homelessness, he told members of a synagogue about to take his walking tour he could understand why some people choose them. "Tired of being a woman or man getting ass-whupped every night at home, would rather be in that tent across the street than being abused every night. They're pushing you out there. So there's a lot of reasons when we see our people out here. Yes, we do have people [with] substance abuse. But what came first?" And as he told a group of Google employees following a walking tour in 2023, people in a tent have more freedom than they would in a shelter.

Individuals who sit and sleep on city sidewalks, in tents or not, may seem to fit no discernible pattern in relation to housed people who walk past quickly. But, according to Del, patterns exist.

"The common thread in our camps is addictions." Crackheads sit with other crackheads, methheads with other methheads, and so on. Some people group themselves by backgrounds. "A lot of the survivalists, the young Oregonians and Washington youths that come down from up north, tend to stick together," he said. "The tattooed and the pierced tend to stay in their own groups. The pit bull people tend to stay in *their* own groups. The parolees tend to stay in their own group." Racial breakdowns exist, he said, as do groupings by gender and age, but not as much as groupings according to more relevant backgrounds. The main criterion for how unsheltered people arrange themselves is where they're comfortable. Del himself, meanwhile, never sat on the sidewalk for long, he said. "I'm a high-energy person."

An inadvertent commonality sidewalk residents share includes rapid aging. "These people here that look sixty, they're really thirty-five. I have a knack of guessing people's ages a lot of time, and you'll be twenty or thirty years off down here."

Along with looking older comes the concomitant loss of self-esteem. "Undoubtedly at one time I didn't have it, when you get to a point you just give up." In Del's case and that of many others, he said, the point happened after getting arrested. "You feel you're going downhill. You can fight one [felony] charge. It's hard to fight two. Once you get three, that's it. You're going to prison. You know that. When you get to five, it don't matter no more." In a wide-ranging discourse about self-esteem when homeless, he said at times he blamed everyone but himself for his situation, other times blamed solely himself, and often felt cut off from "normal" people. "They were invisible to us; we were invisible to them."

In general, he went on, conversations that included self-flagellation along the lines of "How did I get here?" are cut short by others. "It's like me going into a bar to relax, unwind from the day, and having a beer. This happens all the time. A guy sits next to me and"—Del affected a weepy tone—"He starts, 'Man, I'm going to try to stop drinking.'" Del pounded a table. "I'm out of here! I don't want to hear that shit."

Ideally, among other non-whiners congregated on the sidewalks, "We talked about the same things you and your neighbors talk about. Presidential race, the ballgame, how heavy traffic is on the streets outside, who got killed last night, what Beyoncé is singing. Same stuff."

CHAPTER 18

GAMBLING MAN

AROUND 1989, Del returned to Los Angeles and continued using crack until two schoolteacher friends made an offer to help him stop. They had bought a new four-bedroom house in Las Vegas, letting it sit empty until their contract was up in a year.

"They knew I was getting further and further addicted in LA. They said, 'Why don't you go to Vegas and house-sit?'" They might visit once a month for a weekend, but the house was otherwise his. He only had to pay the utility bill. Del agreed.

In Las Vegas, he set to work legitimately, registering at a union hiring hall. Before long he operated a tow truck for South Strip Tow and worked as an electrician for such places as the University of Nevada at Las Vegas. One assignment involved wiring work in the office of controversial basketball coach Jerry Tarkanian, whom Del remembered wheeling and dealing on three telephones simultaneously. At a job for Bob Stupak's Vegas World, a casino and hotel featuring an outer-space theme, later relaunched as the Stratosphere, Del installed security cameras. While making good money, surrounded by people making a lot more, he developed an addiction to gambling.

Later, he realized the casino's "free" paycheck cashing contributed to it. "They put the check-cashing facility in the back, so you got to walk through the whole midway to the check-cashing desk." Del got his money, plus 3 percent of the check as a bonus, in quarters, a free steak dinner, and a free play of roulette. "All of that is 'free.'

But by the time you get out the front door, you spent $200" of your $300 paycheck.

Del's game of choice was video poker. "You get on those machines, and you get hooked." He got so hooked he could not pay the utility bill, some seventeen dollars, for the "mini-mansion" his friends lent him. He winced at the memory. "They came up one weekend, and the power was out."

Then came an event even more painful.

Finishing work at four in the afternoon, he took a shortcut through the bar to get to his car. "There's an older Black man, probably younger than me now, laying down on the bar like this," Del said, sitting at a desk and putting his head down on his folded arms. "At the time I'm spending $1,500 a week on gambling. Both my paychecks. I get paid on Friday; by Sunday morning I could not buy the newspaper." Del went to the man and tried philosophizing. "I say, 'Hey, man, don't trip. It ain't nothing but money. You can't be worse than me.'

"He said, 'No, it's worse than that.'" Del scoffed but bought the man a beer and listened.

The man said he was a schoolteacher in Ohio, coincidentally the same profession as Del's friends, that he and his wife visited Las Vegas months earlier, fell in love with the place and the weather, and decided to buy a house for retirement. They returned to Ohio and put their old house up for sale.

A week earlier, the man continued, the escrow company called to say the house had sold. Del continued, his voice getting somber, "They got the proceeds from the Ohio house. They had enough equity to buy the Vegas house in full." The escrow company said it would send the money, some $225,000 to the escrow officer in Las Vegas.

"He says no. He was an old Black man. 'You're not sending every penny I've got in my life in no mail. You give me the check. I'll hand it to the man, and he can hand me my deed to the new house.'" The man flew from Ohio, but a connecting flight got snowed in, so he did not reach Las Vegas until Saturday morning. The escrow company was closed until Monday.

"Now he's got to goof off the whole weekend. It's World Series weekend. He says he had a couple of hundred dollars cash. He got a room in the tower. He goes downstairs to play blackjack or twenty-one. In about three hours he's broke. It was no big deal because that was disposable money. He said, 'I'm going to go upstairs and watch the World Series.'

"The pit boss says, 'Hey, where you going?' He says, 'Up to my room to watch the game for the rest of the weekend. I'm broke.'" Then he added a deadly coda. "Not really broke. I've got $225,000 in my pocket." The pit boss asked to see the check. "Being, again, an old Black man bragging on his money, he shows the pit boss the check. The pit boss says, 'I can cash this, so you won't be broke.' He said, 'Man, you can't cash that check. That check is from a bank of Ohio to a bank of Nevada.'"

The pit boss replied, "This is a casino. We can do anything we want." He convinced the man to let him cash the check to have money for the weekend. If he bet, maintained the pit boss, the man would probably win it all back. "He let that man cash that check. This was at nine in the morning. I encountered him at four in the afternoon and he couldn't buy a beer."

Del's voice showed the story still affected him. "He says to me, 'If you don't think it's bad—' There was a phone right there. He said, 'You pick that phone up, you call that woman in Ohio and tell that woman in Ohio we have no more life. You tell that woman we have no home in Ohio, we have no home in Vegas. You tell that woman we have nothing. If you don't think it's bad, you make that phone call.' With tears in my eyes, I walked out of that bar."

The following Monday morning, Del repeated the story to his boss, the hotel's security director. The boss asked Del to describe the man.

"I said, 'He was a tall, older Black man, light-skinned, bald head.'

"He said, 'We found him dead yesterday.'"

Del, shaken, asked why he had not heard. The boss said Las Vegas suicides are bad for business. They're not publicized.

"I said, 'That's it. I ain't going to wind up in no hotel room dead. I'm going back to LA." He asked the boss to have his check ready by the end of the day. Later, when he went to collect it, his boss, knowing Del's gambling habit, said he had FedEx'd the paycheck to Del's Los Angeles address but handed him forty dollars to cover gasoline for the trip.

"I cussed and fussed for about two hours, called him every kind of name in the book. But when I got to LA, I called him, said, 'Man, thank you so much.'"

Thankfulness did not last. In Los Angeles, Del resumed his other addiction. "I got back on drugs because it was cheaper."

WHILE THEIR FATHER led his life in California, then Nevada, and then again in California, Deleana and Regina lived for three years in Chicago in an increasingly difficult situation.

As Regina put it, "We used to get abused all the time."

"By [our uncle] and his wife," added Deleana.

"The last beating," said Regina, was set off by some dispute involving a loaf of bread. "We got beat, stomped, all kind of stuff. Then they finally made a connection with my dad."

Did he know what had been happening? "Hell, no!" they said in unison.

"We ended up going back with him," said Deleana matter-of-factly.

When Del and his two girls reunited, Del having again moved to Northern California, he was unable to offer the two a stable home. "At that point," Deleana continued, "I guess was when he was deep into drugs. He was in Oakland running around with our eventual foster mother's uncle. We stayed with some girlfriend in East Oakland. That lasted maybe two weeks. Then she couldn't take it anymore."

"Very mean. And addicted," put in Regina.

The next move, said Deleana, came via the foster mother's uncle, Del's "druggy buddy." "I love [him] to death to this day," she added. The buddy thought his niece could care for the girls. "She was only ten years older than me, twenty something," said Deleana, "and she took us teenage girls in. We didn't see him even that much then. We went into the foster care system but were still with her."

"He was at rock bottom at that point," added Regina.

"Well, he was homeless during Fresno too."

The sisters echoed each other, "We were all homeless together."

What happened, as much as can be reconstructed, is that Del moved back to Fresno and rented a big old house while Deleana and Regina were in foster care. "My foster mother [was] amazing," Deleana said. "At the time, though, I thought I was so restricted because we had all these rules. 'I know you're eighteen. You're still going to have a curfew.' This, that, and whatever. My dad calls. 'You can come stay with me if you want.' All I could think is, 'He's not going to be able to tell *me* what to do.' So [we] hightailed it to Fresno to stay with him. Eventually, I still don't know if it was drugs necessarily, but he did lose the house. He got evicted."

"The house was nice," Regina remembered. "It had roaches."

"It did. But it was still nicer than we ever saw him have."

Del had been earning money in part doing "handyman stuff," Deleana said. "Electrician work. Plumbing." After eviction from the nice house with roaches, the three ended up in what she called "a homeless motel." Not for long, apparently. Regina picked up the story. "The last motel we got put out of, he looked at us and said . . . "

Deleana finished the sentence: "I don't have nothing else for you."

"Yeah. 'You're going to have to call your auntie.' That's how we ended up back with Lovenia again."

Lovenia, in the meantime, had moved to Fairfield on her own. As always, her version of events skewed Del positive. "Del, being on the road all the time, he put them up in a motel. Regina hated that and said her grades were suffering and everything. She asked me, 'Could you please come and get me?' She kept saying 'me'—she didn't say 'Deleana.'" She laughed. "That's because Deleana had gotten herself in trouble, and I may not would . . . take her in. But quite the opposite. I drove down there to Fresno and picked them up and brought them back up to Fairfield."

In Deleana's telling, she laughed too. "I got pregnant while I was out there. That's what happens when I say 'I'm going to go somewhere where there are no rules.' It was a pretty interesting time." She finished high school, had her baby boy, and for a while lived with Lachelle, Del's estranged wife.

The sisters debated where Del went when they returned to Lovenia. Working at the Muslim bakery in Oakland? No, that was earlier, when he brought them pastries. Or was he in the Tenderloin, "between living with some girl in Oakland"?

"He was back and forth," concluded Deleana.

Regina added, "Even though he was different places, he was homeless."

In retrospect, the sisters praised living with Aunt Lovenia. Said Deleana, "I look at both [Del] *and* my birth mother as they made a choice that was unselfish. They could have kept us with them, and we could have struggled with all that happened with *them*. Where I ended up is where I was supposed to be. I came out of it unscathed. Primarily. I don't have regrets like that. I think in [Del's] mind we feel towards him, 'Oh, you abandoned me.' I don't feel like that, though. I feel he had an illness and he made the choices right for us, which is what a parent is supposed to do."

Making right choices for himself proved more fraught.

At one especially low point in Sacramento, Del even rattled his longtime admirer, Lovenia, who had moved there from Oakland. He showed up unannounced.

"He changed overnight, so to speak. I couldn't believe it. I called Regina, and I said, 'Oh my God, Regina. Your dad's laying up here, and I can't have that because when Lynell comes, it may not be a nice picture,' Lynell being my boyfriend. Because he was so possessive." Yes, despite how Del then looked. "He was dirty. He was wearing three pairs of pants. I think if he had taken them off, they would have stood up by themselves."

Yet Lovenia had difficulty grasping the obvious. "I believed in him so much that he would never stoop to that level. I figured he was homeless but not *really* homeless, because Del has always been able to stand on his own two feet. It never occurred to me he was down this low on the ground." As if to reclaim her longtime admiration, she added, "Because he's *very* intelligent."

CHAPTER 19

A DETOX DETOUR

"IT WAS KIND OF A SPIRITUAL THING," said Del. "I was in Oakland. I lived on 96th Avenue and was selling drugs. A guy who lived in Hayward, who's my weekly customer, called and said he had my money because he just got paid." Del knew not to delay. "Because, drugs, you got to get your money right away." Having taken his car's wheels off to work on the brakes, Del decided to go by BART to pick up the money. Leaving his radio on, his dog Satan in the backyard (a neighbor shared care), Del boarded BART . . . in the opposite direction, away from Hayward.

"Some spirit told me to come to San Francisco." From there, Del transferred to a train going to Daly City, just south of San Francisco, then exited. "This sounds crazy, but it's true. I walked over to the 101 southbound highway and started hitchhiking. Didn't know where I was going, didn't know why. I got $250 waiting on me in the opposite direction and had no money in my pocket."

After several rides, he arrived at the seashore town of San Luis Obispo nine o'clock that evening. "I'm hungry as hell. Right at the freeway exit is a Kentucky Fried Chicken. I got maybe forty cents. I go in and ask the lady, 'What can I get for forty cents?' She said, 'You can get out of here, that's what you can get.'" Then she gave Del a whole bag of chicken.

Back at the on-ramp, a highway patrolman warned Del it was dangerous to hitchhike at night and offered to take him to a shelter in the countryside. Del agreed. "They got a very nice place, a couple double-wide trailers with everything, so I got a night's sleep."

The next morning, he started walking back to San Luis Obispo to head south, "where my interior confidence was telling me to go." En route, he saw a comforting sight: "A bunch of Black people sitting on the front porch of this house. Black people!" He approached them, learned the house was a church (since-closed Springfield Baptist), sat down inside to rest, listened to the end of a sermon, and started walking back to the freeway. "[Then] these two absolutely beautiful African American girls pull up in this car. Kind of cut me off. They said, 'Hey! Weren't you just in church a little while ago? What are you doing out here walking on the highway? Get in the car.'"

Del figured, "I'm in heaven right here. Two beautiful party girls like this. I'm sure they couldn't wait to get out of church to start partying. At the time I figured everybody's getting high and doing bad stuff." After taking him to a buffet, they drove not to "a dope house-party house," as Del hoped, but to Bible study. "I'm saying, okay, I guess it's another hour before they put on their party clothes. We leave, drive about another mile." Another house for Bible study, and another. About five o'clock in the afternoon, Del exploded.

"I'm using as much profanity as I can. 'You fucking whores. This is ridiculous.' I was a different person then. I was ready to whup their asses. They'd ruined my whole day with this Bible study bullshit. I get them to drive me back to the highway. On the way back, we pass this church again."

When they promised the stop would take only one minute, Del reluctantly joined them inside. The same pastor, in the middle of another sermon, announced he could not continue. "There's someone in our house that wants to come back home."

Del got up to leave. "I don't have any explanation how it happened. Three seconds fell from my life. I was in the preacher's arms. The whole church stood and . . ." Suddenly, Del teared up in his telling. "What an emotional situation that was."

The pastor invited Del to stay at his house that night. He also made Del toss his cigarettes, stating Springfield Baptist was a faith-based church and Del had to have faith to believe he could quit. "I threw those cigarettes away. Never smoked cigarettes again in my life."

A church member later asked Del if he needed a job. Despite the impulse to continue his journey, possibly to Los Angeles, Del said yes. He then was directed to one George Hartshorn, owner with his wife Laurie of the local Atlas moving franchise.

"He's a Christian. White guy. We went out on the job and moved all day long, like a twelve-hour job. I'm exhausted. We're on the way back in the truck and it's seven o'clock. He says, 'Where do you live? I'll drop you off because you worked hard today.' I say, 'No, just drive me downtown somewhere.'" When George realized Del had no place to stay, he did a U-turn and took Del home with him.

"I don't know this man. What the hell? Especially, I don't know this *white* man. I don't know what's going on here. We drive out to the country. It's like the *Bonanza* estate. A hundred-foot-long ranch house. He pulls up the circular driveway. The whole typical Ivory Snow commercial opens the door. The little white lady with the blonde little white baby with the blue eyes. What the fuck is this? He says, 'Laurie, this is Del. He's going to stay with us.' She says, 'That is so good! Come on in.' First thing she says, 'George, I got plenty of your clothes you don't wear any more. Del, we got your own bedroom and everything.' This complete trust. Man just met me. Now I'm in his house with his wife and brand-new baby. This is not normal behavior. But I didn't know Christian behavior. This is like right out of the Bible.

"We had this elaborate dinner. That's a big thing when Christians get you in the house, biblically you have to make a feast. And someone told them about my conversion the day before. It was all this welcoming back into the Christian fold."

In the middle of dinner, the phone rang. George reported that the Seattle office needed him to pick up a load there that night. To Del's alarm, he insisted not only that Del stay in the house but also temporarily take over managing the business, handing Del car keys and credit cards for expenses. Saying he would return in three or four days, he added, "We got an office manager, but you'll be me till I get back. I know you can handle this."

Eyewitness to the extraordinary tale of trust was Laurie Tamulonis, formerly Hartshorn.

She well remembered her husband George bringing Del home, the latter looking "very skinny, undernourished, under–cared for." The year, she calculated, was around 1991, for the baby on her hip would have been her daughter Becky. Her son David, also home, was several years older. Yes, it would have made sense for her to give Del some of George's clothes and feed him.

But in a phone conversation, after reading a draft of this account, she laughed at Del's description of their *"Bonanza"* house. It may have looked *Bonanza*-like to him but was 1,200 square feet. ("No kidding!" Del laughed when told.)

The main difference between the two accounts involved those first nights in the house. As fundamental Baptists, Laurie said, she and George would not have let another man stay while George was gone. It was a matter of propriety. "We did not see color."

Del insisted he did stay overnight but was so nervous he could not sleep.

Del and Laurie agreed that the next morning he returned to work. "I ran the moving company until [George] got back," said Del. "When we were having dinner he says, 'I can tell you're not comfortable here. Because I know where you came from, and I know what I'm watching.'" He offered to let Del stay in the family's old house they had just sold, which was in escrow. Del did so, became George's new foreman and worked with him as a mover. The daily agenda included an observance new to Del. "We pray when we get in the truck. We pray when we get to the house. We pray when we finish the moving job."

All certainly true, said Laurie, adding that because she helped run the company, she saw Del often. She remembered him as "very, very joyful," funny, a "go-getter." Why wouldn't he be joyful? she mused. He had food, shelter, and a steady job.

San Luis Obispo welcomed Del too. When he was "hanging around downtown" and "probably looking [for some crack]," although he had been clean since Oakland, a police car "swooped" up next to him and stopped. The policeman, instead of hassling Del as he expected, gave him his card with his beeper number and told him to call if anybody gave him trouble. Del was stunned anew in a local store. When he realized he did not have his wallet, then left his purchases to get it, the clerk told him to take his bag and pay next time.

The only downside in the San Luis Obispo wonderland was Spring-field Baptist. Despite Del's memorable initial experience, "It was a hotbed of mess. Everyone's having illicit relationships with their cousins."

Following George's frequent invitation to worship at his and Laurie's church, First Baptist of Santa Maria, thirty miles south of San Luis Obispo, Del accepted, unenthusiastically. In his description, it was an all-white "mega church." At his first Sunday, he felt ever more uncomfortable. Laurie was home with her sick baby. George, who volunteered as the church's bus driver, had to take a group somewhere. "He left me by myself in this church of four thousand white folks." Hardly four thousand, responded Laurie, laughing: maybe four hundred.

After the service, Del headed to the lobby. What he encountered still affects him.

"There's a line of people. All wanted to talk to me. 'Hey! My name is John. George told us he was bringing you. You need to be at our house Monday night at six thirty. Let me get you the address.' 'My name is Mary. Can you be at our house Tuesday at six o'clock?' I was booked for the next two weeks. *Dinner* for the next two weeks. I would go to these people's house and they would have brand-new clothes from Macy's and Nordstrom's for me. Shoes, clothes, hats. Then I would spend the night at their house. That was part of the ritual, part of their—"

At this point, Del, who had been talking with increasing fervor, broke down and sobbed.

When he gathered himself, he said through chokes, "*Real* Christians. They had no motive. It blew me away. They were unbelievably loving people. To invite you in their house and spend the night with their families. They don't know me from Adam. They knew my background. But they completely forgave me, like the Bible says. They did exactly what Christ would have done."

Months went by. Del remained employed by Atlas and clean from crack. He also continued some ties with Springfield Baptist, his sole connection to Black life. After escrow closed on the house he was living in, he moved to a "Christian rooming house" run by a teetotaling parishioner. He still rues that, despite her wishes, he stored beer in her refrigerator. One day, Springfield Baptist's head deacon asked Del to ride with him to San Francisco and visit his son in the hospital. He did not tell Del more than that. "When we got here, his son was dying of AIDS. He died a week after we left. I remember being very, very, very rude, very, very, very cruel. The man couldn't have weighed more than fifty pounds, and the only thing he could eat was ice cream. The doctor put this ice cream bar in his mouth," the dying man unable to use his hands. Del was furious that the deacon "would bring me into a room with someone with AIDS, some fag with AIDS. Then the deacon asked me, because I was sitting right next to the bed, 'Can you take the stick out of my son's mouth?' I said, 'Hell, no! I'm not touching nobody with AIDS.' It took me years to feel bad about it. That poor man."

Del also accepted an emotionally easier request, to drive a church busload of children to an amusement park north of Los Angeles. When, exhausted, he returned them around midnight, he made ready to leave quickly, knowing he had to be at work at six. "As I'm trying to sneak out the parking lot, pastor's wife says, 'Pastor wants to see you, Brother Seymour.' I said, 'Ohh *man*.'" The pastor loved to talk. "We go in, and he says, 'Brother Seymour, thank you *so* much for taking those kids down there. Here.' He hands me this envelope," half an inch thick. "I said, 'Pastor, what's this?' He says, 'That's your pay for taking the—' I said, 'No, brother. I'm doing this for the Lord.' He says, 'Take it.' We're passing the money back and forth. He said, 'Brother Seymour, *stop*! This is a business. Everybody gets paid.'"

"I thought that money went for the missions and the homeless and the sick. He said, 'No. This money for *us*. Take your money.' That was it. I was done."

Furthermore, Springfield Baptist kept stalling on baptizing him. Del mentioned his disappointment to George and his intention to attend First Baptist of Santa Maria again the following Sunday. Based on that news, George planned a surprise.

"They baptized me in front of three thousand people," said Del, the number an exaggeration, certainly. "He had gifts for me. He had flowers." Emotions ran so high and joyous, it might have seemed Del Seymour had found a new home.

He worked for the Hartshorns at least several months, said Laurie. Del did not recall how long it was but did know he no longer sought crack. "I was clean. I've been clean many times in my addiction. If you put yourself where there's no milk, you're not going to drink milk. Sooner or later, you'll get over it. That's why I believe so strongly in relocating. You can't live where the supply is." And, as far as he knew, San Luis Obispo had no crack.

Precisely because he was clean, Del decided to continue his truncated spiritual trip south. "I felt I was ready to handle a real city." He planned to drive to Los Angeles, transportation provided thanks to the Hartshorns. Laurie earlier persuaded or shamed George into giving Del his Subaru, among several cars he owned. Once Del's decision to leave became known, First Baptist of Santa Maria came through again, giving him an affectionate farewell, including a collection of money totaling close to $1,000.

Del drove off in the Subaru, heading south. He stopped for gas in Santa Barbara.

At the gas station, a "beautiful" woman approached him. She said she knew where to get some drugs and suggested they do so, then "kick back."

The curse, said Del, in talks he gives Narcotics Anonymous groups, is human nature. "We want to reward ourselves with the same stuff that did us in."

Del and the woman, a "dope prostitute" in his description, spent much of his First Baptist money on crack. They rented a room at a Motel 6. They got high. One day or more passed. Del told the woman he had to sleep but that she could do what she wanted. He gave her the rest of the stash. She left and sold it: to an undercover police officer. Del and the woman were arrested and taken to jail.

Del later calculated that, after leaving San Luis Obispo, he had relapsed within onc hour.

CHAPTER 20

HUSTLING

SOMETIME AROUND THE LATE 1990s, Del returned to the Tenderloin. Within his own crack epicenter, he did what he long had done to support his habit. He hustled. Del used variations of the word so often and so familiarly: "I had to hustle." "I was still hustling." "I would hustle." It seemed he was speaking about an old friend, Hustle.

"One of the original hustles," he said, was being known as the go-to guy, sitting outside on the steps, ready. "'Hey, man, I need a room I can rent for a couple of hours. Who do I go to?' That's the old Chicago hustle." It translated well to San Francisco. "You need this policeman to get off your ass in the Tenderloin. I'll go talk to him. You stole something from the store, and the man won't let you in the store no more. I'll see if I can negotiate you getting back in. Your landlord just pooped you out because whatever. Let me go talk to your landlord. But I charge for everything. A real hustler don't do *nothing* for free."

Del seemed stunned to be asked if he collected his fee before or after the hustle. "This is the Tenderloin!" Answer: before.

He learned his lesson as a child, he said smiling at the memory of "the chicken man," whom he called a Black version of comedian Red Skelton's character, Freddie the Freeloader. In the hot Chicago summer, the man carried a chicken on his shoulder. "He would go in front of a bar where everybody was standing outside smoking and said, 'Y'all want to see the chicken dance? Cost you a dime.' Then he would stand there. They'd say, 'Put the chicken down.'"

The man's response, "No dime, no show."

Once people put their money in a hat, the man put his chicken on the pavement. "The reason the chicken would dance was not that it was a talented chicken; it was because of the hot-ass concrete." Del did not realize the cruelty until later. It was the lesson that stuck. "No dime, no show."

As for Del's hustles in whatever city, he set his charges in part by a cost-benefit analysis. "Based on looking at you, what I could get from you. I had to do an assessment. How difficult is this going to be for me? What kinds of repercussions am I going to have to go through? How criminal this is? How much risk?" Hot items involved special risks. "Guns or whatever. Something just fell off the truck. I could be an accessory. Which is actually one of the least of my problems, because I would try to take the least risk I could."

"We're criminals," he said at another juncture. "We forge shit all the time. That's what I used to do best. I could forge a college diploma or immigration paper better than immigration. Top of the line!" About one of his prostitutes, he said, "My girl Sheila, she was into identity theft."

Sheila. She clearly meant much to Del. His daughters, however, were not fans. "The love of his life," said Deleana dryly. (Del has indeed called her that.) Regina began a singsong "Sheila, Sheila, Sheila," then added, "First time I met Sheila, I wanted to run her over with my car." But Del was smitten, and Sheila a major part of his life.

Around 2006, at the invitation of Glide's Rev. Cecil Williams, Del and Sheila attended the San Francisco premier of *The Pursuit of Happyness*, based on the book by Del's formerly homeless friend Chris Gardner, played by Will Smith. Del said he considered it just a movie until he and Sheila, returning to their apartment, walked down Ellis Street in front of Glide. "I broke out into tears, because I realized that 'movie' I just saw was not a movie. That was actual depiction of life."

AS FOR DEL'S OWN LIFE, none of his arrests, he said, was for hustling. In fact, hustling was a point of pride. Not for Del Seymour a cup and a plea, "Any spare change?" He might pick up discarded coins, he said, but begging, no. "I never panhandled a penny in my life." Nor, another point of pride, did he ever pawn any belongings, including his signature bling. No begging, no pawning. He hustled.

In the Bay Area, Del's legal hustles included working for several alarm companies, at least ten electrical companies through his IBEW union membership, and a number of plumbers, which he carefully named. Then he got entrepreneurial.

"I had my own plumbing company called Shitman Plumbing. People always laughed," he said, laughing himself. "It *was* Shitman Plumbing. Once I tell you my company's name, when your pipe busts in the middle of the night: 'A plumber, a plumber. Oh, Shitman!' That was a marketing ploy. You could only do it in San Francisco."

CHAPTER 21

THE SUMP PUMP CONNECTION

O F ALL THE PEOPLE WHO HELPED, or tried to help, Del overcome his addiction, perhaps the most unusually effective was a woman who never asked him about it or offered a word of advice.

Marie Duggan owned the fabled Italian restaurant Original Joe's, on Taylor Street in the Tenderloin. "We were doing some remodeling work in the banquet room," she said, "and he was hanging around." She figured he probably wanted to connect with her contractor, a Black man hiring other Black men. "I was going in and out. [Del] was a very friendly and engaging guy." They got to chatting. When she asked Del what he did, he told her he was an electrician and plumber. She filed the information away. "Probably something came up." The year was maybe 2000.

"Little by little, he started to help me out. One of our major problems, we had a sump pump downstairs. He knew about pumps. So, a sump pump would go, because a lot of debris would get in there or the motor would burn out. He'd pull it up." As Del and Marie knew, without a working sump pump, the restaurant would close.

"The more he and I got to know each other, the more I realized he was a very sharp guy done in by his demons and his addictions. It wasn't because he was dumb."

In degrees, Del told Marie, a hearty, amiable woman, about his past, including going to Catholic schools in Chicago, later being a paramedic. Although he had been "bombarded with life," as she put it, "he had stuff *in* him that made it possible for him to build."

Many of their conversations took place after Original Joe's official closing time. "He'd come in late, like at eleven o'clock. He'd say, 'What's up?' 'Go check the pump.' Then, 'Do you want some spaghetti?' All day he was doing whatever else he was doing, and then he'd come in and check."

Intentionally, Marie did not ask Del about the whatever else. "I tried to keep it positive. We were talking about things common to us. The pump. The leaks. We got to know each other more and more. I knew he wasn't totally clear of all his problems. He was always very polite and very on point, but sometimes I wouldn't see him for a couple of days. He wasn't living a nine-to-five life, I knew that. I think he mentioned there were drugs involved. He didn't go into it. I never put my arm around him and said, 'You really got to straighten up.' I *never* did that."

She added, speaking in the new Joe's (the original Original closed after a kitchen fire in 2007 and relocated to more upscale North Beach, where Marie ceded management to her adult children but convivially worked the dining room), "He always presented himself in a pretty good state, because I think he valued his position. Whatever he was going to do, he wasn't going to do it in front of me. And I wasn't cluing in on him as a drug addict or as a pimp or anything. I was very appreciative of his skills as a tradesman. I think what Del appreciated about me was that he could relate as a *normal* person." She figured "he had some semblance of normalcy at times during his life," but it needed to be restored, which she tried to do. "Call Del! We got a leak."

Del learned every inch, sound, and smell of Original Joe's, including the floor above the restaurant, which was an SRO, where Del also started making repairs. He also knew well the building's extended basement. Giving a private tour of it, Del said, pointing, "Ghosts often are over there." They make a whoosh sound, he said. Real fast, *whooooosh*. In fact, they terrified two maintenance women into quitting.

The ghosts did not bother him, he implied, but a few longtime employees did. They seemed upset Marie gave him, not them, keys to the building and that he alone could use petty cash for purchases. Racists, he said.

Marie shrugged at the allegation. "I knew there was a little friction here and there but not that it was racial. Not that I'm saying it wasn't racial," she added with a look. "I trusted him more than I trusted most people, let me tell you that much." To Del, the connection with Marie included feeling like part of her family.

Did her professional respect for him, the reintroduction of normalcy, save Del's life? No, she said. "I helped. I think he saved his own life. But what was provided for Del at Joe's was a safe place where he could go back to being a tradesman. Being able to ply regular skills, rather than these other skills. I didn't know a lot of this stuff, and I didn't look to know. We were operating on a common ground with common problems." The main one was indeed the sump pump. "I'm telling you, I'd be in water up to my ankles. And he was my guy that was going to fix that pump at eleven o'clock at night."

CHAPTER 22

ADVENTURES IN
CRIMINAL JUSTICE

I N HIS YEARS OF ADDICTION, Del's main arrests involved prostitution and drugs. According to San Francisco rap sheets from 2000 to 2004, the first of six noted arrests happened on April 10, 2000, on Ellis Street in the Tenderloin.[1] "POSS NARC CONTROLLED SUBSTANCE," it read. Oh, right, he said, examining the data. He was living in an SRO across from Glide Church. "Til they put me out."

On Ellis, "[I] sold some dope to a cop. It was a sting. I was walking back across the street, coming this way, and a white guy was coming this way. We're in the middle of the block, jaywalking. As I tried to sidestep, *he* sidestepped. I got the money in my hand. Everywhere I go, he heads towards me and tries to snatch the money. I pushed him in his chest and felt the badge, under his T-shirt on a chain. I still didn't realize he was a cop because everything was happening in nanoseconds. I'm thinking he's trying to rob me. Then the other guys come out of nowhere, because they saw me push him. They get me on the ground in the middle of the street. He said, 'This is *my* money. This is city of San Francisco money.' And it was. He wanted his money back so he could use it for evidence."

Part of the arrest was for the shove. "I think I pleaded guilty because there was a fine. Let's see," he said, looking at the sheet of paper. "This is the Municipal Court eleven three fifty [11350 on the rap sheet], Health and Safety felony. I plea-bargained." He was fined, he recalled, two or three thousand dollars.

"This one here," his finger moved down the page, "was on the corner of 6th and Market." The arrest involved another violation of the Health Code, as possession of drugs is listed. "I got arrested for possession, and I also had a warrant out for my arrest."

He moved on to the second page, an arrest in 2002 in the Mission District, about two miles from his usual Tenderloin locale. "I was running from police. They arrested me for a $181 warrant. They charged me $800." He interpreted the numerical shorthand, codes for resisting arrest reduced to disorderly conduct, a misdemeanor. "It was more or less fighting with the police but reduced."

So it went, next arrest at Turk and Taylor, by the same policeman who had arrested him multiple times. On the third page came a heavier charge, from June 18, 2003. "This is possession of base rock. That's different. Raw cocaine. That's a much higher case." During this period, Del said, he was arrested four or five times and jailed in one month.

The final arrest in the sheaf startled him: a 647 PC. "That's when I got arrested in jail." He had gone to visit one of his girlfriends, a prostitute, Zeena (a pseudonym), whom he was annoyed at for getting arrested in the first place. "She was in jail because she sold dope to a friend of mine who was a cop, an African American undercover I knew from the streets." She knew him too. "That pissed me off. He came up to my room, said, 'Man, I just got your girl. What's wrong with her stupid ass? She *knows* me.' He says, 'I kept *telling* her to get back,' because the camera was on the transaction. The other cops were getting ready to pounce, and he was trying to tell her, 'Don't come over here.' He came up to apologize to me for arresting my girl. He's saying, 'I'm so sorry.'"

To prepare for his jail visit, Del drank. "I was always drunk when I would visit. It's the only way I can handle going in jail. I've been in there so many times myself, I medicated to be able to *stand* being in that place."

Jail, he said at another juncture, was his breakdown. "Shelters, yeah, I didn't like it." But they offered the option—indeed, usually a command—to leave the next morning. Del made sure he realized that, telling himself, "When I get out of here in the morning, I'm not going to be here tomorrow night."

Of the lack of freedom in jail, he said, "It don't bother some people. It bothers me." To cope, Del developed a strategy. He got close to people in for a long time. "I can always say, 'I'm getting out next week.' They *hate* me." He also avoided being around prisoners who would be released the next day. "That depressed me."

Whenever in jail, he said, as in a hospital, he never wanted visitors, nor did he often visit anyone in jail. The exception was Zeena, "because she was always in jail."

This time, in the small visiting room, watched over by "two big old sheriff ladies," he and Zeena got into a fight. "She said I was with somebody or something like that. She got up to hit me. I got up, and I hit her first. In the jail." The two sheriffs reacted with opposite commands. One yelled, "Sit down!" while the other yelled, "Stand up and turn around!" Meanwhile, Zeena still tried to hit him. "So I'm fighting three women." Amid continued shouts both to sit down and stand up, Del said, "You all bitches need to make up your mind."

"When I used the word *B*'s to them, they went crazy. This one maced me; this one hit me in my neck. They drug me outside and put me in an elevator, took me down to the men's jail and booked me in there. They did not like that B word."

Some of Del's San Francisco arrests—he tallied fourteen—he attributed to the SFPD being out to get him. From his own descriptions of himself, he could be plenty annoying. "I fought the police all the time. I was doing my community activist 'Why you messing with me? You just arrested me two days ago.'" It did not endear him. "The police would sometimes go through the crowd, grab me, and leave fifty other people selling dope." He shook his head. "Thank God, I'm not in that culpable situation anymore."

And thank God, he might have added, for another part of the VA's Stand Down program. It brought together Superior Court judges from local counties to consider clearing pending criminal charges.

Del became rhapsodic, remembering the volunteer judges. "They take the day off and come out there and administer justice. You sign up and tell them all your charges. Then they go back to the courts and come back the next day with all the records, the bailiffs, the court clerks, the court reporter, and set up a courtroom at the Stand Down location."

Whatever year it was Del availed himself of the program, he was in big trouble, stemming from charges relating to drug sales for which he had not yet been arrested. In fact, knowing San Francisco's fugitive squad was looking for him, he had been hiding in a woman's apartment in the Tenderloin, at Ellis and Jones, feeling imprisoned.

Del managed to sneak to the Stand Down site in the East Bay, where he was assigned Alameda County judge Ronald Hyde, in Del's description "a very well-known, no-nonsense judge" and "maverick," as well as a "dinosaur" in terms of sexism. (Judge Hyde in 2003 was removed from the bench for "improper sexually explicit comments, manipulating a court docket to benefit a family member, and other misconduct.")[2] Del attributed Judge Hyde's difficulties to petty small-town conflicts.

"When I walked into his courtroom in Dublin [in Alameda County], I was sitting on seven active warrants. Possible seven prison sentences." In another telling, Del said it was three warrants. More significantly, he remembered Judge Hyde's surprising verdict on each one: "Dismissed."

"I walked out of there a completely free man. Jumping up in the air and all."

The next day, Del was back in the Tenderloin, carrying a bucket of tools and keys to Original Joe's and in plain view of "the fugitive guy," the county marshal from the probation department. "He looks for wanted felons. They drive through the Tenderloin all day. They only use three specific cars, which is stupid because we all know the car when it's coming."

"I'm still shaky, but I'm not tripping because I know I'm free and clear." The marshal's car, which Del had spotted a few blocks away, appeared. "He pulls up. We know each other. But he says, 'Are you Del Seymour?'

"I said, 'Dude, you know I'm Del Seymour. Why are you playing?'

"He says, 'What's your full name?'

"I'm standing there looking in the squad car, and he's got the book on his lap." The "book" included photographs of people being sought. "My picture's right there, big, in color."

Del's claim he had been cleared led to a testy exchange. The marshal pointed to Del's photograph. "He says, 'You bullshitting us, man. You're right here. We got three of your warrants: two no-bails and a hundred thousand dollars.'"

Del had no written exoneration and doubted it would been believed, given the possibility of forgery. But he insisted he had no more warrants.

"He says, 'Oh, yes you do. You need to come with us today. You know the drill.'" After the marshal drove him to Original Joe's to drop off his tools, Del was handcuffed and taken to 850 Bryant, a complex including San Francisco's main county jail.

There he was uncuffed and turned over to a probation officer, a "straight asshole" who lit into Del, saying "the bounty hunters told me you gave them some bullshit about you went to some court out in Dublin and they cleared you," adding that Del was always trying to con the police, then cuffed him again. "He walked me down and pushed me in the cell. He said, 'Besides all this, you're a fucking liar.' I said, 'Man, check! Check!' He said, 'I ain't never heard of no bullshit named Stand Down. You got three serious felonies.'"

Later, the same officer paid Del a surprise visit. "He came to my cell, said, 'I'm getting ready to retire, and I've never apologized to a prisoner in thirty years, but I'm going to do it right now. Everything you said was the truth.' He says, 'I'm sorry. I never heard of a justice system like what they did for veterans.'"

He added, recalled Del, the program was "'so preposterous, I didn't even entertain the idea. You've got three crimes that could put you in jail for twenty years and some judge dismissed it? Without a trial or anything?'

"I said, 'That's how we do it.'"

CHAPTER 23

DIFFERENCES OF OPINION

LIKE SEASONED WHITE HOUSE REPORTERS who speak of "their" seventh or eighth president, Del speaks of "his" sixth Tenderloin police captain in thirty plus years. Captain Teresa Ewins and Del clashed, at first.

"I remember the day she came down and going to a meeting, wanted to lock everybody up. The entire Tenderloin," Del said, smiling, as he addressed a graduation class of Code Tenderloin and an officer Captain Ewins sent to attend the event. "I said, 'Captain, it don't work that way. You can't lock us *all* up. C'mon, you ain't got room.' She saw what we go through down here. She saw the reason people stand on the corner selling crack, because they can't get into Twitter." Now, he said, she sent such people to Code Tenderloin. "She's been active in job recruitment in this community. She wants to see those folks out there off the corner but wants to see them working." He turned to the officer. "I want you to give her thanks for that." The audience applauded. Captain Ewins, Del added, was the first Tenderloin commander he had known who was "actually trying to do something positive."

Over the years, a cordial, if at times sparring relationship evolved between the two. They have spoken together at various San Francisco sites, including a church in Pacific Heights (Del was astounded it had valet parking) and crossed paths at Tenderloin events. In one community meeting of several dozen people, on the topic of safety, Del suggested store owners in the crowd go back to the old school way of doing things and take care of matters themselves, including by hiring security guards.

Captain Ewins, trim in her uniform, her blonde ponytail neatly pulled back, stood by, exuding confidence. When it was her turn to speak, she took Del on, saying private security was "a dangerous slope," in part because of insufficient background checks. If Tenderloin business owners and residents have a problem with a situation, she said, they should call her. "We'll meet." She also took Del on about a subject that loomed substantially in her work: drug dealing.

In his talk, Del had addressed the subject in a joking manner. "The Tenderloin is maybe not as nice-looking or nice-smelling as the Mission, but it sure in hell's a lot safer, because there's too many eyes watching. There's something I want to tell you about safety in the Tenderloin, and I hope the captain's not listening." He told her, "Close your ears," as the audience laughed and she smiled.

"I was involved in a lot of the shenanigans in the Tenderloin about twenty-six years, until I finally got enough sense to stop it. What most of you all don't know, on every block there's one guy who's paid to make sure that block is safe. His job is to keep folks like you," he addressed the mostly white audience, "from being assaulted or harassed. Because if you walked down that drug block and someone grabbed your camera or your phone or slapped you, *you're* going to call the police. You're going to call Teresa, which means that block's going to be shut down for one or two hours while she does her investigation. The drug dealers can't lose their money. So he pays the guy every shift to stand there and make sure all of you culturally different people walk down that street unmolested." In the Mission, he claimed, "you can be walking from your car to Valencia and two cats will jump out of their cars and snatch every i-product you got. Does not happen in the Tenderloin. We got too many eyes out here."

In response she said, with a raise of an eyebrow, if what Del said were true about lookouts monitoring Tenderloin streets, she would not need her hundred or more officers.

The mild exchange belied her considerably stronger feelings about drug dealers. This issue in particular she addressed later in her office, a few steps off the unadorned—close to shabby—Tenderloin police station lobby, where people in various modes of distress communicate through thick plastic windows and a fixed telephone.

Teresa Ewins saw the Tenderloin not as the neighborly we-help-each-other-out place Del sometimes conjured but instead as a repository of people who have "made so many bad decisions they give up. That's why sometimes they're here in the Tenderloin. [It] for many years has been considered the bottom of the barrel. If you're coming here using, you're coming here buying. You've run out of all ability to find it or afford it somewhere else."

Yet, Captain Ewins mentioned repeatedly that help often arrives via "relationships we build with people. A lot of times we find them places to stay; we find them jobs." Officers recently came across a woman and child in an alley, she said. The shelters being full, the officers pooled their own money to get the two a place to stay.

Officers also intervened similarly, Captain Ewins related, in a situation involving two parents and five children during a torrential downpour. "Both parents were addicts. They got them a couple nights at a hotel. The kids were healthy, probably a little more put together than the parents. We connected them with services. I think ultimately the kids were taken away from the parents because they couldn't deal with their addiction, which sometimes is a blessing, because they can always be reunited.

"We have a homeless car. Every morning they go out and check on everybody, which is important because a lot of people have medical issues. We have ambulances for people. We try to connect them with services at that point, waking people up." The Tenderloin station has gotten a lot of people into St. Anthony's or Glide or Hospitality House. "Those locations are the best thing the city has, because they're always there for people."

Officers and homeless people, she said, are often on a first-name basis. "It goes back to the relationship." A major problem, however, is that after the police connected people to services, people were "not showing up for their appointments, to get services they vitally need."

The reason they did not show up? "Addiction." To her, most bad paths led back to drugs.

A Santa Monica native, Teresa Ewins moved with her family to the East Bay when she was ten. She first noticed "seeing a lot of homeless-ness" as a teenager during a trip with her mother to Berkeley. "I was like, 'Oh, that's interesting. People kind of do what they want to do.' My mom was like, 'It's just wrong. This is the world. You have to be responsible for yourself and others.'"

Her daughter agrees, to a point. "If you're going to make a decision for yourself, it's one thing. But if it involves a child or being responsible for someone else, there needs to be a little more responsibility. Addiction is on top of that. I can talk to people about it, but I can't necessarily understand it, deep down, because I don't have that in my family. We have a bunch of drinkers. I've seen how that affected our family, but I can't imagine the narcotic part. I can't."

When Captain Ewins was offered the job as Tenderloin captain, a draw was the neighborhood's complication. "I like complicated. I like when there's issues we have to tackle and come up with maybe new ways of dealing with it." The police station itself is diverse, with "six transgender members in our department. I have the utmost respect for them."

She was also impressed by "amazing" police relationships with so many organizations and learned that building on those relationships was part of her job. "A lot of the issues are not necessarily police-related. It's really about how do we have conversations with people making the wrong decisions and trying to change their course. We have people that have thirty pages of crimes they've committed. Going to jail is somewhat of a Band-aid, because they're not prosecuting."

Since becoming Tenderloin captain, and after police work in the Mission District, among other San Francisco locations, Captain Ewins said she believes younger addicts came to San Francisco to get free services fast. "I think our willingness to be so open and giving in the city brings people here, and I don't think that's bad."

Homelessness, she said, is changing, with unsheltered people now living throughout the city yet concentrated in the Tenderloin, which itself is concentrated. "We're the densest district in such a small area, which brings complications but works itself out, for some reason. The SROs are very responsible and really try to make it a safe place for everyone. I work with them a lot. The Tenderloin is so different from any other district. I try to tell my bosses, it's very complicated; we have the most amount of services, the most amount of drug dealing, the most amount of SROs, the most amount of kids. We don't technically have schools, other than a private school, but we have a lot of day care and after-school programs. It's an interesting attempt to balance all that, especially when you go to get methadone and there's drug dealing right outside. Which is frustrating. How can we allow that to happen?"

Captain Ewins would arrest every dealer she could. "There are so many drug dealers, I wouldn't have cops on the street if we took on every single drug dealer, there's that many. It's organized crime. We start arresting them, they send more. They inundate the district. To make it unmanageable, basically." Dealers she knows and knows of are not local, she said. "None of them lives in the Tenderloin. It's mainly Oakland [and] Richmond they come from. They use BART or they bring their own vehicles."

Clearly, from her words and tone, she and Del do not see drug dealers in the same light.

His views about drug dealing remain in part pragmatic. Recently, while Del was talking to an acquaintance, a dealer walked by. "I say, 'Hey, you a little late for work.' Because she works this corner here," he said, pointing to an intersection at Taylor and Eddy. She says, 'Yeah, I know. I should have been here ten minutes ago.' We laugh about it. But it was *real*. You expect to see your dealer at a certain time. They have to be here like clockwork. All it takes is one time going somewhere else and it's better dope; you won't go back to your dealer."

In general, said Del, dealing wraps up the end of the afternoon. "All the hustles are closed by six. So why stay out here? The pawn shops are closed. The welfare department is closed. All the money sources are closed by five or six o'clock. Food stamps are closed, but you can still buy drugs with food stamps." Dealers then return to being a family. "First they go pick up the kids at child care," then head home. "This is a job. This is the thinking they're forced to do because they can't get in the Apple Store. I'm not trying to defend that lifestyle, but, yes, I am."

When asked about differences Del suggested the two had, Captain Ewins answered, "Maybe the idea that I have zero patience for drug dealing. I do think people that are addicted at times need to be forced to stop. I don't believe jail is necessarily a bad thing. There's a lot of people that have come up to us and said, 'Jail saved my life. Thank you for arresting me. I'm doing great now.' I think our system is broken a little bit as far as rehabilitation goes. When people go to jail, they should be agreeing not only to go to jail for the offense they've committed but also in an agreement of getting their GED [or] to learn a skill. When you come out of jail, you should actually feel confident in your ability to get a job."

She later added more praise for what in effect was for some people a jailbreak, an opportunity for them to get on "an even keel," adding, "Maybe their family will take them back so they can get them into programs and have a good life. [But] that break doesn't exist any longer." People are not in jail long enough, in her opinion. "We forget about our responsibility to the community. We've had guys that should have been in jail here, then [were] murdered in Oakland. We give so many excuses why people do things and not enough 'We got to save our communities.' Again, it goes back to what are we doing with people that are incarcerated. We're not getting them the mental healthcare they need and also not preparing them for a job."

Drug dealing, she said, makes for a dangerous life. "A lot of times people get killed. A lot of times they get beaten because either they sold too much or they didn't come through for the drug dealer. The majority of our homicides here have been drug-related. We get a lot of guns off the dealers. We get a lot of guns out of people's cars that are traveling through. This is the location everyone goes to, so when you steal something, you rob somebody, or you have a stolen car, they all come this way."

"Everyone always wants to talk about suspects and the hard times they've had in their lives, but no one really talks about the victims in the Tenderloin who *have* hard lives. Young kids who beat up people and rob them or barge into a store and fill a trash bag with loot. [They may have been] victims themselves in their lives, but it doesn't make it acceptable to victimize other people."

"The people Del is talking about, the homeless people or the people trying to go to our [detox] program, they can't, because every time they walk down the block, they get offered drugs. That's a victim, to me. Drug dealers are victimizing. They're victimizing the kids that have to see people shooting up constantly [or smell] that weird smoke [from crack] when they're walking down the street."

Yet she and her officers had similar conversations with dealers that Del did. "We approached drug dealers and asked, 'Would you rather have a job or continue selling drugs?' They're like, 'We want a job.'

'Okay, let's have a job fair. We'll get you a job.' So you give somebody the opportunity, but they don't necessarily have the ability to follow through. The idea of getting up at eight in the morning, going to a job, getting along with others, not smoking pot, and actually having that kind of lifestyle is difficult for people. Job preparation idea is not there."

In a later interview, she elaborated on one challenge, which Del knows well; dealers often have no other work experience. "What they've known their entire lives is how to sell drugs." She looked dismayed and said the "worst case" for her staff was a man now on parole, whose father brought him to the Tenderloin at the age of twelve to sell drugs. "That's all he knows." The situation is similar, she said, to long-term unhoused people. Living on the streets is maybe "their security blanket."

In the cauldron of the Tenderloin, where does Del fit?

She answered as if not for the first time. "Del is a good example of a person that got himself out. He's the first person that's going to admit his own mistakes. He doesn't make any excuses and doesn't allow anyone to give excuses either. He holds people accountable. Sometimes I don't agree on his approach. He can be really aggressive, and that can shut people off. When you talk about racism and bias, of course he gets very upset because he's seen all parts of it, whether it be city government or communities. He gets very worked up."

After two years heading the Tenderloin station, Captain Ewins was promoted to commander of the Muni Task Force, charged with assuring safety on San Francisco's transit system. "It was hard for me to leave," she said in her charmless new surroundings, which resembled her old ones. "The Tenderloin is unique in that you answer to so many different people. I miss that working relationship. Like Del. If Del was pissed, he would tell me. Then we'd talk it out or explain or change whatever we're doing. It's nice to have that other perspective outside the police department."

"[As for] the complexities of homelessness, there's so many different levels. Unfortunately, I think what we've been doing in the past is treating it as if it's at *one* level." The approach now, she said, is to assess differences, some problems being "more extreme than others.

"How do you get around California's laws in regard to you don't have to take medication? Finally we're looking at the fact that conservatorship may be a good answer for some people, which I completely agree with—because some people are not capable of keeping themselves safe, especially women. Women have, obviously, a much harder time, being on the street and being safe. There's some real horror stories. It's heartbreaking." She paused. "Having to exchange sex for a safe place to sleep, or a safe place to stay, to take a shower—rape is not out of the ordinary for a lot of women on the street, just the amount of violence associated with drugs in general. How do you finance your drug habit? Prostitution becomes involved. It's such a horrible place for women."

If unsheltered women exist who are not addicted to either alcohol or drugs, she added, "I haven't met them. There are some women that *used* to be users, as well as men, but they're still homeless. And keep in mind, what they tell me and what the truth is can vary, because they don't want to tell me they're using. You create relationships with these people and sometimes they don't want to disappoint you."

As for Del, she concluded, "He's a great advocate. Most people don't know how many people he's helped individually. He'll be hard on people because he has high expectations for them. He's done a lot of good."

CHAPTER 24

INVENTIONS

I N APRIL 2017, Del paused in his burgeoning efforts to expand Code Tenderloin and welcomed back to San Francisco his British friend, Shash Deshmukh. In fact, Shash returned in large part to see Del again and put their laptops together to work on Code Tenderloin's next steps. Whatever steps already had been made, Del credited to Shash, to Shash's embarrassment. Whenever Shash congratulated Del on whatever piece of news, Del wrote back, in capital letters, "YOU CREATED THIS!"

Shash downplayed his role. "In starting a company, it's not the idea, it's the execution." He added, "If I wasn't there, there'd be someone else," but he added, "When I make a commitment to something, I'm pretty OCD about it. Like this is my vacation, but I'm here. I want to do something, even if it's small, because it works. I've met the people." Blushing, he turned to Del. "I'm not a religious person, but I firmly believe you're doing God's work."

Shash continued to wonder how San Franciscans adapted themselves to the undiminished homelessness in their midst, especially on sidewalks. "It may have happened incrementally," he said softly. "I get why people adopted strange scenarios of walking diagonally or dodging things. But at what point do you actually say, 'No, this is wrong'?"

The situation weighed heavily on how he compared his and Del's enterprises. "Look at us now!" he said to Del, as they opened their laptops for work. "Three years down the line, I did my fancy schmancy, but what have I got to show for it? Created six jobs, made a product—which now is closed down. But you, Del, took a little bit of the ideas we talked about, and in the last three years you got eighty people jobs. *Real* jobs, not just start-uppy jobs. These people woke up with a different life." He added with affection, "You tell me who's more successful."

A MUCH EARLIER ENTERPRISE of Del's has eluded success, at least so far. He, among other people, was living in San Francisco's Transbay Terminal, then a bus depot. The benches served as beds. Because Del was addicted at the time, it is not clear when he set to work scribbling an idea—perhaps wildly lucrative—on scraps of paper. Years later, his voice holding a note of challenge, he pulled newspaper articles decades old from a folder. "That's my invention. Sit back and put your seatbelt on. I, Del Seymour, invented the OnStar system." Go ahead and smile, he said, but look at the clippings.

The first, from the *San Francisco Chronicle*, in the popular Herb Caen column, is dated December 15, 1992. "SF's Del Seymour has a patent pending on a four hundred dollar anti-carjacking device that can be activated by telephone, whereupon a siren sounds and a voice commands the carjacker to 'Leave immediately.' . . . Seymour has the financing, some of it from the Small Business Administration, and hopes to market the gadget early next year."

The front page of a January 1993 *Oakland Tribune* featured the banner "Foiling Carjackers" and a photograph of Del, mustachioed. "Del Seymour Installs an Anti-Carjacking Device." Del's invention, stated the article, "belongs to that rare class of gadgets created solely in response to carjackings. Alarm installer Del Seymour invented it after a carjacking last year left him too scared to ride in a car."

The carjacking occurred one night outside a liquor store in West Oakland. With a laugh of sorts, Del said he had been involved in so many dangerous dramas, especially involving drugs, that having his van stolen at gunpoint "was not the worst thing that happened to me that day."

Police got word of the theft—Del doubted, considering his outstanding arrest warrants, it was he who alerted them—and chased the van some sixty miles, to the town of Dixon. There it flipped off the road and rolled several times. At some point the driver flew out a window and died. In the glove compartment, police found a DMV license issued to Deleano Seymour.

Next of kin was traced to Del's wife, Lachelle. The coroner called to inform her Del had died. Word spread. Knowing nothing of the chase or the driver's death, Del had his own concerns. "I was hiding from everybody." After a couple weeks, however, he made his way to Oakland's DMV to replace his license. In the loud, cavernous place, a woman's voice suddenly screamed his name over the noise. The voice came from a sister-in-law, who ran up to him and shouted, "You're dead!" She told him the entire family thought he had been killed in an accident, with one friend so distraught that he had not eaten.

The incident led Del to figure out what to do if someone tried to carjack him again. Consequently, he said, "I invented the OnStar system. In the Tenderloin."

As his invention progressed, Del received grant money from the Urban League, the Black Chamber of Commerce, and the city of San Francisco. "Mayor Frank Jordan gave me a big-ass check, this big," said Del, holding his arms wide. The amount eludes him: $10,000 or $100,000? He shrugged. Doesn't matter, at least now.

The invention—"100 percent my technology" —came to the attention of General Motors. "To make the story long, I was flying back and forth to Florida, dealing with their engineers [who] approached me to buy the technology." At the time, he said, Florida was a center of rental car carjacking. "I gave them all the information. I was young and dumb. Or younger and dumber. They wined and dined me, brought prostitutes every night to the room. I was staying in a three-room suite on top of the Hyatt in Fort Lauderdale. Oh, they knew what they were doing. I'm the one didn't know what I was doing." (And, added Deleana and Regina later, the story would have ended differently had their father not been on drugs, smart as he is.)

Del spent his grant money on production. "Paying developers, photographers, to prepare the projects to get the prototype boards made and all that." He realized GM knew he could not finance full production. "So you got this system and you ain't got enough money. I'm General Motors. What I do, I *steal* your system. *All* companies do this." Del assumed GM planned to take a dollar off every system it sold and save it to pay him off when he sued. He did get a lawyer, with the unforgettable name of John F. Kennedy, but Kennedy, who had his own issues, never filed a lawsuit and later committed suicide.

As Del summarized his situation with General Motors, "They weren't interested, but three years later my device comes out in their cars." This from *Wikipedia*: "OnStar was formed in 1996 as a collaboration between GM, Electronic Data Systems and Hughes Electronics Corporation."[1]

Del gave up fighting but continues to hope someday he will be compensated.

CHAPTER 25

A BUSINESS ADDRESS

AS VIRTUALLY ANY urban business owner will attest, especially the owner of a business with a street-level entrance, local homelessness and the panoply of conditions associated with it constitute major challenges. In San Francisco, at one end of the equation, owners of hotels and restaurants that cater to tourists are upset because the tourists are upset: aghast at witnessing incoherent wraiths, or repulsed by filth and open drug use, or frightened by angry and seemingly insane behavior, perhaps all of the above. The tourists go home, vowing not to return.

In neighborhoods where tourists less frequently venture, homelessness may take on a more intimate character. The same raggedy-looking man slumps over a coffee shop table evening after evening, until closing time. A woman in apparent distress squats by a shop door, her bundles nearby. A specter of a man lost to himself wanders the middle of a street, yelling. In the Tenderloin, multiply such scenes, add drug dealing, not necessarily by people who are homeless but by people who prey on those who are.

To cope, some small businesses joined forces. One example, the Tenderloin's Larkin Street Association in May 2017 invited Del to address its members about his expertise. Del, of course, planned to promote Code Tenderloin.

While ten or so people, mostly middle-aged white men, sat at a long table in a Larkin Street restaurant, while employees in the background prepped lunch, Del introduced himself and Tenderloin dilemmas with almost brutal candor. He started with his familiar riffs: of arriving in

San Francisco on a highway one day, soon living under it, of his addiction and homelessness. He went on almost in a cadence. "I've laid on every sidewalk in the Tenderloin. I've been arrested fourteen times by the San Francisco police for drug sales. So I know a little bit about what I'm talking about."

Addressing the Larkin Street group, he continued, "When I kind of got my act together about eight or nine years ago, I decided to try to give back some of the resources I took *out* of this community for those mad eighteen years I spent going to jail, going to court, fighting with the police, getting shot, getting stabbed."

Del's audience looked riveted. After listing his current endeavors, from the walking tours and Code Tenderloin to being on various boards of nonprofits, Del turned the subject to local business. "A lot of the things I'm trying to do is make this a neighborhood not to avoid." Recognizing a recent spate of violence there, he said the "immigration department" had eliminated a lot of "South American drug dealers" around Larkin, but violence was coming from a new group hawking a "dirty nasty heroin" fourteen times cheaper than what heroin had previously cost. "It's causing a reaction of people not getting high. They're getting crazy. So they're going back to the dope dealer. That's where the fights and the murders and the massive trauma injuries are coming from. We're trying to work with the Department of Public Health to educate people more about their choices. This may sound silly, but we got to keep it real. They're actually encouraging the people that *are* on heroin to try to stay with [their] dealer," that is, to trust their usual source.

A related problem, Del said, is that addicts without homes do not want to go to shelters because they can't shoot up there. They prefer putting up a tent. The combination of tents and cheap "dirty nasty heroin," said Del, with detail his audience may not have expected, "makes the poop problem worse, because 90 percent of the time, heroin is cut with fentanyl. They mix fentanyl with mannitol, which [is] baby laxatives. So when you put that needle in your arm about halfway down, you got to poop right now. If this is going in, that's coming out." Apologies for talking about the matter in a restaurant, he said.

The discussion moved to violence. The Tenderloin contains more than just the people you see on the street, he said. "About 70 percent of people, you never see. Little old ladies and little old men, like me, hiding up in their rooms, terrified to come out on the street. They're sending their neighbors to the store, who're ripping them off, because they send them with two dollars," and are told the item cost three dollars. Do not forget the frightened elderly, he said. "We got to give the Tenderloin back to those folks. This is their neighborhood."

With that, Del segued again to Code Tenderloin, saying with emotion, "[People I try to reach] don't know how to come in here and ask for a job because they can't pass the interview." He imitated a person slouching, hat on sideways. "'Man, you can't wear your hat sideways when you're in an interview!'" He said he coached new employees how to behave, how to talk to the boss, and how to leave tough street talk behind.

If a boss gives an insulting command, like telling someone hired for another job to sweep the floor, Del's counsel is to "do whatever silly thing he asks," wait a couple hours, then address the matter with the boss. Other lessons: "Keep the street swagger, but don't bring it to work. When you get off work, leave that work there. Don't go home, 'Man, the boss did this.' Because in the morning, you're really pissed off."

Finally, he urged the merchants to hire Code Tenderloin graduates. "You don't have to break down your standards whatsoever. My people will be at your standards. Then you got me to be there for you, different than hiring someone off the street. I'm their mama, their daddy, their probation officer. I'm all of that. And they know it."

Del noted that Code Tenderloin graduates seeking work are scared to approach a non-Black business. "They automatically figure, 'Well, they're not going to hire Black people.' I'm keeping it real. It's a cultural fear we have that we're trying to break." He suggested if any Larkin Street businesses opened their doors to meet Code Tenderloin students Del would introduce them to, business managers would see "how remarkable they are," and those students in turn might be able to recognize potential places of work. Half his battle, he said, was trying to make Code Tenderloin students believe someone would hire them for a good straight job.

To a question about fund-raising, Del's answer included a message he would repeat for years. "We are very frugal. We work our butts off with what we got. We're really good stewards of money. We don't splurge on anything. Our buck goes a long way, man."

Those bucks would increase enormously. At the time, Del also told the group that Code Tenderloin had mostly volunteers, along with "1.75 employees." That number would increase enormously too.

CHAPTER 26

AN ALLY AT THE HILTON

WHEN JO LICATA ARRIVED in San Francisco in the mid-1970s to work at the new headquarters of Hawaii-based Dillingham Corporation, every day on her commute she saw men she assumed were homeless.

Both of them.

"One was an evangelical minister with a Bible, and he was constantly at a high pitch, admonishing people." The other "gentleman," as she referred to him, had no legs, sat on a wheeled cart, and sold pencils in front of a department store.

Fast-forward to 1988. Jo began a job in community relations at the artfully misnamed Hilton San Francisco Union Square, which stands in the Tenderloin, blocks from Union Square. Across the street is Glide Church, with its many-in-need clientele who sleep on sidewalks fronting the church. (An unspoken rule one Tenderloin police captain did not know, to alarming effect, is that Glide's sidewalks are sacrosanct for the desperate. People should not be rousted from sleep and made to move.)

Jo knew things had changed since the 1970s. "There were certainly more people living on the street. People who looked like they were using drugs, who seemed non compos mentis, really out of it."

To her, the Hilton was out of it in another way. "Here we are, the largest hotel on the West Coast. We have nonprofit social service agencies all around us. Tenderloin Neighborhood Development [Corporation] is starting to grow. St. Anthony's is having a bigger voice in the neighborhood. Glide is certainly getting national if not international recognition. What are *we* doing? Our reputation as a business was sort of a corporate monolith. It didn't seem like we were a good neighbor."

Jo, a large, smiling, pale woman nearing retirement, expounded in her subterranean office, the walls covered with testimonials praising her work. The impetus to be a good Tenderloin neighbor came from the Union Square Hilton's general manager, "very progressive in his thinking," who tapped her to become the hotel's first community projects manager. Having already organized volunteer events, Jo was delighted at the assignment. She summarized it: "Go out there. Do stuff. Tell us what you think is right."

Immediately, she introduced herself to various like-minded people. "My first project, I think, was putting together volunteers to serve lunch and dinner at Glide." Her volunteers soon helped out at homeless shelters, including one for women. "We used to go there once a month, play bingo with the ladies, bring and serve dinner, and have dinner with them. We would see them graduate and finally get into supportive housing or get out on their own."

"Pretty soon we got a reputation as not just sitting there on the corner." Despite her modest budget, Jo got the Hilton to sponsor fund-raisers such as a community pool toss. She sent the hotel's maintenance team to paint and renovate schools. "I saw what groups needed." Pointing out her door, she said, "You see we're here on the garage level. We're also on the loading dock level. I saw things going out of the hotel like furniture and mattresses [headed to the dump]."

After much effort and many calls, Jo found recipients to retrieve the bounty. Eventually, she connected with "a like-minded concierge at the Marriott. We're the two biggest hotels. We got together and said, 'If our hotels have stuff to give away, let's go to all the other hotels and see if we can work with them.' That's how the Hotel/Non-Profit Collaborative got started."

Her program works in two directions. The hotels get a tax write-off for their donations. "[In turn,] the organization gets a needed product. And I mean wonderful furniture, china, glassware, linen. Sometimes a hotel just changes the design. Things have been languishing in storerooms and all of a sudden people say, 'Get rid of this stuff!'"

Much goes to programs that help the unhoused. Jo sends used sheets and towels to the Next Door shelter on Polk Street. "Glide Housing is picking up some linens this week. We have donated to Delancey Street, to shelter programs, to the chef's program at Episcopal Services."

Thanks to Jo, the Hilton became the first corporate sponsor of a now defunct anti-trafficking organization, SAGE (Strategic Alliance against Global Exploitation). "We worked for a while with the vice squad. A lot of women in prostitution were being exploited by families and by their pimps, and a lot of them wanted to get out and had no way out. *No* way out." She has donated to San Francisco Safe House for Women for former prostitutes and heard "horrendous" stories. "I didn't know young girls are often put into prostitution by their families. And their boyfriends." She added sardonically, "Aren't they wonderful."

Working late at the Hilton, she also saw some guests bring in with them women she believed were prostitutes. There was nothing she could do about that, she realized.

Of all Hilton contributions, perhaps the most consistent has been food. "Every day San Francisco Food Runners is here. They pick up food that's remaindered from our Grab 'n Go restaurant. Sandwiches, entrée salads. We don't waste food. If there's food left over from functions, we donate that. Glide is a recipient of a *lot* of food from us." The list goes on. "This past weekend we donated hot dogs and buns for the Tenderloin Family Fair. Every holiday we donate dinners for Safe House. We donate box lunches for veterans' events. We just donated canapés for a senior event. We do a lot."

Word of Jo Licata's outreach reached Del Seymour.

One day he appeared at her crammed office and introduced himself. "He told me what he was doing." The subject centered on finding Hilton jobs for Code Tenderloin graduates. In their conversation, Jo told Del the Hilton did hire graduates of various job programs. "But one of the problems was that people will go through a program, they're given a job, then they're kind of let on their own. I said, 'We didn't see much success with that.' He said, 'That's right.' I said, 'Why is this happening? We really want to help people get back on track.'"

She added, almost in a whisper, "They're not used to being successful. They're not used to having that money. And nobody was following up to see how they were doing. We would have people come in, and they hadn't worked for a while. They would work in culinary or something, and they'd come back down to me two days later. 'Your chef doesn't know what he's doing.'" Such complaints clearly masked other issues.

Jo would respond, "Technique we can teach you. The recipes we can teach you. But what we can't teach you is how to be a team member. Regardless of what you think, the chef is in charge. You follow the instructions to the best of your ability and do your job.' That was a different concept for them. Simple things, like getting to work on time. Del knew all this stuff I had been struggling with. I was impressed."

"I was so taken with him right from the beginning; we established this friendship," she said and laughed. "I work with him as much as possible." Initially, she got the Hilton to pay him to address national salespeople. "He has such a compelling story." She pointed to various piles of goods, including clothing. "A lot of the stuff in here I'm saving for Del. He'll come occasionally and pick things up."

After years of Jo's largesse, Del agreed to take part in her benefit stunt for Outward Bound. It involved being harnessed as if into a parachute and dropped down the side of the Hilton, forty-six stories high. The stunt proved frightening. "The wind was blowing, and . . ." Jo paused. "He didn't go straight down. Afterwards he comes to my office. He says, 'You no longer get an immediate yes from me!'"

Jo glanced around her office, at the numerous plaques, proclamations, and framed certificates of thanks, many mentioning her efforts to combat homelessness. "I have no wisdom about this," she said softly. "I just know we need a type of leadership here in the city that will recognize this is an emergency and desperate times. The Navigation Centers are helping somewhat, but we still have way too many people on the street. And making sure there's a safety net for people who are almost there, especially women and children. They're so vulnerable. There shouldn't be any reason to see children on the street. [Homelessness] does affect us. It's a scourge. It's a waste of human life. You do the best you can."

CHAPTER 27

CONFRONTATION

S EVERAL YEARS INTO the Tenderloin Walking Tours, journalist Leslie Katz interviewed Del for the giveaway newspaper, *San Francisco Examiner* in 2013. "I slipped and made a mistake, talking to her as a friend rather than as an interviewee. I *know* better. 'Well, she's not going to put that in there. She *knows* the streets and she knows better than put something like that.'"

The first sentence in the article, "Walking the 'Loin," reads: "Leading a tour of San Francisco's Tenderloin, Del Seymour shows where heroin dealers do business (under trees), where fences wait for hot goods (near a BART station exit) and where women wearing black sell crack (at Turk and Taylor streets)."[1]

That sentence hit the Tenderloin hard, particularly its young women dealers.

"The kids didn't like that at all," said Del. "It gave away some of our neighborhood things that we, as a code, don't give away. That the girls standing on Turk and Taylor are selling drugs for the guys. And they're all dressed in black because if you buy some drugs and then go tell the police, 'I just bought some drugs from a girl dressed in black on the corner of Turk and Taylor,' police roll up . . . twenty-five girls dressed in black. They can't do anything. They *sure* can't take it to court. Because you say, 'Your Honor, there was also twenty-four other women in black so why did they pick me out?'"

"That was one time I felt a little threatened, even though they knew who I was and they know I ain't no joke either. They stopped me in the middle of the street and says, 'We need to talk. Right now.'

"I says, 'Well, I'll . . .'

"'No. We need to talk right now, Bro. What the fuck is wrong with you?'

"I said, 'That was not supposed to come out like that.' I fubbed a little bit. I said, 'My agreement was that the journalist would not publish what she and I personally talked about.' They backed down. Then that's when the conversation started about jobs."

First, the women demanded to know what Del told his white tourists, whom they had seen traipsing behind him through their streets. "That's when they say, 'Why didn't you tell them we don't want to be out here? Why didn't you tell them we are dodging the police? Why didn't you tell them we need to put Pampers on our babies just like they need to? Why didn't you tell them we got to pay rent just like they need to, but we can't get a job? No one will hire us.'"

Among the women who confronted Del, one stands out. Del described her as someone who could be on the cover of any magazine. "She is a dark-skinned Beyoncé. One of the most beautiful girls you've ever seen in the Tenderloin." She was about twenty-eight, he said. "She's been out here maybe ten years."

Her story still moves him, of her going into a downtown Apple store to apply for whatever job she might get, seeing nobody who in any way looked like her, and feeling unwelcome, no matter that she herself used an iPhone. She simply left.

"She was *the* person who inspired me. She's the reason for Code Tenderloin."

In fact, during some of his tours, there she is, on the corner. Del will introduce her as the reason for Code Tenderloin. "Then she'll speak to us a little bit."

Whether the tourists guess why she stands on the corner is a matter Del does not address. He knows, though. "She's still selling drugs. She slowed down a lot because she got indicted." A federal indictment had come months earlier, he said. "She's not ready yet financially, because she makes a lot of money. It would be quite a sacrifice for her to change her careers. *She's* the boss. She probably clears $500 a day." Del figured she herself is not selling drugs but oversees people doing so.

If she ever wants to join the organization she inspired, though, Del is ready to welcome her.

CHAPTER 28

AN EVICTION AND A STABBING

OF ALL THE TIMES DEL HAS BEEN EVICTED ("It's been a bunch," he said), one stands out. He and his girlfriend Zeena were living in a room above Original Joe's restaurant on Taylor Street, thanks to his connection with Marie Duggan. He and Zeena had a fractious relationship. "We used to fight upstairs all the time," Del said. They also fought in the building's basement and on the street, not to mention in jail.

In 2003, or thereabouts, Del received an eviction notice for nonpayment of rent. As he knew, San Francisco evictions—at least absent acts of violence involving residents—took ninety days. "I never told her we were getting evicted, those whole ninety days. She kept asking, 'Are we okay with rent? Do you need me to go hustle some money?'" I said, 'No. We're okay.'"

They were not. Del relied on "a last-minute plan which never came to fruition," he said. "Because I was using then, heavily, when I had the money, I wouldn't do it right. I kept figuring, when it gets close to that day, I'll go out and get a bunch of money and take care of it. When the guy knocked on that door that morning, she said, 'Who in the hell is knocking on the door this early?' I already knew. That was her first notice we were getting evicted."

When Zeena realized what was happening, she asked, "Where are we going to go?"

Del's response still pains him. "I said, 'I don't know where *you're* going to go. I'm going somewhere.'" They went downstairs. Del took off. "She stood on this corner yelling at me. 'You motherfucker!' I can hear it all the way down to Market Street. We still talk about it when we talk, because it was real hurtful to her." He added, "We both treated each other bad, [but] that was the epitome of treating somebody bad."

Painful as that memory was, Zeena also figured in a story he told earlier, as a joke. He said he was in the Tenderloin, leading "about thirty tourists from England or somewhere" on a walking tour. "One of my ex-girls, prostitutes, she's laying on the sidewalk, completely bad shape." It was Zeena. "As we're walking by, I'm trying to ignore her. Then she comes out of her stupor and looks up. She says, 'There's my husband!' She's pointing at me. And she sees the group and says, 'I bet he didn't tell you that when we was together, he cheated on me with everyone in the Tenderloin, including two dogs and a cat.'

"I turned to her and said, 'Zeena, the cat was lying.' The group just fell out."

Now he laughed.

In all the time Del spent in the Original Joe's building, fixing the sump pump for Marie Duggan, living upstairs with or without Zeena, then, post-addiction, holding Code Tenderloin classes in the Piano Fight areas and hosting various events there, such as a luncheon for veterans, the building nonetheless contained memory of his cruelty to Zeena. "I always think of that day. Out of everything that happened in this building, that was the worst."

AFTER KICKING AROUND THE BAY AREA and other parts of California for years and getting kicked out of countless places for years, Del got his own place for the first time in a long while. Granted, the SoMa (South of Market) stucco building at 1080 Howard Street, off 7th Street in a semi-industrial mixed-use area of San Francisco, is not outwardly impressive. Three stories, a shop on the ground floor. But in a way, the small kitchen-less apartment was hallowed ground. And it came with a monthly rent reduction of fifty dollars or so in exchange for Del's being "more or less site manager," he recalled.

Swords to Plowshares had stepped up yet again to help. Thanks also to Swords, Del received money to furnish the place. His first night there still makes him glow. "Oh, it was very emotional and wonderful." The reason was basic. "I had my own key that no one could take away from me. Because I was getting put out of all these other hotels, on the whim or wham of the manager."

Del later disclosed that in his first nights in this, his own apartment, he did as many formerly homeless people do: despite having a bed, he slept on the floor.

The Howard Street building manager later told Del of another available apartment, one with a kitchen. "Of course, I would jump at that." The building was located at Bush and Hyde Streets, an area north of the Tenderloin sometimes dubbed, waggishly, the Tendernob, more often called Lower Nob Hill, as distinguished from Nob Hill itself. Del shared his new apartment with two long-time girlfriends, Sheila and Jasmine, if not at the same time.

One day, he and Jasmine got into an altercation. She was high, he was drunk, and, for whatever reason, she attacked him. "She stabbed me and ran." Del passed out.

When he woke, he was lying in what he figured was half an inch of blood and losing more. "I fought for my *life* in that room." He staggered outside. Serendipitously, the apartment building stood across the street from St. Francis Memorial Hospital.

"I crawled on my hands and knees. I couldn't walk. I left a blood trail all the way across the street. People actually looked at me like I was a drunk. Because I was so exhausted, so drained, I said, 'I'm going to lay here for a little while, and then I'll get up.' I put my hands down, and I could hear the flapping of the blood. I said, 'I got to get out of here. I'm dead.' The security guard who was standing outside smoking a cigarette saw me in the middle of the street and ran out and put me in something, I don't know what. A block away, I would be dead. My blood pressure was down to twenty six over eighteen. Doctor said, 'Five more minutes, we would not have to deal with you.'"

That night, Del underwent surgery. "About a week later, they did another real serious operation. I wanted to go home. The doctor says, 'You can't go home until you can walk up a flight of steps.'" Using a walker, Del tried but could not even reach the steps, instead falling in the hallway. He remained hospitalized three weeks, his mood bitter.

Police interviewed him repeatedly. "I had cops and cops and cops." From the beginning, Del wanted to prosecute Jasmine. "I never had to think about it. The cops said, 'We go through all this, you *are* going to prosecute.'" He reassured them. "She wanted to kill me. She had murder in her eyes."

But Jasmine had vanished.

In the course of the police interviews, an arrangement was worked out. If and when he was in touch with Jasmine again, he would let them know. The homicide detective gave Del his card, told him to call him anytime, day or night.

About half a year after the stabbing, Jasmine phoned, acting as if nothing had happened. "She just called: 'Hey, what's up? I want to see you. Where you are? Let's go get high.'"

Del was not getting high at that point but acted agreeably. He arranged to meet her back at the Hyde Street apartment in fifteen minutes. He then called the homicide detective. "He says, 'We'll be there. You come on over.'"

When Del's cab arrived, police had surrounded the area. Jasmine was lying handcuffed on the ground. "She said, 'Del, what are they *doing*? Tell them to take these handcuffs off.'

"I said, 'You done, girl.'

"'What are you talking about? I didn't do nothing to you.'"

As promised, Del pursued the charge of attempted murder to trial. Complicating the dynamics further, Jasmine, he said, belonged to a gang family in the often rough Bayview district of San Francisco. "Her whole gang threatened my life. They were going to kill me." It did not matter that Jasmine had almost killed him, he said. Their view was, why would a pimp prosecute? And so what if he were stabbed? It just means she won that time.

From the stabbing to the trial, Del figured about two years went by, Jasmine in custody throughout. By the time the trial started, her family's threats had not abated.

"I went in like I was the Cosa Nostra," escorted by court marshals, while most of Jasmine's family glared at him ("like 'We can't wait to get your ass,'" he said). The family was not completely united, though. "Her sister was one of my girls also. Even in court, she was always on my side."

Jasmine's lawyer planned for her to plead self-defense.

"The prosecutor had these colorful graphics of the wound, big charts with the blood all over the walls. He came in with a *very* well-prepared case. He had *every*thing. Close-ups of the blood, the operation, me in the hospital with tubes coming all out. The defense still was saying, 'How could a pimp claim self-defense?'"

"I'm a very colorful storyteller sometimes. When it came for me to testify, I got into maybe thirty seconds of the story, and the defense guy came up and says, 'We want to sidebar.'" He offered a deal. "Because he *knew* the jury was believing everything I was saying."

Jasmine was sentenced to five years for aggravated assault. She served her full time, released after three years, having served the first two in pretrial custody.

Watching her being led off back to jail following the plea deal, Del had an epiphany. He did not want to pimp anymore. Actually, the case brought on a second epiphany many years later, also involving Jasmine.

"She and I have talked. I've admitted to her I don't know what happened that day." He does not recall whether he hit her first or, as she charged, tried to strangle her. Therefore, if her assault conviction came up when she applied for a program or a job, Del told her he was ready to say he was not sure what happened. Furthermore, if the trial were held today, he told her, there is a good chance he would not prosecute.

CHAPTER 29

THE SEARCH

SITTING AT A RESTAURANT patio table in Fairfield, California, Del's daughters Regina and Deleana got deeper and more painfully into reminiscence, trying to figure when a certain wrenching event happened. Both women had young children, so could it have been in the late 1990s? Somewhere around there?

"He stayed with me for a little while," said Deleana, calculating that happened off and on between about 1996 and 2000. She turned to Regina. "Did he ever live with you?"

"No. He would just come to my house and detox."

Deleana adjusted her calculations from "a little while" to "quite a while," recalling. "He would go back and forth, but he would do too much with the drugs, and I'm, like, 'I can't have you here.' When somebody's on crack really bad, there's an awful smell that comes out of their pores. He would have some good times and some bad times. When he was having good times, I'm, like, 'You could stay here.' Because he would help me with the kids." Her daughterly dance, however, proved complicated. "He kept living with me and putting me through stuff. Then I had a *huge* situation where I had an ex who tried to kill me."

Del stayed to help. But, Deleana said, "[he] would make my trauma worse because I [would] end up having to take care of him. He started driving a cab in Vallejo, and I'm, like, 'That's the worst thing for you to do. That cab life is all over the drugs, and you're in here with my kids.' Because he'd keep my kids for me during the day and drive the cab at night." When he got "so deep into drugs," she reluctantly told him to leave. "Regardless of what he does, he's still my dad. That's hard for a daughter to say: 'I got to kick you out of my house.' And you don't have anywhere to go."

Regina remembered, "One thing he always did is try to hide how bad he was [from] us. When he was staying with her," she said with a glance at her sister, "he would try to make it look like he wasn't really that far gone." Whether far gone or not, she said, "even when he was on drugs really bad, one thing you could always say is he never stole. He wasn't like the drug addict you had to watch at your house. He kind of always held his own."

Del's addiction also had an inadvertently positive affect on the sisters: drugs appeal to neither. They spoke almost in unison. Said Regina, "We were *not* in the least bit interested."

"*Zero* desire to ever even try a drug for me," confirmed Deleana. "No D.A.R.E. for us. We lived D.A.R.E."

When she saw Del in the period she called his worst, "I was at *my* worst." Only three days after she told her father to leave, while assuring him her ex would not harm her, the ex broke into her house, held her at gunpoint, and attacked her. "My dad knew about this. He probably still holds a lot of guilt for it because he stayed with me a lot during the stalking period."

Deleana's decision for Del to leave, telling him she would be safe, matches her longtime family role: strong daughter. "Even going through everything I was going through, I was probably looked at as, because I was older, the stronger one."

"One year older," said Regina, shaking her head. She felt Deleana knew more about their father's ups and downs than she did because of their being "a lot closer." "This is his twin," Regina said, pointing to her sister. "They read everything. Even to this day, they have a competition on who read the news story first. He'll call her and try to tell her about something he saw on the news."

Deleana laughed. "It frustrates him, and I get enjoyment because he's not scooped me yet."

Regina steers clear of such contests. "They argue all the time. They're very intellectual people. It's not that I'm not an intellectual person, but I'm more street smart. That's how I analyze it."

While the sisters chatted about family dynamics, they edged closer to the subject of a particular night sometime in the mid to late 2000s. During the years of Del's addiction, the sisters went to the Tenderloin a few times to look for him. Deleana said, "All we would have to do is go ask on the street, 'Have you seen Del?' Everybody knew him."

At times, when his drug use was not at its worst, Del even had some of his grandchildren visit the Tenderloin for overnights. Deleana said, smiling, "He was really close with my kids when they were little. Not that he's not now. One of the things exciting to him was having grand-boys, because he had girls. He used to be able to clean himself up and say, 'Please let me bring my grandkids down here.' They would spend the night in the SRO. I would check it out and make sure it was [okay]."

"Not *my* kids," interjected Regina. "My husband wasn't playing that. At all."

Deleana had her rules. "'You get *one* night.' But it got to the point everybody knew my kids, especially my oldest son, who ended up hanging out down there a lot as he got older." He looks so much like Del, she said. "[Del] used to be really proud of walking around with him because he'd be flattered the ladies thought that was his kid. I'm like, 'You can't tell people that's your son. That's your *grand*son!'" she laughed. When the boys were little, Del took them to Glide Church activities. "They'd come back and [say], 'We had *free* lunch.' I thought, 'Oh, my God.' But it was an adventure. I'd be amazed at how he could clean himself up. He gave them such a good time. They never knew the conditions they were staying in. 'You know it was one bathroom, Mom?' I would be, like," she affected a fast command, "'Make sure you don't touch anything in there.'"

Adventures with the man they called Grandpa petered out as Del fell so far into his addiction he no longer contacted his family. After he had been incommunicado longer than ever came the memorable night Regina decided to search for him.

"I've always been the gullible one that would put up with a lot more. Or try to believe something wasn't what it was." This night, she took a girlfriend, and they drove from Fairfield to the Tenderloin to look for Del.

"I literally picked up homeless people and had them in my car, helping me find him. We went to all kind of SROs. We drove around, asking about him. This person running this SRO sent us to another SRO, and then we went to another SRO." The SROs got worse as they went along.

Regina earlier had met her father at the entrances of Tenderloin SROs, but not much farther inside. "He'd never let me come all the way into the elevator. I never got to be exposed to that. But I swear that day it seemed he knew I was out there looking for him. Every time somebody said, 'Oh, I just seen him at this place.' We'd get there. 'Oh, he just left.' I said, 'I think he's running from me.' I took that as a challenge. 'Okay. I'm going to be here until I find you.'

"He used to always tell me, 'Be careful when you come out here. Don't trust people.' Because I was always kind of non-fearful. I picked up this one homeless guy; I can't remember his name, but I love him to death. Every time I ever went out, he'd always help me. He got in my car. Oh, God. Smelled like urine. He smelled like my dad would when he'd get at *his* worst. And he took us to the last SRO." By then, it was two o'clock in the morning.

"It was the worst situation. I went up the elevator, and it's like they pee in the elevator. It was so funky. It was so nasty. But I wasn't by myself. We went up to I think the third floor. I had never been in an SRO all the way in, so I didn't know how bad it looks, but it was really dark, really gloomy. You couldn't see where you were walking down the hallway. And they had one bathroom at the end."

Regina and her girlfriend Terri made it down the hallway and knocked on a door said to be Del's, the memory still so palpable, Regina paused and took a deep breath.

"I have *never* seen him look that bad. Like *ever*. He looked like the dope fiend you see on TV. And he stunk. It was the worst I'd ever seen him. You could tell he was so embarrassed I found him."

He wore, Regina remembered, what looked like six layers of pants and "a whole bunch of jackets," an army-green trench coat of sorts over them. "He wasn't shaven, and he's always normally pretty shaven. He doesn't let it get out of hand, but it was out of hand. Whatever hair he does have left on his head," she giggled almost in what seemed relief, "was out of hand. He looked very dirty. He smelled bad. In his face he looked exhausted. I've never seen him like that. He looked *horrible*. I remember telling my friend, 'My dad is not going to be here very long. This is it.' He was going to die. I knew he had really hit rock bottom."

While Regina stood mutely at the door, taking in her father's state, Terri spoke up. "She's so loud. She was like, 'What's up, Del? What are you doing, Pops? Come on out, Pops.'

"He was like, 'Hold it, hold it, hold it. Let me get myself together.' He came right out and, 'Come on, let's go.' He wanted us *out* of that SRO right away. He took us walking around the TL. We took him to get him something to eat. I said, 'Daddy, when was the last time you ate?' He damn near was in tears. I've never seen my dad show any type of sign of weakness, and it just hurt me to my soul."

Regina began to cry. "He might have showed *her*," she said, glancing at Deleana, "but he never showed me. Like being weak and wanting some help. But he said he hadn't eaten. He was hungry. I took him to Burger King, got him something to eat. He didn't want me spending my money, so he was really trying . . . I said, 'Daddy, just order what you need.' I'd never seen him like that. He was tearing up. He always played tough, 'I got everything in control.'"

After Del ate, Regina urged him to go back to Fairfield with her. He refused. "He said he had to go to church in the morning. I said, 'Okay, we'll leave you. Daddy, don't disappear like that, because I'm going to keep coming back to the Tenderloin. Keep avoiding me if you want to, but I'm going to come back.'"

The scene, seared in Regina's memory, was also seared in Del's. In his speeches at events where he is being honored for his Code Tenderloin work, with either or both daughters in the audience, he will say yes, this happened, but they never saw him again like that, did they?

They will shake their head, no.

CHAPTER 30

QUITTING

A Two-Sided Tale About a Dealer

DEL ATTEMPTED MANY TIMES to quit smoking crack. Apart from his desire to free himself from it, other factors motivated him, including drug-chasing fatigue. "I analyzed it topically," he said. "At one point in time, you get tired. Pele got tired of playing soccer. Michael Jordan got tired of playing basketball. Loved it to death. Got tired of it. We addicts, sooner or later, get tired of it."

Hustling for crack he remembered as exhausting. "We should have got paid to do that!" Del laughed. "Because that's more work than any job in the world. And you got to be on your job. You can't miss a chance to get high. You can't roll over. If you don't get up by ten and you want to get high, you ain't going to have no money. I just got tired of it. That's where I analyze my recovery." In part, as it turned out.

Del also recalled his drug-chasing fatigue after trying to help an overdosed friend he was sponsoring in Narcotics Anonymous (NA). The friend lived in an especially awful Tenderloin SRO. "I'm trying to get him out of the place. He don't think the place he is in is a danger, but it's a *big* danger. He had a crisis. I got a call three o'clock in the morning—this guy relapsed the night before and was completely off the chain. So I got my car, and I drove down here [from Fairfield, a good hour plus away]. It's just a zoo, which completely brought me back to 'Man, this used to be me.' Three o'clock in the morning, running around in these crazy-ass hotels. Everyone's running around like it's three o'clock in the afternoon, doing their thing."

Del's speech became rapid-fire. "I'm watching people go over here to get a hit, take it over here smoking it. Finding out, it's no good. Going over here to get something else. Taking it. Smoking it. It was good. Now they got money, go outside and hustle. Get some money. Break somebody's car windows, steal something. Come back in, get a hit from here. Now the dope man has gone off. He's on the third floor. They got rum on the third floor. The dope man is in the basement. Go down to the basement and take a hit. It's no good."

During the rescue mission for his friend, Del got into a fight with the SRO's manager.

His voice in imitation turned to a harsh shout: "'What are you doing in my building?'

"'Hey, man, fuck you. I'm going to check on someone in harm's way.'

"'I don't care about that. You need to take him out of here anyway because he's nothing but a dope fiend.'

"'I got nothing to do with that, but I'm going to his door.'

"'Over my dead body!'

"I says, 'Well, you called it.' Then he says, 'I'll whup your ass right now.'

"I says, 'You don't know who I am.' Because I don't take no ass whupping. Then he realizes I'm not paying attention to his idle threat.

"He says, 'I'm calling the police.'

"I said, 'If that's what you need to do, call the police.' Then I go to my guy's door, and I'm knocking. 'Michael, you all right?'"

The door was broken. Del walked in. The first thing he says, 'Who are you?'"

"I said, 'Put your clothes on, man. I need to take you to the hospital.' He was so out of it he didn't know who I was. I took him to St. Francis, emergency room."

During his years of NA sponsorship, Del kept checking up on Michael and getting him various jobs, such as a security guard. Once he persuaded Michael's wary supervisor to give him another chance, arguing to her that one relapse was tied to diabetes, that Del would take him to a doctor to get a physical and review the medication. After an hour-long plea, she finally agreed to give Michael only a two-week suspension. Michael never knew of Del's intercession. "It would be like blowing a horn."

But when the relapses continued, Del threw him out of the NA recovery group. "Cannot let someone make that many mistakes and always be forgiven," said Del. "Brings the whole group down."

Weeks later, Michael overdosed and died. Del helped arrange a proper funeral.

IF A PANOPLY OF CIRCUMSTANCES—fatigue, disgust, embarrassment, tastes of bygone "normalcy"—constituted some of the reasons Del quit crack, he also cited, in more detail, "one main factor."

That factor's name is Alonzo Fluker.

Del relayed the tale from his onstage perch at Piano Fight on Taylor Street, gesturing out the window toward intersecting Eddy Street, where Alonzo stood some ten feet away at what then was his usual station, outside a convenience store. "I used to get dope from him on credit." In two different tellings, Del said he owed Alonzo either ten or twenty dollars and arranged to pay him the afternoon of a certain day Del expected a check. "Alonzo is a very moody person. He lets things bother him, and he brings the baggage over everyone. You never can tell. One day he'll be, 'Hey, man!' Just jolly, jolly. Next day, 'Man, what are you talking to me for?' His business affects him."

In Del's two versions of the tale, on the morning of the arranged payment Alonzo saw him on the street and not only demanded the money immediately but also "completely went berserk."

"He said, 'Man, where's my motherfucking money?' I say, 'I'll get my check this afternoon.' 'No, you going to pay me *now*, motherfucker.' We got into a big knockdown, drag-out fight right there on that corner. Alonzo was thirty, something like that." Actually, he was in his late forties. "I'm rolling around on the ground. I realize, I'm sixty years old. I am fighting a teenager. I still call everybody 'teenager.' This is nuts. I got to listen to some shit from a dirtbag like this over ten [or twenty] fucking dollars." Del pointed upward. "I looked at the Lord. I said, 'You'll never see a pipe in my mouth again.' And he hasn't. That was the last hit I ever had."

For about a year after the fight, Del and Alonzo did not speak. Eventually, Alonzo started offering Del his usual wares. When Del told him, "I don't get high no more," Alonzo, said Del, replied, "Bullshit."

"That pissed me off, because he wouldn't believe me I was clean. We went through another year of that." Yet Del understood the attitude. "Dealers get that a lot. Someone'll go clean for a couple weeks, and they'll be right back."

While Alonzo continued to scoff, Del was so annoyed at him, he did not tell him their fight on the sidewalk sparked his recovery. "I'm still pissed off at him, years later. I would not give him the benefit of the doubt by saying, 'You're the reason why.' He didn't do it with the *intent* to make me clean. But he was the party that made it happen."

Once Alonzo realized his former customer really had changed, however, so did Alonzo.

By the third year, said Del, Alonzo not only started bragging about how Del did what he said he would; Alonzo also set himself up as a barrier to Del's possible relapse. "If I walked up to him right now, 'Hey, man, let me buy twenty dollars [of crack],' he wouldn't sell it to me."

ALONZO GREW up in Hunters Point, a then predominantly African American neighborhood considered an impoverished and industrially polluted section of San Francisco. At one time, Hunters Point was infamous for its gang-controlled housing projects but later became known, in part, for its extensive artists' studios. Alonzo'sgrandmother, who helped raise him, taught him to cook, but that was not a skill he used to earn money. Instead, when living in the Hunters Point projects, Alonzo started dealing. That he sold to people with young children now pains him to the point he grimaces when talking about it. "It affects me *bad*. I think about that all the time, the corruption I did, the food I took out of kids' mouths." It did not affect him then, he said. "Don't nobody think about nothing when it's going on."

Alonzo said he had smoked crack himself. But, in an odd twist, he moved to the Tenderloin to get away from it. "I called my social worker at General Assistance, told her I needed a place to stay. They got me up out of there that same day." The year may have been 1989. "It was

easy for me to stop using crack, because I didn't like using it *no* way."
The first night in his new room, he did take another hit ("just a test
of me to see if I was really tired of it"), decided he was, then threw it
away. "That was it for me."

Dealing was another matter. So was the Tenderloin clientele, from
his point of view. "You don't really deal with parents with kids." That is,
he clarified, "You don't really have a vision of seeing them not dealing
with their kids."

In the Tenderloin, Alfonzo mentally adjusted to what he was doing.
"It don't affect you to where you can't live with yourself, because, the
thing is, people going to buy drugs from somebody. Me, myself, I felt
it was okay for people to buy, because I never mistreated nobody. I
never sold them bullshit. A lot of people told me they would rather
deal with me than other people. Some people don't care what they sell
you. I had a conscience. I was real trustworthy."

Perhaps one reason is that Alonzo became what Del called a "pure"
dealer, a seller who does not use. "If a person is using," clarified Del,
"I no longer call them a dealer. You don't get that so-called honor, by
street code." Yes, Del called himself a dealer and certainly used. "But
I would not be called a dealer by a real dealer," he said. "By the other
people on the street, people I sell to, of course I'm a dealer." But a
"pure" dealer, to him, is clean. "You're a businessperson. A dealer
would never touch drugs because that's a separation. You're no longer
respected or trusted anymore." Dealers who use their own drugs, he
said, start selling smaller packages or diluting the product.

Furthermore, he said, "Dealers are addicts to their trade. Sometimes it's not even money; it's the behavior. The swagger. Your status
in the community. 'There's Bob. He's a big baller.' Then people look
at you funny when you're not a baller anymore. 'What happened? Did
you get addicted? Busted? Did you snitch on somebody? Did you run
out of money to be able to buy?' In the community, a dope dealer is
looked at like a basketball star or rap star or movie star. On the *same*
level. Even the highest people in community, the lawyers and doctors
and probably the preachers, still honor that guy."

Alonzo figured he first met Del in the Tenderloin's Boeddeker Park.
By about then, the park no longer was a bucolic place featuring trees,

grass, benches, and raised brick planters but had become a drug haven. Used syringes tossed into the park from windows of adjoining SROs piled up. One park walkway featured so many drug offerings it was called "the gauntlet." (By the time its multimillion-dollar overhaul started in 2012, some called Boeddeker the worst playground in San Francisco. Boeddeker now looks so upscale, Del says it "has psychologically displaced a lot of homeless folks.")

Alonzo's connection with Del came via a woman they both knew. "Over the years me and Del became good friends." Asked what Del was like, Alonzo looked respectful.

"One thing, he was working. Even though he was, you know . . . Something must have happened in his life to make him . . . start using drugs. He used to come through all the time buying. But you would have never knew Del was going through struggles. You would have never even knew he was homeless. He was always polite. He was a user, but he wasn't taking stuff from people and manipulating people. None of that." Yes, he was "spending a whole lot of money" on drugs. "[But] I didn't see Del really bad off as a dope fiend or a junkie. I never seen him raggedy." At Boeddeker, continued Alonzo, the two sometimes talked of personal matters. "He was telling me about problems with the females and stuff like that."

One female may well have been a firecracker named Jacqueline Mitchell.

A pretty and curvy woman whose voice resembles a high soprano with a sandpaper chaser, Jackie was born in Arkansas the same year as Deleana. Her route to the Tenderloin involved her parents' divorce and a foster home before living with Del in the Coronado SRO, sometimes ferociously. One measure of her anger, which Del more than Jackie found humorous in the telling, involved her throwing their television out the window.

"No," she confirmed, "Del was not Mr. Faithful."

"My memory isn't all that great from back then," she said. "I think some stuff I choose to block out." Like Del, Jackie became addicted to crack. She described the Coronado as "a pad, like when people are on drugs," and "guys like girls. That's sort of how we met. I wouldn't say it was a prostitution thing. It was just the company." Del liked the company of women, she said, laughing. "A lot of different women. I do remember that's how that TV got out the window."

"He took very good care of me, I'm going to say that. He would make sure when he came home, he brought food. And if I wanted something to drink. He would have, of course, his beer." Del then worked as a plumber. Jackie's role was homemaker. "I would try to have everything together. I was all about taking care of him. That made me feel good about myself."

They were "fine" for a while, she said, looking sad. "But I guess he must have got bored, or temptation was out there. I don't think he was truly faithful *ever*." They would argue. She would leave and then return to break up whatever relationship he had ("I'm baaack!"), and the cycle repeated. Jackie said that despite Del's philandering, she was not worried about STDs. "For the most part, we did use condoms in the beginning. That's always the best. And I would like to say he used them with other people."

Jackie laughed high, her memories then expanding into their inadvertent reunion in 2017, when Del recognized her voice on Market Street. "He's still making drama where there is none. Just the life of the party, full of energy. He's still the same guy. Just not in jail." She smiled. "He likes to be in control of everything."

Jackie estimated their initial time together lasted "about a year, and that's a long time in drug addict time."

After dramatic events of her own, including jail for stabbing a woman in a fight, Jackie managed to quit drugs in 2001, years earlier than Del did, he said admiringly.

She launched a career in medical data research and was doing a temp job when the reunion with Del took place. It clearly affected her. She figured he "hit rock bottom" after she left. If she had seen him sleeping on the sidewalk, she said, she would have taken him home. "Del has always had a soft spot in my heart."

She teared up. Then, recovering her composure, she said that perhaps among Del's current girlfriends, she was now "one of the top three up there." She added impishly, "And hopefully the other two are gone."

Yes, it seems possible Jackie was one of the females Alonzo heard about.

AS FOR ALONZO'S TRAJECTORY in the world of drugs, he seemed far removed from the "big baller" portrait Del painted of some dealers.

Alonzo's self-portrait depicted a man who was small-time and easily intimidated. "I was coming out here at least for the last two years, hoping I could make forty or fifty dollars [a day]. Shouldn't even have to *think* about that. You see other people making thousands of dollars in a day, in the same amount of time *you'd* be out here. But I wasn't that aggressive. I was out here scared for twenty years. Because I was risking my Section 8. I was risking my medical." Alonzo has had severe arthritis in his knees and elbows for decades, he said. "I was risking my SSI. Everything."

One reason he did not deal a lot of drugs, he said, was because he did not deal with a lot of customers, nor did he compete. "When people got in my way, I walked away. The money wasn't that important to me. Even though I need it, I wouldn't get into no confrontation about a sale. I did a lot of credit. And that don't really make no money because you have to wait the whole month, then you got no money to buy nothing else. I would leave my house with probably a hundred and fifty dollars' worth and probably end up [returning home with most of it]. I know people out here," he said with a laugh, "[who] wouldn't even think about bringing a hundred and fifty dollars' worth. It's *way* too small."

Alonzo did not put in long hours either. "I was gone by one or two o'clock. That's another reason why I never made no money. I always used the BART for an excuse. I don't like getting on crowded BART trains, but it was no reason for me to leave before three."

Around 2008, dealers Alonzo knew were getting "maybe forty and fifty thousand dollars a month," he said. "I was probably getting four or five." In those days and earlier, he said, big Tenderloin drug money led to a lot of shooting, including among gang members from Los Angeles. "Then you got the Asians and the Mexicans having shootouts. It ain't *nothing* like that now. This is a nursery school compared to what it used to be. Serious."

Although Alonzo was arrested once for a parole violation, stemming from an incident the night of the Rodney King riots in 1992 (when someone charged him with stealing a camera, which he maintained he did not steal and therefore refused to cop a plea, thus was in jail when his only child, a daughter, was born), he said police never arrested him for dealing.

"I knew a lot of them, and a lot of them knew me. I was afraid of a lot of cops, but a lot of cops didn't really care nothing about me because they knew I wasn't trying to do too much. They knew I wasn't harming nobody."

Alonzo's view of himself as somewhat innocent, a Ferdinand the Bull of drug dealers, includes his stated antipathy toward guns. He said he did not carry one. "I don't like guns at all. You don't need no gun to protect yourself. You protect yourself by staying out of trouble. I know how to walk away if I see somebody got an attitude. I apologize quick and go my way. Some people refuse to do that." He shook his head. "I'll be more tripping on how does a person live with killing somebody? Once you shoot at somebody, your whole life is ruined. You can't rewind that. I really don't understand about shooting a person. But drugs, you can get over that."

It was time to ask Alonzo if he knew he was a major reason Del stopped smoking crack. Once he heard the story as Del had relayed it—their argument over the money, the name calling, the knock-down fight on the sidewalk—Alonzo shook his head.

"I don't remember bad things. I don't like bad things at all."

CHAPTER 31

BEWARE THE SPARK,
AVOID THE SNAKE

DEL HAS A FRIEND, years clean, whose wife called Del in a panic. Her husband had disappeared, his phone traced to a dope house somewhere in the Bay Area, not far from the family home. The snake had bit him, as Del put it. "I'm not personalizing the danger. But I'm generalizing that danger, because it *is* a danger."

The danger is the pull of the dope high to a vulnerable and recovering addict. Del barely skimmed the surface of the topic, including about his friend, then stopped, as the snake suddenly inched closer to him. "I'm not feeling comfortable with getting into the details." As an advocate for the Narcotics Anonymous groups he attends, if not as frequently as he once needed to, he said, "I'm practicing what I preach."

Del has attended twice-weekly NA recovery groups at Glide Church for more than two decades, during and after active addiction. At one meeting (which he did not attend), held in a tranquil upstairs room, people sat in a circle, confided with apparent trusting ease about such matters as triggers, then moved to get immediate medical intervention for one attendee. After the group broke up, one man laughed ruefully about someone who planned to get clean but only after a twenty-dollar crack sendoff.

"Now, this is really presumptuous," Del said of the group, "that I don't necessarily go there for myself anymore. When I used to go, I needed to hear from the people clean for a long time. Now I'm the voice of the clean person. In our present group, everyone else has been clean a maximum of weeks or months. I'm the old man. So I need to go there when I can, to put my voice in."

"That's my family," he said. "I gave them my five-minute encouragement speech on the moment I got clean" (the sidewalk fight with Alonzo), that "it was so unexpected."

"Because I know those folks in my group. They won't tell you, but 90 percent are not clean. They'll sit there and wonder, 'When am I going to be clean? Will it ever happen?' Mine was the morning I got up not planning to be clean for the rest of my life by the end of the day, but I was. It came out of nowhere, more or less. They got it. I'm saying, 'Have hope, brothers and sisters, today might be your day. Be ready.' Because they're sitting there thinking, 'How I'm going to deal with this? I want to get high right now.'"

Del delivered his 360-degree mantra to them. "Anywhere I'm at, I can stand and do a three sixty," he stood and circled, "and I will not see a dope fiend; if you want to get clean, you got to be able to do that."

"They really took that well. It's a moving monologue. But make it hopeful. As addicts, we have to have hope, because you don't see *any* light at that tunnel. You're sitting in these bullshit meetings that make you want to get high, because you're sitting there for an hour listening to people talk about crack cocaine. How silly is that?"

Another staple of Del's counsel, including to his errant friend, comes down to two words: "So what?" Yes, you messed up, fell off the wagon, got high, ended up—according to your cell phone data—in a dope house. Yes, you feel ashamed, and your wife is beside herself, and you're worried about your job. But your slip up was yesterday. Pull yourself together. This is today.

For decades, Del knew a particular woman in the Tenderloin as a "using partner." She got clean before he did, he said, became a facilitator at Glide NA meetings, then had what Del termed "a short relapse," got clean again, and became a drug counselor at the San Francisco jail. He figured she does her work well. "She is as real deal as can be."

"Most counselors in San Francisco," he added, "are ex-users. There's two different schools of thoughts on that. One is, if I have a truck-driving school, I may not necessarily hire a guy that's had fifteen accidents. I'd rather hire a guy who's *never* had an accident and tell these people how you never have accidents." Yet the fifteen-accident guy might have helpful input too. "We look at that the same in recovery. Do you hire a guy that's never got high? Or do you hire a guy that's been getting high all his life? Who's got the best wisdom? Naturally, you could say the guy that's *never* got high, because he could say, 'I never got high because I never hang around dope fiends. I know how to say *no*. And I'm not curious.'"

"The other guy says, 'Don't get high because you're going to lose your house. You're going to lose your car. You're going to lose your wife.'"

"Who knows? Maybe you need this guy on Monday and this guy on Tuesday." More than maybe, Del concluded. "You definitely need both sides."

He saw two sides as well in the question of whether it was good or bad for addictive drugs to be cheap or expensive. "There are so many variations. If it's more expensive, there's more crime, more break-ins. Because the drug desire is not going to diminish." In "certain cases," people stopped because they could not afford to continue. But when Tenderloin supplies dropped and crack "cost four times more than normal," Del did not stop. "And I don't remember too many people that did," he said. "[If drugs are] too cheap, it'll lower the crime but also may make people who stopped using, because they couldn't afford it, go back to using." Cheap drugs may also attract people "who thought about doing it but were afraid of the money." Del added, "There's many pros and cons on each one."

"They ask the question all the time, how would it look if we gave them away free, like some countries do. I don't think that's a good idea." Del has been suspicious of anything labeled free since Las Vegas casinos offered "free" check cashing that fed his other addiction.

Meanwhile, he had spoken again with his remorseful, snake-bitten friend, now "doing fine." The nonprofit organization the man works for had kept him on and gotten him help, help he was taking.

QUITTING—FOR GOOD—WHATEVER drug you're on, said Del years later, is only one step. "You got to build up two different steps in the cleanliness program, as I call this. From my mouth only. There's one day you decide not to use anymore, [a] very important day, but that's not the most important day. The most important day is being able to say, I don't *want* to use." He continued, "Sometimes they're a day apart, sometimes ten years apart."

In Del's case, they were about four years apart. He was in a money-order and check-cashing place in San Francisco's Mission District, wiring $30 to somebody. He paid the cashier with a $100 bill. She gave him a receipt and change; he walked outside, and he realized she had accidentally also given him back his $100. He went back inside, pointed out her error, and returned the $100. Outside, it hit him: as an addict, he would have kept the $100 and immediately bought crack with it. But now, although he was low on money, he was not even tempted.

His epiphany occurred as a member of his church happened to walk by. Del immediately relayed what had just happened. The two embraced and wept. To Del, the incident remained memorable. "You're striving to get to that second date, *that's* the one."

DEL MIGHT BE DESCRIBED as someone who cannot say no to someone who needs help, at least to a point. About the same time he was trying to help his friend Michael, he was checking up on the daughter of a friend in Solano County, not far from Del's Fairfield home. The daughter, seven months pregnant, homeless, and using drugs, was with her father, "both sleeping in the bushes." On hearing about her situation, Del asked a favor of a pastor who runs a shelter, then contacted his friend. "I told him, 'I got her a bed in a wonderful place.' I knew she was hard-core. I said, 'Here's the address. She can find her way there if she wants to go, because I'm *definitely* not going to take her."

As Del also put it, she had to do her part. "You got to get the hookup, which she can't do. But getting over there, she can do. If there was dope, she could get there."

Similarly, a man from Del's church asked him to help another man get into St. Anthony's drug program in San Francisco. "I called him back. I said, 'Look, I made all the arrangements. He needs to be at St. Anthony's eight o'clock in the morning. See Sister Marion.' He says, 'Okay, I'll get up and take him.'

"I said, 'No. No, no, no, no. San Francisco. Buses on every street. *Don't*. Let him know he's got a place. He's a grown man. At this point, you need to step out of it and let him get aggressively into it. Again, if you were chasing dope, you would own your responsibility. You won't need nobody to wake you up. Prioritize. This is *clean up your life.*"

To Del, the old saying about not helping people get over an addiction until they want to rings true. He remembered he and a friend trying to help an addict in San Francisco. "We took the guy to drug rehab and signed him in. Our car was two blocks away. We went back to the car, got in, and just happened to drive back past. He was all the way out the door. He didn't last five minutes. He wasn't ready."

Meanwhile, Del was also checking up on a woman in semi-recovery. He had paid her rent to help her get back on keel, even though she admitted she lied to him after he went through an intricate plan to deliver a check to her at a BART subway station during his fifteen free minutes between meetings, so she wouldn't have to leave the subway and pay a second fare. She never showed. He was miffed but undaunted.

"It's a drama a day," he said with a shrug.

Many of Del's neighborhood dramas involve money. He knows the vagaries of Tenderloin banking well. "I live that street creed. I can't walk through here being a sustained person and one of the guys I used to drink with asks me for a dollar, I give him a dollar. 'You moved up and got yourself economically together. Don't forget about us.'"

If someone pretends to forget, watch out. "Uh-oh. You're on their radar. You got two dollars, and you're not going to help us out? Because this neighborhood helps each other out all the time. 'I just got my check on the fourteenth of the month, I got everyone around me until I run out of money. You get a check on the twenty-first, then you help me and everyone else.' That's how we do down here. I don't let them misuse that trust. I had to check a guy the other day. I says, 'Man, every time I pass you by, you ask me for a dollar. You're not pimping me out like that. You need to back up. Give it some time.'"

Most days, Del estimated, he gives out between $10 and $15 to a variety of people. He also hands out $25 gift cards from the HandUp organization, which people can redeem at such places as Safeway, Walgreens, and CVS. "This is for the lowest of the lowest." The organization in turn is connected to the city's health department, so if people want more gift cards, they are offered extra help, such as a blood pressure check.

When Del hands out his own money, recipients say they'll pay it back. Some do, most do not. Others, after Del got clean, made him their de facto bank. "They would get their paychecks and say, 'Man, I'm trying to get clean, keep my money for me.' Then all of a sudden you get calls at two o'clock in the morning for $20 and then three o'clock for $20. Finally, I would wind up, by the third call, 'Here, take all your money. I'm done.'"

Requests for Del as lender and banker continued, though. "One girl, by the end of the month, I will have given her $25." Next she tried to deposit money with him. "She'll say, 'Here, take $50. That way I got some money banked up with you.'" Del refused. Apart from early morning wake-up calls, he pictured forgetting about the money, then going out of town. "She'll walk around the Tenderloin, 'That motherfucker left with my money.'"

When Del next saw the woman, she was angry and broke. All his fault for not keeping that $50 for her.

Del again reached for his wallet.

CHAPTER 32

A FREE SUIT, A FREE ROOM

SOMETIME AROUND 2009, in Boeddeker Park, when Del was wearying of his own dramas, he met Walter Hughes, whom he later referred to as "my sobriety buddy" and "my best friend." Walter's trip to the park came at the behest of his pastor at the enormous San Francisco Christian Center, located in a blue-collar southern part of the city.

Decades younger than Del, Walter gleams with good health and prosperity. His mixed Black and Mexican heritage bestow a bronze glow under freckles, his black hair curly and shiny, while his upscale-looking open-necked shirts reveal a glimpse of a tattoo, mention of which can make him blush. Walter is an independent financial advisor based in San Francisco, as well as a homeowner and married father of five whose cell-phone family photos are never far from display.

But in his youth, Walter knew Boeddeker Park well.

The middle son of three boys his mother had with three different men, Walter grew up in a small two-bedroom San Francisco apartment. He described his mother as "a beautiful young woman that men took advantage of." She was also an addict, he said. "She bartended, sold cocaine out of the house." Sometimes she brought friends and customers back to the apartment at 3 a.m. to party and dance, waking the boys. Walter shook his head. "I knew about drugs before I knew how to multiply."

His mother, herself physically abused, including by Walter's father, extended her experiences to her children. "She would beat us with belts, extension cords. It was *really* bad. It got way worse as we got older." One punishment Walter especially remembered. "My mom would line us up and turn the stove on and burn our hands over the open flame. I used to have to watch my brother get burned, which was almost worse than me being burned. Then *knowing* you're going to come up next."

After Walter's older brother ran away at sixteen, their mother intensified her abuse of Walter. One day she hit him with pots and pans while her brother visited, thus giving Walter an audience and a witness. "I'm *embarrassed* that my uncle is watching me getting beat. I'm a thirteen-year-old kid. My mother leaves to go somewhere. I'll never forget, my uncle comes up to me . . ." and whispered he would not blame Walter if he packed all his clothes right then, called his father, and never returned. "It was the first time an adult stood up for me."

The counsel gave Walter courage. "I went in my room, and I took a big Glad bag and threw everything I had in there. I called my dad. My stepmom answered, and I couldn't hold it—I started crying. 'I got to get out of here. My mom's beating me all the time.'"

Life with Walter's father and stepmother worked well at first, but a secret from her past intruded. She confided in Walter she could not have children, following a back-alley abortion in her youth. "A coat-hanger type deal," Walter described it. When she saw Walter's father being happy and proud about his son, the emotional pain of her own situation kicked in. She gave her husband an ultimatum: choose Walter or her. Walter lost.

He and later his older brother went back to their mother, who had grown oddly passive, or perhaps tired, working three jobs. Now her sons drank and took drugs themselves. The family got evicted. In Walter's telling, their mother simply forgot to pay the rent, although she had the money. The landlord would not budge; the apartment had been cheap, thanks to rent control. He could make a lot more from new tenants.

Eviction led to the family splitting apart and becoming homeless. Walter's brother took off to stay with a friend, their mother lived out of her car and slept on friends' couches, and Walter moved in with a girlfriend, then with other friends for months. "When you're young, it's almost like a sleepover. Then you realize, I can't get up and go in your refrigerator." Finally, he bought a car and slept in it, surrounded by his few possessions. Some friends let him shower at their home when no parents were around, but that opportunity did not happen every day. "You start to get into this reality of 'I got to get some stability.'"

Walter managed to contact an aunt only five or so years older than he was. She lived in a small studio apartment in the Tenderloin, close to Boeddeker, and invited him to stay with her. He arrived about ten o'clock at night, a moment he recalled clearly. "Her place is a *wreck*. There're clothes everywhere." He cleared out a little area to lie down and sleep. "Thirty minutes later, the doorbell rings and she buzzes somebody up. This guy comes in, all super-energetic," talking a mile a minute. Walter's aunt introduced Walter, the man paused to say hello, then pulled out a glass pipe and started smoking.

He passed it to Walter's aunt, who started to say Walter did not know she used. "Before she could even complete that sentence, she's grabbing the pipe and the lighter. I found out it was crystal methamphetamine. It was a crazy introduction to the Tenderloin."

The next morning, after his aunt and visitor left, Walter cleaned and organized the whole apartment. His next step, motivated by not wanting to end up like his aunt, was to look for work. Yet he was living no clean life himself. "I was young, but I was already snorting cocaine. Then I found a job, and I would go out and party with my friends. They would also take the crystal meth and *snort* it. Each of them, after they'd do it, they scream, they hold their head, tears coming down their eyes. I'm like, 'What the heck? Why are you doing that?'"

In his drug world experience, said Walter with a shrug, "We minimize our drug of choice." The "pinnacle," he called it, is shooting heroin. Drug users would say at least they didn't do that. Or they snorted cocaine, but at least they didn't snort crack. Or, down the line of usage, they just smoked marijuana, he concluded during a talk stoked by three shots of espresso from Starbucks. Walter Hughes's current drug of choice is caffeine.

Once when out of other drugs, Walter tried crystal meth too. "It felt like little metal shards shot into my brain." He was up for two days. That was not his sole misstep. He stole from friends, was incarcerated multiple times, and took advantage of girls, "being a bad boyfriend," he said. "I've left girls with a lot of debt." At thirteen and fourteen, his male influence came from neighborhood toughs who convinced him it was an honor for a female to be with them. "I'm taking life lessons from nineteen-year-old dudes!"

Walter's future seemed to face downward. His best friend, stabbed by the friend's drunken girlfriend, died in his arms. At one point in his early twenties, Walter, again in jail, prayed to accept whatever sentence he would receive. As if in answer to his prayer, the prosecution lost a key piece of evidence. Walter, set free, resolved to change his life.

He landed straight jobs, including being a "lumper" (unloading enormous packages of frozen meat at a San Francisco warehouse) and working as a landscaper, sometimes in affluent parts of the city he had never seen. Jobs in office services, thanks to his older brother, led to a career in document management for San Francisco law firms and later passing an exam in finance services. "That was all God."

By the time Walter was thirty, working, and married to his second wife (he has two children with his first, three with his second), an older friend, who to Walter's amazement had been sober and clean two years, urged him to attend a Bible study class at the Christian Center. Walter went and soon peppered the teacher, "Pastor Joe" Taybron, with so many questions Taybron became Walter's mentor, exemplifying male "virtues and values" new to him. "I didn't have a role model of Black men in society doing honorable things." Walter said he told the pastor, "You're like a unicorn and a leprechaun to me. I didn't know you existed."

One day Pastor Taybron approached Walter for a favor involving people of Boeddeker Park. "He asked if I would come with him to the park with the church and give *my* testimony on what happened in my life." Walter agreed.

"I didn't know what to expect. I went down there and spoke from my heart about my life experiences. Unbeknownst to me, the people in the park were responding to me sharing my story. I guess because I was a young guy in jeans and a t-shirt, just saying, 'This is what I've been through."

One of the people listening was Del.

Walter remembered him sitting on a rear bench, then moving forward. After Walter's talk, church people passed out donated hygiene packages as well as new clothes, some still with their price tags. At one point during the distribution, Walter tried to divert a man, apparently an addict, who was bothering a woman, apparently an addict too, both fidgety. Walter distracted him with the offer of a free suit, then gave him a card with the church's address and a map. At that, a voice yelled out to the fidgety man, "Look here, partner. You got a suit, you got a business card. Come Monday morning, you have no excuse."

Walter looked over, saw "this light-skinned older brother," and told him, "I think I have another suit."

"Really?"

"What size are you?"

Walter looked at the man, six feet tall and skinny, went to the stock of clothes, and found a prize. "One suit left and it's his size."

"Do you have another one of those cards?" the man asked.

"'I was waiting to see if you'd ask.' I gave it to him and said, 'Brother, what's your name?'"

"Del."

"I'm Walter. Nice to meet you.'"

Walter said he thought no more about the exchange.

Del did. To him, Boeddeker during the week offered a place to deal drugs in one corner and use them in another, maybe drink in both. When various church people came by on Saturdays, the agreement was, he said, gesturing like a referee keeping two sides apart, you do your church thing over there and leave me alone with "my forty ounce," then a "watery" Miller High Life. Del imbibed E&J brandy heavily, too, he remembered, but he no longer smoked crack after the sidewalk fight with Alonzo.

"I think I was clean when I met Walter. I was still hustling, selling dope, and doing crazy things." And he lived with his girlfriend, Sheila, who was not clean. "So I was still dirty," he clarified. As for Walter Hughes's gift, the suit he gave Del was a new three-piece Pierre Cardin.

Del calculated. "That was easy! These are *marks*. What else can I get from these cats?" He decided to attend the church the next day and work them.

Walter attended too. "It was a very moving service," he recalled. "Emotionally heavy. They allow people that want to come forward to have prayer if they were moved by the word. I was on the verge of tears." He told his wife he was going forward to get prayer and stood waiting for a pastor to pray with him. He felt somebody lay a head on his shoulder, figured it was another parishioner, and turned.

"It's Del Seymour. He's just wailing." Walter stumbled in his telling. "I meet people all day long. I don't know why I remember his name. 'Del!' I don't know if it was me recognizing his name or what, [but] he collapsed in my arms. Now I'm crying, he's crying." Walter said Del kept whispering, "Thank you, brother. Thank you."

Walter got Del's phone number and called him repeatedly to join him for lunch in the Financial District, where Walter worked. "I could hear reservations in his voice, but I don't take no for an answer." When Del finally agreed and showed up, Walter sensed he was uncomfortable. Small wonder. San Francisco's steel, glass, and stone Financial District lies one easy walk but a whole different world from the Tenderloin.

Walter decided to spare Del the possible discomfort of going to a nice restaurant and instead bought food to go. In a scene that repeated itself, the two then walked to a park. "We'd sit down and talk," Walter said. "And talk and talk and build and connect and talk."

Both men had "similar upbringings," he added. "A generation and a half ahead of me, eerily similar stories." Especially similar was the lack of a reliable father. The similarities helped deepen the friendship, but clearly Walter had outpaced Del in terms of recovery. "When I first saw [Del], he looked, for all intents and purposes, homeless. He was missing teeth in the front of his mouth. Some of the teeth were rotten." Del since has gotten a dental plate he often wears. "Clothes was kind of tattered and had an odor. I think when I would take him to go eat, that was part of the shame. I didn't care. It doesn't bother me, and I don't care if it bothers other individuals. I didn't *know* him that well, but I saw a guy with a great heart. So we continued to meet."

With each meeting, it seemed, Del Seymour was leaving behind the chokehold of addiction as well as its corresponding punishment of homelessness. And thanks to that "great heart" Walter recognized, Del was about to begin a remarkable path to what might be termed redemption.

That was not Del's plan at all.

HIS FOCUS IN PART became finding a drug-free place to stay. Witness to the effort was Jason Albertson, a psychiatric social worker for the San Francisco Department of Public Health, who supervised an outreach team of case managers. A burly head-shaved man with an unsavory Lower East Side New York past (he stole car radios for drug money) that still troubles him, he speaks with bureaucratic precision, street slang, compassion, and a bucket of fishing analogies.

His "outreach and engagement team," he said, "was the wide end of the funnel. Our job was to find the people who needed the care, establish that they needed the care, and sell them to the care provider. Then go back and find another fish in the pond. We weren't the fish processors. We were the unit that finds the people, packages them, presents them, and then a longer-term caseworker would take them."

Jason heard about Del before meeting him: "I think one of the outreach team members found him in an evening and placed him in one of our protected shelter beds for a while. We had a routine process for people who wash up on our shores, of saying, 'Who are they and what do they need?' At that time [about 2009], a 'protected' shelter bed that didn't go away was a pretty scarce commodity. I was invested in having us use them for a purpose. Not just as a shelter resource but [also] as an engagement tool and a way to develop a relationship and do some goal setting with people. Either we were going to throw you back in the pond or we were going to keep you until you could get on General Assistance and get a shelter bed from that program—or we were going to pile on as many additional resources as it took to help you get stable."

Sitting on a downtown San Francisco park bench during a noon break from his assignment helping administer the city's COVID vaccinations, he continued, "If you bounced into one of our shelter beds on an overnight shift or a result of a direct outreach, within about a week the case manager's job was to interview you, figure out what your circumstances were, and present the case to the team with a recommendation [as to how to proceed]."

Every once in a while, caseworkers told Jason of someone in a shelter bed, "You got to meet this guy. He's one of yours." This time, the guy was Del Seymour. "I got the specials."

What made Del stand out?

"He probably had a lot of presence and gravitas and asked for the supervisor. They were much more used to folks who sort of accept the process for whatever it is or should be, rather than somebody pretty emphatic about what they need and want."

A meeting was set up. By then, Del must have looked in better shape, at least sartorially. To Jason, Del presented as "a tall, somewhat thin, African American man." "I remember saying to him that he moved well and his pants dropped just right. They 'drapped' well. His shoes were in good condition. He was sustaining a public persona while in difficult circumstances. I was certainly, to some extent, impressed by that. But it's also part of my professional stock in trade that I find something about the person whom I'm talking to that allows me to provide them with compliments or ego goods. Something to feel good about today."

After the meeting, Jason said, "we decided to keep him." That meant offering Del a rare commodity: a free hotel room as long as needed.

"The Department of Public Health had at one point about 240 hotel rooms the homeless outreach team administered," he said, eyeing a seemingly drugged-out young man stumbling along a park path. "They were a strong intervention, because we could meet somebody and make a decision to place them in the hotel room that day, that week, or whenever. They would have a place to live and stay, which they didn't have to pay for. It was aid-blind. And it meant the caseworker could find them to have appointments with them. It was really key for stabilization of homeless folks with substantial challenges.

"At that time, the methodology of transferring people to a stabilization hotel room and putting them on full-service case management was a little bit more possible than it is now. A lot of capacity challenge has made fewer of these available hotel rooms we could [use later] on, and much more demand for them because of the high numbers of very sick people. So we were able to be fairly liberal." The room assigned to Del was in the Civic Center Hotel on Twelfth Street off Market, near City Hall.

Jason trusted Del was clean. "I have to accept what people tell me. He did tell me that he was. It was a point of pride and also concern for him, that he not have too much risk of relapse." He also recalled Del expressing a wish to return to taxi driving.

Weekly meetings with his caseworker—Del professes no idea who it was—would have been away from the hotel, said Jason. "We tend to discourage having meetings of significance in a person's room, especially because a lot of our caseworkers were themselves in recovery. You don't want your caseworker walking in on somebody who's taking an unknown white powdery crystalline substance in a glass pipe and having that part of the experience," Jason said. "We would ask people to come to the office, or we would meet them in community."

Caseworkers are expected to stay connected to their clients. Some clients slip the net, though, avoiding appointments. "But with a lot of warning and a series of defined come-to-Jesus talks and interventions," Jason said, "we didn't have to end people's stay."

No such problem marred Del's stay, according to a log Jason later perused, with Del's written permission. The record shows Del Seymour spent well over a year in the Civic Center Hotel. He then opted to find housing the Veterans Administration subsidized. Jason recalled being impressed that Del did not want help in that regard but instead took on much responsibility himself, such as contacting someone in then senator Barbara Boxer's office for assistance.

By Jason Albertson's count, Del had sixty-three interactions or meetings with Public Health Department personnel in roughly a year. That was not an unusual number, he said. All in all, he noted, from the time Del "turned up in the net" to when he left the Civic Center Hotel, "I think he got good services."

CHAPTER 33

HOW TO STOP HOMELESSNESS

WHEN DEL IS ASKED how the government can help solve homelessness, his answers are pragmatic, his opinions set. Anybody who has attended a monthly meeting of the Local Homeless Coordinating Board knows he is not shy about expressing those opinions. And what he says during board meetings echoes what he says away from it.

"I'm not 'housing first.' I'm the only one on my board that's not housing first. I'm probably one of the only prominent homeless activists in the country that's not housing first. I'm 'issue first.' Before I make you a tenant, you need to know how to be an acceptable tenant. I'm not going to ask the landlord to take a drug user into his building. It's not proper, and it's not fair. It *should* be illegal. It should be contractual. *Any* landlord should have a right for his place to be a drug-free place."

What about people who say they cannot get clean until they have a place to stay?

"That's what they say. 'Let's get them in off the street first.' *Then* what? Now you've given them a haven to do their thing in, behind closed doors, making it easier. You're co-depending. They need to go into an in-house program, then come out of that program and get into their own unsupported housing." His words proved prescient; during the COVID pandemic, addicts provided rooms in hotels or SROs died at what the *San Francisco Chronicle* called a "disproportionate" rate from overdoses.[1] In part, people were not only lonely but also alone and therefore unable to reverse an overdose, even if accidental.

A related issue was the controversial establishment of "safe injection sites," where addicts could shoot up illegal drugs legally, with help if they overdosed . . . or wished to consider getting clean. Del initially balked at the idea.

Speaking during a 2019 forum at a café in the Mission District, he said, "I am not against the safe injection sites, but I damn sure ain't for 'em either." As a former addict, he said, "It's hard for me to support legalized drug use. I can't wrap that around my head. We've talked about it in recovery groups. Hardly anyone in recovery group will say 'Yeah, let's go for it. Safe injection site.' That's so against everything that killed us, that took eighteen years out of my life and my family's life and my kids' life. I can't see supporting someone else getting in that miserable situation I was in."

Regarding a 2021 San Francisco demonstration in favor of the sites, however, Del was quoted as saying "This is real"—rapid fatal over-dosing from fentanyl occurring in San Francisco. The contention was that overdosing could be reversed with Narcan if the addict used in a safe site. By year's end, Del said he "completely embraced" such sites. For much of 2022, a city-funded Tenderloin Navigation Center, since closed by Mayor London Breed, included an unpublicized safe injection area. Del and others railed against the center's closing, but he also said people trying to recover from addiction should not be in the same line for services as people about to use.

A side benefit of the sites, supposedly, was fewer discarded needles. Del suggested paying people a nickel a needle to turn them in. If it works for soda cans, why not needles? The idea got no liftoff. Within a couple of years, furthermore, discarded needles were less of a common sight; many drug users switched to meth, then even deadlier fentanyl, both ingested various ways, including smoked from a piece of tin foil. The sight of crumpled, burned foil on city sidewalks was joined by the sight of crumpled people.

To Del, drug use is not always the major scourge in the Tenderloin. That distinction goes to liquor stores that sell in volume everything from beer to vodka. Distributors from southeast San Francisco make morning deliveries. "You see them coming out off Highway 280 in these eighteen-wheel caravans. Liquor trucks. That's *our* weapons of mass destruction. They double-park and take over the streets. They unload cases and cases of these weapons. And in these liquor stores, they just keep it in cardboard box[es] on the floor and sell it. They don't even have a stocking procedure because it goes so fast. When that store opens in the morning, they'll go through two or three cases of vodka within the first half hour.

"That's why people's lives are *so* messed up down here. I would say, of the people addicted to drugs and alcohol, 80 percent of them are alcohol. The other 20 percent is drugs. With a lot of crossovers." His solution to the overabundance of liquor stores, especially in poor neighborhoods?

"Eminent-domain those damn places! Nobody even wants to talk about that."

Instead of liquor stores, every few blocks "put a treatment on demand center" or a wet house (where homeless alcoholics may live and drink) or a harm reduction center. "We need [these] reasonably all over the city, so we don't cluster that character of a person in one neighborhood."

Del believes, however, that the vast majority of the unsheltered population nationwide are not addicted to drugs or alcohol. In San Francisco, he claims, 82 percent of that population is on the streets for other reasons. Actually, "on the streets" is misleading. By HUD definition, he said, homelessness means you do not have a key to your own dwelling. You are technically homeless even if couch-surfing, a phrase he called "white." "In the Black communities, we don't necessarily let people sleep on our sofas. You come here [to sleep], make you a pallet. Get some blankets and make it on the floor. First of all, an older Black person would never let you sleep on their sofa because, 'That's not an adequate replacement. That's my living room.' Years ago, in a Black home, you could not even *sit* in the living room. You sat on the patio or in the kitchen. Living room was for when Uncle Charles came from Chicago. Or the preacher. No one's going to sleep on the sofa. Barely can *sit* on a sofa."

What about non-addicted people who are homeless? What about housing first for them?

"They could have other issues they need to address before I would put them in a place. They need their mental health addressed. They need their anger management addressed. They need their tenant unsuitability addressed. They need to know they can't play their radio all the way to the top just because they paid their rent. That's problems we have. 'I paid my rent!' Which is only like a hundred dollars out of their pocket. The rest is subsidized. 'I'll play my radio as loud as I want. It's *my* place.'

"No, it ain't your place. You're *renting*. You need to go to the dictionary and look up renting. This is *not* your place. When you buy your *own* land in middle of Oregon and you put your cabin out in the woods, you can play your [radio]. The only problem you got is with the bears and wolves, and they're not going to trip."

Furthermore, exclaimed Del, getting more wound up, being a suitable tenant also means "you can't bring all your cousins over here in the morning and shoot dice on the front porch" or have "people waiting for you to come home, sitting in the hall smoking weed."

Del would like to get HUD to bring to San Francisco its suitability training program for new tenants. Issues are basic. "You don't pay your rent on the sixth day. You pay it on the first day. When you get your check, the first thing you do is pay that rent. Buy all that *other* shit later. If you haven't paid your rent, don't avoid the landlord. Go see him the first day when you *know* you're not going to pay it and work out a deal."

During a talk following a 2023 walking tour, it was clear that timely rent payment continued to be an issue for Code Tenderloin graduates. "We teach priorities. A lot of our young women on the streets we bring in here, we get them a good job. They'll call me two months later and say, 'Del, can you help me with my rent?' I said, 'Well, what happened to your paycheck?' 'Oh, Del, I *had* to get my hair done.' I said, 'No, you didn't!' 'Oh, yes I did! I'm a young Black woman in society. I had to get my hair done.' Your hair is like $300. I said, 'But you needed to pay your rent first.'

"The guys too," he said. "'Man, the new Jordans came out. I *had* to get them shoes. I'll pay the landlord later.' No, you don't do that. Of anybody you don't pay later is a landlord."

OVER THE YEARS has loomed the enormous question of where people without homes, but with various problems, can live. One of Del's answers: San Francisco's county to the south.

"San Francisco has chartered land in San Mateo County. I would build villages there for the homeless. I would have onsite job training, onsite computer labs. You can't just warehouse people. That's what we're doing in these shelters, with no exit plan." People cannot get their lives together in one month, he said. Yes, they receive a respite, but they need more time. Navigation Centers let people stay for three months, but, according to Code Tenderloin volunteers, that amount of time is not enough for people to figure out more permanent solutions. They start panicking well before the three months are up.

"My place would have exit plans. If it turns out that they need clinical care the rest of their life, I'll build places that'll be like a board care. For clinical or mental illness. Mental illness cannot be cured, but it can be managed better." Del had his eye on an old prison in San Mateo County he figured could be repurposed or torn down for housing.

For recovering addicts, he pictured dorm rooms with chest-high dividers providing semi- privacy between beds. Once residents become drug-free or alcohol-free and have solved other issues, they would get how-to-be-a-good-tenant training and move into their own room.

He also favored regional plans. At the National Coalition of Homeless Vets meeting in Washington, DC, in 2016, he was impressed by Terry McAuliffe, then governor of Virginia. "He has designed this homeless program to be statewide. He's one of the first people in the nation looking at homeless[ness] on a regional [level]."

Del said he would use other sites in San Francisco too. "I would take our piers—Pier 80, Pier 70, Pier 90—and make them gigantic homeless shelters. Immediately! A seven-day build-out: Start work this Thursday and be done next Thursday. Move in Friday. Bring in all the Porta-Potties and [portable] shelters." Use "gigantic event tents" such as were used for Navigation Centers. "Boom! Have the chef's program [of] ECS [Episcopal Community Services] prepare the food every day, cater the food in, three meals a day. Have that gigantic yard part of the pier, the outdoor area, and fence it off so people can't fall in the bay. And, kumbaya, it would make a beautiful setting. Have all the mental illness folks, the substance abuse folks, the VA folks, the welfare folks, everyone, have satellite offices at every shelter." Again, beds would be separated by dividers. There would not be complete privacy. "You don't want that."

Del has gotten nowhere with his ambitious plans, he said. But, he asked rhetorically at a Local Homeless Coordinating Board meeting, look at the situation this way: what if a tornado hit San Francisco and made thousands of people homeless?

It has hit, he said. "It's called homelessness."

The solution is not money, he says repeatedly. San Francisco's fiscal year 2024 budget for the Department of Homelessness and Supported Housing is $636 million. The great majority funds subsidized housing and services (such as mental health and hygiene programs) for more than ten thousand formerly homeless people and includes money for shelters, homelessness prevention, and outreach.[2] "We got plenty of money," said Del, if in flusher times, "and there are no rooms for rent. So it's not money. It's space."

A less tangible factor includes the actions and reactions of other people. Del's advice for what a housed person might do to help an unhoused person was so basic he rolled his eyes as he spoke. "I guess a smile. A wave and a smile," he said, as anyone might do to a neighbor sitting on the porch. "'Hey, how you doing? Have a great day.' Maybe you don't even want to ask how you're doing, because you may not want to open yourself up to an answer." But say something, he urged. "*Something* to acknowledge that person lying there. 'Hey, hear about the Giants today?' These people listen to sports probably more than most people because they got the time to do it." And such questions demonstrate you are "not trying to be uppity."

In short, treat someone like a human being. At a sermon at Glide in 2021, Del said what people without homes want as much as anything is a conversation. If possible, develop a relationship with one person. Maybe, eventually, you might offer that one person something more, such as a shower. Or a job.

Only a tenth of the time, he calculated, do unsheltered people ask for money, but he does not suggest giving it. "First of all, you don't want to stop [walking]." In the Tenderloin, there may be "a higher density of crazy people," he said. "I use the word 'crazy.' A lot of people are on me for that, but that's the *word*. So don't stop. That's an old New York technique. Never break a stride."

But if someone shaking asks for a quarter, that is another matter. "He needs a drink. I been there. You're only twenty-five cents away from that drink, man. I'm asking you for a quarter, you tell me no, now I'm *really* shaking."

Del also opposes offering food, especially to people in the Tenderloin. Institutions such as Glide and St. Anthony's are so well-established and well-run, he said, people without homes are not starving. They need jobs, not "strawberry candies," as he once put it. And they need clothes, he said in a December 2022 address about the Tenderloin's dual addiction and homelessness crisis. Collect those ugly socks and the ill-fitting coat you never wear, he told his audience, and take them to drop-off places, including Code Tenderloin. People who are homeless wear clothing unwashed, unchanged, until it shreds. They would love to put on anything clean.

Such people also need connections out of homelessness. If you work for any business, including nonprofits, he said, avail yourself of organizations such as Code Tenderloin—unique though it may be in the United States—and hire its graduates.

Be advised, however, that in the Tenderloin, when you see people on the street, maybe playing cards on top of a trash can or leaning or sitting against a building, alone or with a group, talking, arguing, laughing—or drinking or using drugs—they are not necessarily homeless. They may live in a tiny depressing room in an SRO and go outside to escape. The sidewalk, says Del so often he all but chants the phrase, "is their living room."

Del also has advice for the unsheltered people who do not even have an SRO room. That advice might be summarized as "Get your act together to find a job. You cannot do without a paycheck." And consider "the whole package." "I tell this to people every day on the streets. Get plugged into services. You spend eight hours a day, forty hours a week, two weeks in a row, I guarantee you'll be where you need in eighty hours."

Work on it all, he urges. "The sheltering, the hygiene, the clothes, the job interviews, your health, everything. You can't just do one thing a day and say, 'Okay, I went to social security today; tomorrow I'll go to the [hospital] and make sure I get a health card.' You've got to be on it constantly." You cannot take a break. "I tell them, 'You did not take a break when you were smoking. Right now, you don't have a right to take a break, because that's going to be the difference between you and that person who doesn't take a break.'"

As for people who cite "a bullshit myth" in saying they are "only a paycheck away from being homeless," Del showed obvious impatience. "No, you're not. I don't know anyone a paycheck away from being homeless. Most people got last month's rent. So it ain't no paycheck away." In his opinion, "Our homeless neighbors out on the street, they're one paycheck away from being *housed*."

Does a person without a home and in need of help, simply move to San Francisco—or whatever city—to take advantages of its services? Many housed locals seem to think so. Del does not. Asked during one of his walking tours about the belief, he said, "Let me explain how homelessness works. You're not going to go to another city just because they got a better hotdog. If you're homeless in San Jose, you know where the police are. You know *who* the police are. You know the services around there. You know where the dope man is. You know how long the liquor store stays open. You know all your pertinent information in your neighborhood. Then you come up here, you're not going to be welcomed by this homeless community because you're San Jose homeless."

The biennial Point-in-Time homeless count, mandated by the Department of Housing and Urban Development, bears out Del's observation, at least as related to the Bay Area. In the 2019 count, for example, only 15 percent of the homeless population had lived in the city less than a year. In contrast, 43 percent had been residents more than a decade.

Another urban legend posits that some people prefer to sleep on the street. Wrong, said Del. "No one, unless they're mentally ill, wants to be homeless." Some people, he added, "have legitimate phobias about being inside. They're *seriously* claustrophobic. They wouldn't go in a mansion if you gave them a key. You can't do nothing about that person."

Among people who choose the streets are veterans. Sonja Scott, a friend of Del's, was program manager for a downtown San Francisco residence that houses veterans who had been living on the street. Del said when he and Sonja once walked through the neighborhood, she spotted a resident, Larry, she had been looking for. He was clearly sleeping rough. She said veterans' PTSD sometimes made them skittish about any sense of confinement. Larry, among other residents, went to the residence once a month to pick up his mail but never slept in his room. (Del has a separate issue with veterans who, once housed, settle for a modest monthly pension and do not try to supplement it with a job. As he sees it, they limit their own lives and those of their families.) Absent PTSD or claustrophobia, many people who sleep in the street, Del said, find it a better option than some shelters. "Who wants to be in that nasty-ass shelter? Nobody. You'd rather be on the street. 'Hey, you want to go to the shelter?' 'Hell, no!'" he shouted. But what would be the answer, he said, if asked, "Would you like a decent one-bedroom apartment in the Lower Haight?" "'Hell, yeah!' That same person."

Other restrictions come into play, too because shelters forbid "active" drug use, addicts and others may prefer the privacy of tents. Shelters—unless they are so-called wet houses—generally forbid heavy drinking. And this is California! No smoking!

Yet most nights in San Francisco, some one thousand people on a waiting list for a shelter bed (or cot, as they are sometimes more accurately called) do not get one.

CHAPTER 34

A PSYCHIATRIC EVALUATION

THE TOM WADDELL Urban Health Center on Golden Gate Avenue in the Tenderloin describes itself as providing "health care to mostly poor, disadvantaged and homeless persons." Clearly, funding included aesthetics. The lobby offers comfortable chairs, artful lighting, and a LEED designation of green building practices. Aesthetics go only so far, however. Taped to one window is a sign, headlined OVERDOSE ADVISORY, which reads, "San Francisco's fentanyl supply is very strong right now, containing more fentanyl than we've previously seen in other samples we've tested!" It advises users not to use alone and to have Narcan on hand.

One morning, a pale thin man walked quickly through the clinic's front door, looking agitated. He made his way to a Plexiglas-partitioned counter. An intake clinician apparently asked him a question. The man yelled, "Everybody in this town wants to know my fucking name! My fucking business!"

Everybody in the tastefully furnished waiting room turned toward him. Someone got him to calm down.

The outburst, said Dr. Pam Swedlow later in her office down the hallway, was "pretty typical." Actually, "acute" situations usually happen later in the day. "In the morning, not so much," she added with a small laugh. "But you see a range of things."

Because of that range, the Waddell clinic upped its security. "We finally lobbied to have a sheriff's deputy here. We have private security, and they know a lot of the clients and give a sense of order, but they're not armed. They're there to de-escalate people."

A psychiatrist who has been treating poor and marginalized patients for twenty years, Pam understands that challenges inside the clinic originate outside. "It's a neighborhood where the rule on the street at times is 'might makes right.' If people are homeless or living in pretty chaotic or intense situations, sometimes aggression is how you set boundaries and keep yourself safe." It is "a big ask," she said, for people to drop such behavior at the door. Another complication: aggressive behavior may be delivered "inequitably," aimed at lower-ranking, front-desk staff, not the clinic's doctors.

When people know an armed deputy is among them, escalation is down. Yet, Pam noted, "A uniformed officer here means different things to different people." She herself welcomed having a deputy in the lobby, as she has been threatened by the kind of man who just vented.

Nonetheless, she extended empathy toward him and other patients being asked a lot of questions by someone masked behind a partition (COVID was then raging). "It *is* frustrating. Especially if you feel unwell or, as so often happens, you're probably expecting to get a big fat no in the first place. I think sometimes people gear up for a fight because so frequently the answer is no or 'you don't qualify' or 'there's not enough to go around.' Aggression is something we use in the United States of America to get our way."

That day, outside the clinic in one direction, people lined up for free clothing. In another direction a couple blocks away stood a center, under construction, to help struggling but enterprising women cooks. A bit farther on, an epicenter of drug sales was open for business. Tents and debris lined the fronts of virtually every building. One man staggered up to a seemingly passed-out prone man and took what looked like a crack pipe from him.

Back on the Waddell clinic block, a middle-aged man employed by the civic organization Urban Alchemy kept watch, his Narcan pouch attached to his shirt. One man recently told him that Narcan had saved his life from overdosing death eight times.

"Why do they keep doing it?" the Urban Alchemy man wondered out loud.

Although many patients who come to the clinic are housed, many others either live on the street, in a shelter, or with a friend. The latter are considered "marginally housed," sometimes because of what Pam Swedlow called "behavioral reasons."

The majority of her patients are chronically homeless. "Our age range is probably forties to sixties." Few live to be older. "This is not a population that ages well."

Asked what she believes to be the primary cause of homelessness, she hesitated not a second. Leaning forward, she said, "Trauma." A pause. "Trauma."

She sat back. The extenuating problem, as she sees it: "We have systems of care to catch people who have fallen down, down, down, [but] . . . we don't really have any social structure to help people early on when their lives start to fail. Extended families and stuff like that aren't the norm, I think, in America."

She brought up the ACE score, an acronym for "adverse childhood events." They include parental divorce, mental illness, substance or sexual abuse, incarceration, and poverty. "The higher the score, the more likely you are not just to have issues like depression but [also] increased rates of cancer, increased rates of heart disease, increased rates of COPD [chronic obstructive pulmonary disease], increased rates of substance use. There's a direct correlation between what happens to people in their lives, especially early on, and how their bodies and their minds do later on." Traumatized children, in sum, become adults who may become homeless.

Getting a subsidized room off the streets is no guarantor of recovery, at least in San Francisco. "The buildings where we house people, every effort is made, but they're tough places to live. A lot of noise. [And] there can be a lot of drug use, when you're sharing bathrooms. Kitchen is in short supply anyways. It can be pretty unpleasant, to say the least. And there's no way to overstate the role of trauma in people's lives that bring them to the point where for whatever reason, they're unable to work and earn a living and manage their money and maintain relationships." That situation, she said, "speaks to years of trauma and intergenerational trauma as well—there's no quick fix."

She added, forcefully, "I don't think there's any way to overstate the role of institutional racism that plays into also what is trauma. People who look like me"—she is a slim strawberry blonde—"have a very different experience walking through the world. If you think about our patients who are African American, who are Latinx, the experiences they have, wherever they go and try to be part of this system, I can't underscore that [difference] enough."

Then there is bureaucracy. "A shockingly high" number of organizations try to help unsheltered people in the Tenderloin. "First of all, both the Department of Public Health [which administers Waddell] and UCSF together and separately are the big providers of healthcare in the city of San Francisco." The city's many nonprofits, she added, include the Tenderloin Neighborhood Development Corporation, or TNDC, which owns the building that houses not only the clinic but also some 170 apartments upstairs. The rooms may be small, but what an entrance! This building used to be a grand YMCA and features an elaborate marble stairwell that rivals a Hollywood movie set.

Pam continued listing providers, adding Mercy Housing and Episcopal Community Services and nearby institutions St. Anthony's and Glide. "The Department of Public Health also contracts with a lot of CBOs [community-based organizations] to provide other services." Then there is the Tenderloin Outpatient Clinic and various substance abuse programs, including for methadone dosing and counseling, subcontracted by the city. "Just off the top of my head, there's a lot.

"We are first and foremost a primary care clinic who have a pretty strong, robust mental health staff. Meaning psychiatry providers, social workers. A lot of times this is where people end up. We aim to refer them to programs that probably have more favorable staff-to-patient ratios, where they could get mental health services, but people often don't make it there. So we end up seeing a lot of people for whom making it here is as much as they can do, at least for now." Navigating from one agency to another "can be so tricky," she said. "It's hard enough for anyone. All the more so for people who are disenfranchised or whose life situations makes it hard to be organized or even just have a phone." Cell phones are essential but may get stolen or cut off for lack of payment. "A lot of logistic barriers get in people's ways [before they] can start to take the steps to better their own physical health and mental health, then achieve housing. We're also talking, of course, about a system that doesn't have a lot of housing."

Yet housing, in Pam Swedlow's opinion, may not be the most important component in ending homelessness. "People need relationships with other people, whether they form it with a case manager, whether with a nurse or a doctor or whatever other people they happen to live with. It takes a long time for someone who's experienced a lifetime of trauma to trust [anyone]." But trust, she said, is essential. "We are pro-social creatures. When we don't have relationships, we don't make it."

A TANNED COMPACT MAN with a neatly trimmed beard, Dr. Josh Bamberger works as a primary care provider ("from womb to tomb, cradle to coffin," he put it) at a Veterans Administration clinic in San Francisco's South of Market area. In his several decades as a psychiatrist, he has paid special attention to treating people experiencing homelessness. In that work, he has won fans but ruffled feathers too and paid the price at least twice.

One ruffling involved the well-publicized $30 million Homeless Housing Initiative begun in 2019 by San Francisco billionaire Marc Benioff, founder of Salesforce. "What I wanted [the initiative] to do and what it ends up doing? That's one of the reasons I'm not there anymore.

"Getting enough housing for everyone who needs it is a much bigger problem than $30 million. Government-sized problems need government-sized solutions." As an example, Dr. Bamberger said, "At the VA, we pretty much ended homelessness for all veterans in San Francisco. Very few veterans end up being homeless for long. That's a great example of a government program that provides housing and services and can pretty much accomplish the goal of giving everyone a place to live. Once they're living there, they have to *live*," he said, with a small laugh. "So they have many of the same joys and challenges [that everyone has]."

The point was, they got housing.

The Marc Benioff rupture followed one that took Josh Bamberger off the UCSF faculty. It started, he said, with his admiration of an eight-hundred-acre facility in arid southeastern Colorado called Fort Lyon. The facility had been a tuberculosis hospital but lain fallow for years until then governor John Hickenlooper "turned it into this place where homeless drug users can go and recover without any expectations or prerequisites. You literally can be on the streets of Denver on a Monday, call a phone number, and a van will come by and pick you up that evening and take you out to Fort Lyon. You can spend as long as you want. The only thing you have to do is *be*. Just can't use drugs there. Not that you can get them easily. Can't drink. So if you are wanting to be sober, that's a place you can go. And if you choose, you can get a degree at the local community college that has classes on campus."

When visiting the facility, the doctor was struck by a remark from a resident. Not until he had been at Fort Lyon eight months, said the man, did he realize birds were singing. "When you're so traumatized from life on the street, it takes a huge amount of safety and peace and kindness to see that there's a world outside your nose."

He was so impressed by Fort Lyon, he looked for a similar setting in California. And there it was, in wine-famous Sonoma County: an empty site that had been home to the Sonoma Developmental Center in Glen Ellen. "Very nice, huge campus with five hundred buildings." He claimed his lobbying for it to become like Fort Lyon cost him his job—apparently the idea upset major vintners. A final resolution took place in late 2022, when local officials voted to turn the property into basically standard housing.

He now favors a site in San Mateo County, which Del also has mentioned as a place to build housing. "It's another rural, isolated, beautiful part of the world. You could have two hundred small houses where people can learn a trade. They can code, they can learn how to build buildings. Self-governed, set their own rules, and get off drugs."

How many unsheltered people has he known who would welcome such a facility? "Some." He pictured those opposed having a range of reasons, including wanting to stay in a familiar and urban place, perhaps to use drugs.

Absent a large facility to treat unsheltered addicted people of the Bay Area, he touted a smaller place in Seattle, called 1811 Eastlake, "a nine-story building [with] beautiful architecture. The ground floor is an open floor plan [with partitions] about six feet high. There's a gap between the wall and the ceiling." This mirrors the model Del described. "Everyone has their bed and their armoire and their sink. But no one is in an enclosed space. So if they're going to have a seizure from withdrawal from alcohol or they're scared to be in an enclosed setting, they go there first. After they've been there for a month or two or ten, whatever is their desire, they can go upstairs to their own apartment in the same building with the same staff and the same community. We have nothing like that in San Francisco. There's no one in a place of authority who has any imagination or innovation or trauma-informed policies at this point. It's a real desert. We used to be the early adopters. Now we're . . . not."

Josh Bamberger echoed his colleague Pam Swedlow. "I often say the one common thread for all people who've experienced homelessness is trauma. Whether it's sexual trauma or psychiatric trauma, physical trauma, economic trauma, discrimination, racism. There's rarely a person who's been on the streets who hasn't been exposed to an inordinate amount of trauma that creates pathologic response."

He asked rhetorically, "What is the treatment for trauma?" His answer: safety.

"Knowing you have a place to live, that you can shut the door or someone won't exploit you, so you won't be re-exposed. And after you've established the sense of safety, you need to know that feeling for a long time. To get better, it takes long, slow improvements. At Fort Lyon, eight months before you hear the birds. Two years before you have enough sense of self-esteem that you are confident enough to get back into the workforce." Del concurs. Long-time homelessness to acclimation as a housed person, he has said, takes two years.

It may take much longer than that, if ever, to get over the effects of PTSD on homelessness. In a 2023 sermon at Glide, Del said, "I served in the Vietnam War, served the streets of South Central LA as a firefighter paramedic. Saw a lot of stuff, man. I saw a lot of stuff. You know what my nightmares are about? Being homeless in the Tenderloin." He began to shout. "I think I'm homeless again. I'm homeless again! I wake up in a sweat, running out of the room. How can this happen? I'm homeless again. That surpasses all that trauma, is being homeless."

AS FOR JOSH BAMBERGER, if he had unlimited resources and the power to end homelessness in San Francisco, he said would focus on one issue. "Housing. Making sure everyone gets a place to live and where they live provides adequate support for the illnesses they live with and opportunities for earning an income and feeling they're useful members of society." He does not believe people without homes simply give up. "Everyone I take care of has a great drive to live. Everyone has hopes and desires. Opinions."

He had nothing good to say about shelters or about conservatorship, committing a person—in the general opinion, someone filthy, raving, jumping in and out of traffic—against that person's wishes, to some institution. "You wrestle the demons and give them a shot of an antipsychotic medication. You hold them in a facility with high walls for a month or two or four. Then what? You're not going to do that forever. After four months, what do you do? Well, you send them back to some crappy program, and in two days they're exactly where they were four months ago. Or you send them to an architecturally beautiful facility with onsite services, psychiatric care, decent place to live, with a sense of control and free will. That works really well. Why don't you do that from the beginning? Conservatorship just kicks the can down the path."

By Dr. Bamberger's calculation, some 20 percent of people who are homeless have a diagnosed mental illness. "Another 30 or 40 percent on top of that have a primary substance use disorder." Yet, he claimed, "the majority of people who spend at least a night on the street are there because of economic reasons, not because of medical ones."

As it was time for the doctor to get back to his patients, he said San Francisco's Department of Homelessness and Supportive Housing offers "excellent quality, permanent supportive housing that can serve as a wonderful place for people who are suffering, to heal from their trauma." He added, "It works for the vast majority of people, but it's an inadequate supply."

There is another problem. "The people who are getting it are not necessarily the ones who need it the most." They may have been homeless for years, but that "doesn't necessarily mean you're the person who's sickest. You still might only need a shallow rent subsidy and a decent place to live." People with severe medical or psychiatric problems need the full gamut of supportive housing, he said, but "we don't necessarily prioritize" them.

His priorities in providing services for such people include trust, relationships, and free will. "You can create programs that might have a lot of rules, but if people are accepting those rules because they want to and they're not being coerced, those rules can be very supportive. Many people on the left think we have to do things without rules. I and Del are probably in sync in this space. Rules are important when you are fearful and untrusting and traumatized. You need to know what happens if you do something, what the consequences are. The problem is, we don't have alternative choices, so people feel coerced into these programs and end up living in places where they feel constrained.

"On the other hand, if you have a 100 percent, very crazy, various-substance-using people all together in one building, [that is] not a very good place to live or to work." He pictured a ratio of thirds. If twenty people out of thirty in a group home have "severe and persistent mental illness and substance use, [that] would probably be fine," he said. "We're good at it. We've been doing it a long time. And the more beautiful the building is, the more the community can tolerate the severity of people's mental illness. If you put someone in an SRO with a bathroom down the hall, the community doesn't tolerate even a small percentage of people." He cited approvingly "a beautiful building" in San Francisco called Mission Creek. The modern apartment building is home to low-income elderly people. "You can throw pretty much anyone in there and they do great. They themselves feel they're probably being cared for and cared about."

Del would agree: Getting a home is one thing. Feeling you matter is at least as important.

CHAPTER 35

PAM'S SONG

WHETHER BY WORD of mouth or constant hustle, Tenderloin Walking Tours hit enough of a stride that Del had to hire another guide. By trial and error, he learned he needed someone with three basic qualifications: punctuality, familiarity with the neighborhood, and anger management control. One new guide, despite Del's careful coaching, exploded into what he called "ghetto talk" during her first tour, hurling expletives so aggressively at a drug user, she alarmed nearby children.

Enter candidate Pam Coates, a gray-haired, fair-skinned, blue-eyed British woman in her sixties, with an accent formed in part by training with the Royal Shakespeare Company. Credit Del for looking beyond stereotypes. Pam may not have fit the part of anyone's presumed Tenderloin resident, but she had lived without shelter there too, also because of drug use . . . although not her own.

Her descent into homelessness began after she married, in 1998. "We'd been together a few years. As soon as we got married, the whole thing turned around." Her husband became her stalker. "He used to follow me to work. He was all over the place. It was a mess." Speaking in her sunny, memento-filled Tenderloin SRO room, she said that to this day she cannot figure how she got in the situation she did, but . . . "I know I'll never be there again. The odd thing was that I'd stayed in it so long because I was scared of being on the street. That actually proved to be the least of the worries."

Pam's husband was a member of the longshoremen's union. He developed "a *huge* cocaine habit." Pam tried to get him to "organize" himself and his addiction but was unsuccessful. "I actually had an alcohol problem. It's something I still have to be aware of, just in case." Drugs were not a lure. "His use was the biggest deterrent I could ever have, because I needed to be on the ball with him. He'd be coming round with a knife at three o'clock in the morning," while she tried to sleep, "looking for somebody who was hiding in the mattress. You can't reason with that."

Meanwhile, she held "all sorts of temp jobs," including in a Chevron office. "Any amount of money that came in, hammer over the head! 'Gimme.'" Pam did sense her salary was not being used as planned. "The fact I give him money to pay PG&E [Pacific Gas and Electric] and we get cut off a week later, it's a clue." She and her husband often were evicted for not paying rent.

Thus did Pamela Coates, a singer and once an acting colleague of such people as Diana Rigg, Ben Vereen, Matthew Broderick, and Paul Winfield, became on-the-street-homeless in the Tenderloin. The most difficult time on her own was the sopping wet winter of 2008–2009. "I spent a lot of time in and out of these [SRO] hotels. Got to meet some people who are still friends, who'd done their recovery. You don't know until you're there, how your survival instincts will work. I used to go out to the beach a lot. I used to travel on BART when they opened in the morning." Like Del, Pam tried to rest without sleeping. If she did sleep, she might wake up to find a couple of dollars left for her. Or not. "I made the mistake of falling asleep in a bus shelter once, and I lost my purse. With my passport and my green card." Pam also availed herself of charities. She lunched at St. Anthony's and slept at St. Boniface.

Regarding the question of money, she raised an eyebrow. "We have our routines. I used to do a little bit of conversion here and there, to get food." She air-quoted the word "conversion." "Because general assistance when you're homeless is $59 a month, and some food stamps." She also spent nights in doorways but never alone, thanks to a new male friend. In a gentlemanly impulse, he put Pam on the inside, next to the door, while he slept protectively on the outside.

During the day, Pam faked her situation. "I had to go to the expense of trying not to *look* homeless. Every little penny I got went to

Goodwill, in a way. Just to keep decent shoes on. A coat. It was raining that winter, and I had this heavy black velvet coat, which I still have," she said, with a nod to her closet. To freshen up, "I was able to nip into the Hilton and use their bathroom. I've had many a strip-washing," she said, laughing and pantomiming a quick splash of armpits.

One day in 2008, after buying provisions with her food stamps, Pam boarded a bus. "It stopped and then jerked and shot me into one of the back seats and broke my leg." An ambulance took her to St. Francis Hospital. There she received morphine. But her medical carrier through her ex-husband was Kaiser, where she was sent next. Kaiser maintained her leg wasn't broken because she was not in enough pain (thanks to the morphine). "They sent me back on the street with a broken leg." Eventually, unable to walk, she made her way to San Francisco General Hospital. She was told her leg had indeed been broken, but because of the passage of time it was too late to set it.

Her caseworker, whom San Francisco's Human Services Agency had earlier assigned Pam, found her a room at the Boyd SRO, around the corner from St. Anthony's. "The landlord took a chance on me," Pam said, despite past evictions with her husband. She knew she was lucky. "A lot of people on the street do go flaky. But without that, I would have been waiting for years. I might not have survived."

The Boyd is among other SROs administered via then San Francisco mayor Gavin Newsom's Care Not Cash program. The program essentially nixes monthly lump-sum payments to indigent people and substitutes financial support of services. It's a program Del says he was for. "That's how I got housed," said Pam. "They take you in, your general assistance comes up from $59 a month to $422 if you have accommodation. They're not going to give you four hundred dollars to spend on the street. Heaven forbid you might want to get a room."

Under Care Not Cash, an organization called the Tenderloin Housing Clinic basically trades services for a cut of the rent subsidy. "I had a hundred dollars a month and a room, and two hundred dollars in food stamps. Then, because they have this agreement with the city, they have to staff it properly. That's why you have all the security down there."

Indeed. A few steps into the Boyd's open front door stands a barrier surmounted by a thick metal screen, behind which sits a guard. For a visitor to gain access to a resident's room, one must phone the resident, who must come down to meet the visitor, who must show a photo ID. Finally, visitor and resident must both sign a log. Only then may the patchily painted elevator be approached, the journey upward commenced, a landing reached, a door opened. The overall impression of the Boyd, from the lobby to Pam's floor, is shabby, clean, and safe.

"This is the best one I've stayed in," said Pam, sitting on her neatly made double bed that took up much of the room. After years of being terrified of her paranoid husband, she sleeps in peace. Arrayed around the room's perimeter are posters from her late-in-life career as a cabaret singer and an actress with the Tenderloin's Recovery Theatre, which bills itself as "composed mainly of people in recovery."

She rose to extend the brief tour to her home's rare feature: a private bathroom, with a bathtub. A bit of laundry soaked. Because SROs generally have neither kitchens nor enough electrical current to support a refrigerator, keeping food in one's room is discouraged but difficult to monitor. How can one dissuade the formerly hungry from hoarding? Pam's small stash of fruit had led to some fruit flies; she pointed out a dish of apple cider vinegar, a practice she learned in England to combat them. Pam appreciated the Boyd. "They have a case manager, a property manager, the janitor."

Once Pam was partially healed emotionally and physically from the accident and her marriage, and safely housed, she began thinking beyond survival. "I happened to be walking up Golden Gate [Avenue] at the time the Community Benefit District had offices there. They were advertising for board members. I thought, 'That's exactly what I need.' I'd always been really politically active. My mother saw to that, and of course we European students in the sixties, were a force to be reckoned with! I thought, 'Well, this is cool.' I knew the community. I knew the situation." She got on the board.

She met Del in 2010, she calculated: "Through being on the board, because he applied for a grant from the committee I was chairing. For Tenderloin Walking Tours."

During the city's annual Sunday Streets event for nonprofits, Pam and Del were assigned to share the same booth. "I said, 'How are the tours going?' He said, 'It's funny you should ask. I need somebody to help me with them.' We were obviously on the wavelength because

I was thinking that's something I would do." Thus, Pam Coates took over some of the tours, and punctually, and without exploding.

She landed not only a home and a job. After joining the San Francisco Recovery Theater and singing jazz through the group, she made a CD. She all but shouted, "I get *paid to sing!*" then added, "It's a bizarre thing, but maybe it was meant to happen, because I wouldn't have discovered I have the balls to do stuff like this."

Pam's rosy picture, however, belied local violence.

In 2014, "I was attacked on Jones [Street]," she wrote in an email, "right by the police station (yes, really). I was attacked coming home from a gig. The girl who attacked me was 7 months pregnant. I fought tooth and nail to keep my purse, and though she eventually pushed me to the ground and I was knocked out, I had made enough noise to attract both the police and 2 girls passing through who videoed the attack. I did go to hospital for MRIs etc. The girl was arrested, allowed to stay out to have the baby and was given a court date which she didn't keep. She was arrested on a bench warrant, but the judge felt sorry for her (he is the legal representative on Glide's board of directors) and let her go. 34-year-old girl attacks a 65-year-old woman and is given preferential treatment. I had a severely damaged right knee which is still troublesome and although the previous judge had given her a hard year sentence if she went wrong, she walked away Scot free."

Their paths have not again crossed.

The attack, and other street activities near the Boyd, prompted Pam to try to move, as Del hoped she would for her safety. In 2017, about to have an intake interview for Section 8 housing, she emailed, "Keeping fingers crossed!"

Meanwhile, she remained at the Boyd, tended to her painful knee, then limping, headed out to give a Tenderloin Walking Tour.

CHAPTER 36

A DIFFERENT DIRECTION

IT MAY HAVE BEEN inconceivable to many people in the Tenderloin, including Del himself, but despite the measured success of the Walking Tours, he decided to move not only out of his apartment near the Tenderloin but also out of San Francisco.

Reasons were adding up, if only to two. Del downplayed the importance of one: the family of Jasmine, the woman who stabbed him, whom he sent to prison, had not retreated from its announced intention to kill him. San Francisco's district attorney, Terence Hallinan, via the Victim Assistance organization, stepped up to get Del out of immediate range.

Del had no special desire to move to the semirural town of Fairfield, halfway to Sacramento, but Deleana and Regina and a number of grandchildren lived there. Regina told him there were places for rent on her block. Del agreed to try. "I went and talked to the landlord and presented myself very well. And I came back and did all the paperwork."

It was a bureaucratic maze, getting his Veterans Administration housing voucher for San Francisco to be used in another county. "Ninety-nine percent of the people would have given up," he said. Not Del. "I'll get this handled." He did and moved to Fairfield.

As for Jasmine's family's threat, Del said later, he was not really scared, being from Chicago, after all. He wanted to leave San Francisco anyway. The main reason, he mentioned frequently, was to escape crack. That is, to live miles and miles and miles from the Tenderloin. If anybody in Fairfield dealt crack, he said, he did not know them.

"I don't want to deal with the Tenderloin at night. My use was mainly at night. Some people call that cheating and [say] I'm running away from my addiction. I don't care. But in the five years I've been in Fairfield, I woke up three times in the middle of the night and said, Fuck it. I'm going to get high." In each case ("three major trigger nights"), he planned to drive to San Francisco, but the distance stopped him. "As I'm putting on my clothes, I said, 'Hell with this.' Because I was so determined." If he had been living in a Tenderloin SRO, he would not even have to light his own crack pipe, he said.

Once Del moved into his modest duplex in Fairfield, he got involved in local life to some extent, beyond his family. He found a restaurant he liked. He managed a woman's reelection campaign for supervisor, offloading donated hamburger patties in the sweltering heat. He waved to neighbors. He visited the ducks at a civic center pond.

He had escaped not only a vengeful family but also an even more powerful adversary: the crackling Tenderloin.

CHAPTER 37

FILLING NEEDS,
AND MORE NEEDS

CODE TENDERLOIN TOOK OFF slowly and then accelerated.
Del could hardly keep up—121 emails in one day, he complained.
That was a record, at least for him. Please call, he often said. It's easier.

Year by year Code Tenderloin gained more and more traction, not only in the neighborhood but also in local, national, and international media, after Del added the component people kept asking for: coding. Yes, Code Tenderloin was born of hospital terminology, but why not teach coding to disenfranchised people who wanted to get into the tech industry, an easy walk away? It made sense, but it also made for more challenges, such as finding more teachers.

Then, with $84,000 in Code Tenderloin's account, one volunteer requested an $80,000 annual paycheck. Del exploded. "Trouble with millennials, they think they're the best and only seat in the house. That's not how we roll out here. They came on board, all Mother Teresas: 'We just want to be part of this.' It's completely laughable! Someone here demanding $80,000? Did you fail math in school? Unless I'm missing a zero, that's not possible, Bro. This is little Code Tenderloin working out of a bar. That should tell you something right there. Yes, I could get a storefront around the corner for $5,000, but that's not the mission. The mission is to put this money back into these folks on the street."

The more he spoke, the more he got in a lather. Thousands of volunteers at St. Anthony's and Glide do not ask for a paycheck! Why had Del been working for two to three years and not taken a penny? "What part of the word 'volunteer' do you not understand?"

He was equally outraged about a trip to Haiti planned by the San Francisco Christian Center, with which he has a sometimes contentious relationship. In a guest sermon, Del objected so strongly that he invented a verb to fit his reaction.

"I bambosted my parishioners for ignoring the homeless. I said, 'At least wave at us when you fly over. You're flying eight thousand miles away to help some people the whole international community is falling head over heels to help, because it looks good to say 'We have people in Haiti.' Your brothers and sisters and cousins are languishing down in the Tenderloin, and you're ignoring them. That's fiscally irresponsible and spiritually irresponsible."

They went anyway. And of course, when years later a church toilet broke, it was Del the plumber who fixed it.

By the late 2010s, Code Tenderloin had a formal board of directors, later turned into an advisory board, including none other than one of Del's rescuers, Walter Hughes. Several tech people were voted on the board too, as Del was invited to other boards.

All along, many Code Tenderloin graduates landed work in civic or health-related organizations, some continued their education, and a few even attracted media interest because of high-paying tech jobs. One, Shelley Winner, challenged her dismissal from her new employer, Microsoft, which fired her when they learned she was an ex-felon. Microsoft not only caved and rehired her but also eliminated from its application form the standard damning "check this box" line about criminal history. (Ban the Box is the name of the movement to end that practice.)

Additional matters, personal and professional, kept Del's life full. There were the Local Homeless Coordinating Board meetings, which demanded a working knowledge of federal, state, and city regulations regarding funding for homelessness efforts. There were countless people who counted on him. There were family situations and health situations, usually not mentioned. And a close woman friend was jailed on charges of organizing a hit team that murdered her rival in the then illegal marijuana trade. Believing in her innocence, Del scrambled to hire an expensive defense team.

It was a lot. "Put a fork in me, I'm done" became a typical expression.

Meanwhile, Code Tenderloin both stumbled and galloped along. Of an effort to raise money from one society matron, Del commented, "She didn't slam the door in our face, but she closed it pretty hard." A similar woman of wealth never returned his emails or calls until she wanted him to endorse something. (Del has called San Francisco "socially twisted" and at odds with its liberal reputation.)

Code Tenderloin's finances were on a rollercoaster. One year the organization had about $130 in the bank, Del mentioned. At such low ends, he said his approach to potential funders was upbeat. "We don't want them to see we're struggling. It scares them. 'If they're struggling now, a hundred thousand dollars is not going to help.' We want to keep the posture that we would like your *additional* assistance so we can serve more people, not that we need your assistance to keep the lights on."

The year after the $130 low, Del reported that Code Tenderloin banked some $300,000. Larger grants had come through. He had been "kissing booties" all week at City Hall for one effort, he confided. Unexpected dividends happened too. An admirer from Southeast Asia, distressed that Code Tenderloin lost a $100,000 grant, offered to write a conciliatory check for $50,000, and she did.

Code Tenderloin's office space reflected the up-and-down fortunes. More space was needed than the small tables in Piano Fight's main room, where the Piano Fight team also worked. Del rented space down the street, at 55 Taylor, from the Center for New Music, whose lobby features "unusual and newly invented musical instruments," according to its website. It would be difficult to imagine an odder coupling under one roof, but both shared the commonality of being nonprofits. They figured out the space.

In the building, Code Tenderloin first occupied an upstairs mezzanine area of sorts, then, when the budget faltered, a shared upstairs area, then a downstairs windowless room, then two downstairs windowless rooms. The donated furniture was on the lower end of utilitarian, along with some pieces that might be described as past prime opulent. Del learned from Glide never to turn down any gift, whatever its condition or usefulness. Otherwise the donor might not offer anything in the future.

One night, the building was burglarized, some fifty donated laptops meant for Code Tenderloin students stolen. Publicity about the theft led to such an outpouring of support, including replacement of the laptops, Del was overwhelmed.

At some point in 2019, although many people continued to volunteer, Code Tenderloin started paying salaries to some who worked more or less full-time. Virtually all were Code Tenderloin graduates themselves, a great many of them formerly incarcerated. The salaries would not be considered handsome. Del's talented new executive director, Donna Hilliard, initially kept her other job at a mattress factory in Berkeley. Del started taking an income too, one he called "commensurate" with other leaders of nonprofits. He also had learned his IBEW union pension was peanuts.

In September 2019, Code Tenderloin joined the pop-up trend and went outside. To attract potential recruits, it set up a white plastic canopy about ten feet square, shielding volunteers who sat at a table, brochures and sign-up sheets at the ready. Where did Code Tenderloin's pop-ups pop up? Not only on the most drug-heavy spots on Market Street but wherever there had been a recent shooting or stabbing. A seven-foot-high scroll of sorts attached to one of the canopy's upright supports listed what Code Tenderloin offered under the heading "Community, Education, and Empowerment":

- Job Readiness & Interview
- Code Ramp & Code Ramp ++
- Youth Internships
- Media Bootcamp Lab
- Computer Skills Training

As the *San Francisco Chronicle* reported, in just the first hour after the first pop-up appeared, more than a hundred people signed up.[1] It confirmed what Del had said all along: people want straight jobs. Both he and Code Tenderloin were on a roll, with more and more media attention and potential funding too. Foundations were seeking *him*.

By October, Del professed that at age seventy-three, running the day-to-day operation, with attendant crises, was not something he wanted to continue. Leave that to the staff, especially Colorado-born

Donna Hilliard, who went through Code Tenderloin training herself after rough years on her own and proved to be an innovative administrator. Del called her "the brightest star that has entered my life," the person "responsible for the amazing success of Code Tenderloin, with an almost unbelievable capacity for operational leadership."

Even before stepping down from quotidian work, Del had gotten almost too popular for his own good, invited to various events, simply to attend or to speak. One evening, San Francisco assemblyman David Chiu (since then city attorney) tapped him to moderate a town hall meeting with him. Del did so with aplomb, saying his goal was that someday people would look at the Tenderloin not with pity but with jealousy. He also referred to an emotional fact. While working on the first of Chiu's campaigns for San Francisco supervisor, Del lived in a tent, something he had not told Chiu. "I was embarrassed," Del said later.

Code Tenderloin kept adding and adding. A new program called S.O.A.R., a "sales and recruiting training program," joined the offerings. It posited, "If you sell drugs, then you can sell software. If you can sell stolen items, then you can sell tech solutions," and it added, "We know from experience that the soft skills are transferable."

Next came word that Code Tenderloin was partnering with its officemate, the Center for New Music, to offer "a free five-week music and technology workshop." "Build your skills," the partnership announced.

Then COVID hit.

To the astonishment of no one connected to Code Tenderloin, classes continued, although not in person. More laptops were donated to students who needed them. Donations of clothing, new and used, started piling up. Code Tenderloin also expanded its reach outdoors, dragging out tables and coffee urns, setting up sites to hand out masks and hand sanitizer in addition to food and clothing. An indication of what Del had created with Code Tenderloin can be summarized in a May 2021 flyer. It listed seven efforts under an "All Programs Brief Overview," starting with the original 2015 sole offering, Job Readiness, described as a "4-week class [in] Resume Building, Interview Preparation, Professional Networking, and Basic Computer Literacy."

Del's reputation increased. "Welcome to the Del Seymour Community Room!" read the poster on the festive opening day in 2022 for a new Tenderloin apartment building. Speakers included Del and Mayor

London Breed. (Del arguably has a closer relationship with San Francisco Rep. Nancy Pelosi, riding with her in a gay pride parade, for example, and conferring with her about Tenderloin issues. In terms of celebrities, he is still starstruck from meeting Michelle Obama at a White House conference about homelessness, and savors his cell-phone video of the two Chicagoans high-fiving each other, saying "South Side!")

At the event in the new "Del Seymour Community Room," members of Del's family came too, including Deleana and Regina, and quiet twenty-one-year-old Princeton, or Prince, Smith, whom Del newly learned and confirmed was his son. Prince, whose birth mother had died, was raised by a woman who attended the ceremony too.

By 2023, Code Tenderloin employed some eighty people, including many Code Tenderloin graduates. The vast majority of employees were part-time, and every one of them, said Del, had experienced homelessness. The budget, aided by more grants, including from the City of San Francisco, reached close to $3 million one year. Additional office space was rented on Mission Street in the South of Market area and was again furnished with a hodgepodge of donated furniture—plus a used Stairmaster, in case anyone wanted to work off stress.

How many people does Code Tenderloin help a year? Tens of thousands is the closest answer Donna Hilliard came up with. Inside of a month, Code Tenderloin's Facebook site announced yet another means of helping: a local hospital donated a van. Now Code Tenderloin picked up people in distress, especially at night, and took them where they needed to go.

In the meantime, speaking invitations to Del reached beyond the Bay Area. In Washington, DC, he addressed a 2023 National Council on Ending Homelessness conference on the topic of restoring the dignity of unsheltered people. They have not lost it, he said, but have only misplaced it. Back in San Francisco, another interview awaited, this time by a Swedish film crew.

Over the years, more students with more problems availed themselves of Code Tenderloin classes. Instead of the initial breakfast fare, doughnuts and water, long-time volunteer Brenda Davis put out a variety of cereals and snacks as well as cups of instant soup, for which she plugged in an electric kettle. Some students work all night, she confided, and do not have time for breakfast. And about five of the fifteen students she plugged in for were homeless. They, too, could have worked all night. That there are people with full-time jobs who have no home is one appalling fact of San Francisco life that Del imparts to tourists and potential funders. He mentioned watching a uniformed security guard carrying a backpack into a shelter, the man clearly not earning enough to sleep anywhere better.

Two of nine men in one Code Tenderloin class used canes to get to their seats. A woman brought her two small children, whom the teacher, Justin DeMartra, himself a Code Tenderloin graduate, pointedly welcomed. He also assured the students, "No question in this class is stupid." Some questions, though, were challenging: How do you model a resume that has a thirty-year gap due to a prison sentence? Today's lesson plan turned to credit scores: how to learn them and improve them. Tomorrow's plan was for students to try out their elevator pitches for potential employers. One man expressed nervousness about rehearsing his.

Del had become an infrequent visitor to the classes, much less teacher. He faced instead more grants to apply for, more interviews to give, more of everything. That included more sadness. Cornell Dodd, who had joyously proclaimed he was going to "do a Code Tenderloin on them" and been featured in the organization's promotional film *Crossing Market*, suddenly died of a heart attack. Everyone was upset, especially the ex-paramedic who had come across many such victims in his career.

Another year, during COVID, Del got a call telling him his treasured friend and tour guide Pam Coates had died. She was found in the Section 8 apartment she finally had got. Among the speakers at her memorial service in the Tenderloin were members of her beloved Recovery Theatre, and Del.

ALL ALONG, Code Tenderloin offered more and more classes. They included Community Health Worker (a "12-week course studying doing Case Management and Community Outreach work," according to the website), Code Ramp (teaching "the basics of Front-End Web Development [JavaScript, HTML, CSS]"), and Code Ramp + + (a six-week course focusing on intermediate JavaScript). The core remained JRP: Job Readiness Preparation.

Code Tenderloin also responded to the Tenderloin's all-too-present dangers. Del used the term "Calming Corners" for his approach, to de-escalate tensions at locations where, to cite an extreme but not uncommon example, someone had been murdered. "Calming Corners Ambassadors" consisted of "Neighborhood Outreach walking around building relationships and conducting referrals." Those referrals meant, of course, lessening the chance of violence by offering job training. Similarly, the "Calming Corners Pop-Up" was described in organization literature as a "tabling event where we hand out food bags, face masks, hygiene kits, Education and Job Training information, plus other resources." By the time Covid became rampant, Code Tenderloin employees and ambassadors wore identifying white vests with reflective stripes.

One afternoon on a sketchy block around the corner from Code Tenderloin's offices, vest-wearing volunteers dragged out a table, complete with anti-Covid Plexiglas partitions, a pile of flyers, a huge urn of coffee and paper cups, and a large folding table on which large bags of donated clothes were emptied, then separated and folded. Passersby, some looking shabby, some sparkly, some both, pulled out items, held them up, then took them.

"Any for men?" asked a tall man pushing an older man in a battered wheelchair.

"Nope, today just women's and babies," replied a volunteer.

"Fuck," said the man. "And thank you," he added as he pushed on.

A couple weeks later and blocks away, a recent graduate of Code Tenderloin's Job Readiness classes, a man in his forties known as Howard T., was shot to death. An employee of Code Tenderloin referred to him as smart.

No, said Del, a day after speaking at an outdoor memorial held at the shooting site. If Howard T. were smart, he would not have been there. In fact, Del told some hundred people at the memorial, his message remained: "Get off the block." You cannot play in both worlds, as he put it later. It's a mistake too many people make, to do whatever, such as deal drugs, make enemies, go off to prison, and return to the same place. That's what Howard T. apparently did, although the exact reason for the shooting remained unclear. The murderer was arrested a few days later, said Del, who figured he'd be freed soon, a reflection of San Francisco's controversial (and later recalled) DA Chesa Boudin, who Del joked acted more like a public defender.

"Calming the Corners" efforts continued too, as did street violence. A sampling of 2021 headlines, apart from those about Howard T., included "Second Suspect Arrested in Fatal San Francisco Tenderloin District Shooting of Community Worker," "Tenderloin Shooting Leaves 17-Year-Old Dead, Others Injured," and "SFPD Battling Tidal Wave of Crime and Illegal Drug Sales in the Tenderloin Neighborhood."[2] One Saturday-night shooting happened only steps from Piano Fight. It finally shut down, after valiant post-COVID attempts to stay viable.

Meanwhile, Code Tenderloin "ambassadors" in their distinctive vests visited unsheltered people to offer help of various kinds, sometimes starting with a cup of coffee and a recognition of existence. Think about a red tide washing thousands of crabs onto the shore, Del has said, and an eight-year-old boy washing the sand off them, trying to save them from dehydration, and putting them back in the water, as wave after wave wash up thousands more. Think of a man on his porch watching the boy for hours, then walking over and asking, "What does it matter?" And think of the boy, indicating the crab in his hand, replying, "It matters to this one."

MAJOR FINANCIAL AID to Code Tenderloin for its growing varieties of efforts, including COVID-related help, arrived. In 2020, Twitter head Jack Dorsey, a yearslong admirer of Del's, donated a whopping grant of $1.6 million. And there were more grants from the city of San Francisco.

Code Tenderloin's own efforts, reflecting Del's one-by-one approach, varied in size. When reports surfaced that many Tenderloin youths were not vaccinated for COVID, Code Tenderloin held an event offering a vaccination and, for a bonus, a marijuana cigarette. Staffers were thrilled that sixty-five people got the shot-and-joint combo. Del preferred a cash bonus but yielded to his staff. Media coverage about the action was positive, as it has been from the start.

Adding to the upbeat mix was a film by documentarian Brandon Krajewski called *Crossing Market*, the same title as Code Tenderloin's earlier promotional film. Its message circled back to what Del sought from the beginning: that people without much, including homes, might cross the impediments in their own streets and minds.

Code Tenderloin's address, 55 Taylor, became a drop-in center. Some in-person classes resumed in a repurposed hallway of sorts, depending on the COVID situation. Others were still virtual. A fact sheet Code Tenderloin issued stated that more than ten thousand people had been reached by the classes, with an 87 percent job-placement rate. That figure, of course, did not necessarily include Tenderloin residents that Code Tenderloin reached in other ways.

Clearly, needs went beyond Del's original intention. The building's lobby offered a chair or two to anyone, masked, who needed a rest or maybe information or coffee. Hospitality must have gotten out of hand, for later a table blocked the entrance, although a volunteer sitting at it offered what help he could, counseling one young man not to put up with whatever it was, saying that there were "other places to stay" and providing a list. On a Code Tenderloin wall, a pinned scrap of paper offered a short list of places with free showers.

CHAPTER 38

A RECRUIT, RECRUITING

"**I** KNEW WHO HE WAS, but I hadn't interacted with him," said Terrill Jones of his early days working at Code Tenderloin and observing Del Seymour. "Honestly, I was intimidated. Because when I saw him, he was always commanding people. 'This needs to happen like this,' or 'That needs to happen like that.'" Terrill tried to avoid Del's attention, a challenge for someone six foot five. "I was, like, 'Please don't let him say nothing. Make sure I do everything I'm supposed to do.'"

Terrill's caution paid off. "My job title is 'senior program manager.' What I do on a day-to-day is pretty much juggle people. I attempt to meet them where they're at. And putting the right people in the right position to have the best overall effect for us and them." His basic assignment, he said, includes coordinating "the different students, potential employees, as well as the partnerships" Code Tenderloin has accumulated. "We work with a lot of different organizations."

He also helps oversee some local initiatives, including Safe Passage, which Terrill described as a "walking school bus" that guides children past the obstacles and challenges of Tenderloin sidewalks. "This morning, I met at the walking school bus first, to make sure I have the staff to walk the children to school. If they're not here, then I myself or whoever may be able to walk the children. Then I make the morning huddle at the Linkage Center [San Francisco's then-new, since-closed all-in-one drop-in site] to get the daily agenda of what's open, what's not open, what resources are available." He added, "In the transition from using and housing, we catch a lot of people looking for resources for different things." Sometimes for help he calls his contact at TAP (Treatment Access Program), an experienced nurse practitioner.

Terrill's first foray to Code Tenderloin came at the urging of a friend who taught its advanced Code Ramp course. Enthusiastically, Terrill went. "I quickly found out I was out of my actual depth." He also attended a Code Tenderloin job fair. "It was more geared towards coding and tech fields. It still highlighted I wasn't ready."

Terrill's situation came to the attention of Code Tenderloin director Donna Hilliard, who told him he should first take the Job Readiness class, like other students. "But I needed the work right now. I can't take a six-week Job Readiness [and then other courses] because a condition of parole is that you have to work."

At long last, Terrill was almost a free man again.

He and his older brother grew up in South Central Los Angeles, their father a carpenter who did drywall installation, their mother an employee of the Department of Motor Vehicles. Terrill's downward trajectory started when his father died. "I was fourteen," he said, then paused. "Now, I know as an adult that mental health in a Black community is taboo. People don't talk about it. We don't deal with death in a proper way, especially in terms of how it affects youth, to remain in the survivor's house.

"Right away, my grades started sliding. Right away, my achievement started suffering. Right away, my focus wasn't there." Terrill's brother was already out of the house, leaving Terrill and his mother. "I appreciate everything she did for me, but she couldn't be there enough. Plus she was dealing with her own pain of separation." Terrill dropped out of high school and got a job in construction doing drywall, as his father had. "I was always at work, coming home tired. I would see my friends, and they always were having fun. 'Man, you got all that? It took me all week to get what I got.' They're pulling out big money wads. One thing led to another and I committed my first robbery. Did it several more times in a span of a couple of months. Did that time."

The prison sentence put Terrill behind bars for some four years, until his release in 1995. He moved home, as did his brother, because their mother was sick. Terrill only learned later the sickness that killed her was from HIV. "Everybody kept that a secret." She did not use drugs, he said, but "as far as I could tell, she was with a man that was a user."

Apart from caring for her, Terrill got a clerical job with Health Net insurance company. And, contrary to the terms of his parole, he owned a gun. Meanwhile, California's draconian three-strikes anticrime law had recently been passed. Essentially, anyone convicted of a certain offense (a list since greatly reduced) that increased the offender's two crimes to three, or "three strikes," faced up to life imprisonment.

Terrill had two strikes from earlier convictions. "Three-strikes law came about before I paroled. Had a weapon. 'Possession of a firearm.'" He added flatly, "The only crime I committed was I had it." He received an additional prison term: a quarter of a century.

"I did twenty-five years. Well, twenty-four years, eight months, two days." He calls the years "erased time." Most he spent at Soledad State Prison, situated some two and a half hours south of San Francisco. In lieu of other instruction, "I took/take spiritual courses with the Savior, if that makes sense," he later wrote in an email.

After his release, Terrill was paroled for eighteen months, to the transitional halfway facility at 111 Taylor Street, a block from Code Tenderloin. One day, tired from working two jobs, he had "a hiccup." He returned to 111 carrying a marijuana joint. He knew it was against the rules. The hiccup extended his parole to three years. "It frustrated me, but I get it."

The joint also made him lose his spot at 111. "That actually turned out to be a blessing in disguise because it moved me to Treasure Island [in the San Francisco Bay]." A merged Walden House/HealthRIGHT 360 program landed Terrill a two-bedroom apartment. "I only had one roommate, all the room in the world, no police oversight. It was about me and what am I going to dedicate myself to?" Terrill got busy, in part caring for his roommate. "He was disabled, so I would help him out." Terrill's paying jobs included a place called Civic Pit Stop and being a dishwasher and a DoorDash driver and a desk clerk in the Tenderloin.

"I ran into Donna on my way out of work. She took one look at me and said, 'What's wrong?' I had to put a family out. I didn't agree with putting a family out on the street. This was when COVID started, and everybody was getting put out or turned away. I was frustrated. She saw that and said, 'Well, I think I've got something for you.'"

It was a "Care Team" that partnered Code Tenderloin with a Downtown Streets Team, which offers job training through civic engagement of literal street cleaning. Terrill accepted, despite a cut in pay. "But we got to actually serve the community."

That led to more work with Code Tenderloin and finally getting to know Del. "Staying under the radar but doing my job." Their exchanges of pleasantries led to Terrill's trusting him. "I know if I have an issue or whatever it may be, I've got somebody I can actually talk to and be real. It may not always be what I want to hear, but I know the feedback is going to come from a genuine place."

"Del is a scientist. My first one-on-one with Del was not as nerve-racking as it was cut and dry. I brought my problem to him"—a private matter—"laid it all out. He gave me an honest assessment along with a solution. It worked."

In the meantime, Terrill advanced at Code Tenderloin. He attended various meetings, too, where Del spoke. "I got to sit in and listen and absorb. At this point in my life, I definitely try to emulate a lot of the things he does, because it takes a certain kind of fearlessness to speak openly to so-called power, if that makes sense. Sometimes I'm a little bit brash, though, and I get carried away. My heart is in the right place. I attempt to keep it in the right place," he added.

Thanks to Code Tenderloin's connection to various housing options and an adult probation program, Step Up to Freedom, Terrill got a good-sized apartment at Candlestick Point, which he shares with his girlfriend Aja, whom he knew earlier as a friend, and her son, Amari. The arrangement includes a 50 percent initial subsidy, then 30 percent, then none—toward a $3,300 monthly rent. Terrill is contemplating something less expensive. He had been working two jobs, one for HealthRIGHT 360 and one for "Code T," but the long hours "created tension in the household because I was always gone." He quit HealthRIGHT. "That was two checks. This is one check. Oh, I notice the difference. Trust and believe that, but it's okay. I'll be all right."

Terrill has a thirty-year-old son. "I was not a part of his upbringing," he wrote in an email. "We're currently in a weird time in our relationship. We do talk when he feels like it. I call and he will answer sometimes and sometimes not."

He is clearly connected with Amari, who is now the age Terrill was when his father died. Code Tenderloin became part of Amari's life too. "When he's out of school and we have an event, he comes and volunteers," Terrill said. "He took the OFA—Opportunity for All—class last summer." Terrill named more programs he looked forward to Amari participating in, including computer literacy, then he paused. "He's not my biological son, but I've taken on that role as father. He's been doing great since he's been up here. Grades, he's on the honor roll."

Terrill Jones may be one of Code Tenderloin's major recruiters. He has been trying to get his brother to move to San Francisco and join too. Furthermore, Terrill's current relationship with his parole officer is such that the officer sends him other people from the 111 Taylor lockup site. "Right now, I have on staff maybe twelve people from 111."

Meanwhile, Terrill faced eleven more days of parole. True to Donna's assessment of prison programs, they typically offer inmates little preparation for modern connectivity. Not only had Terrill felt out of his depth at a Code Tenderloin computer course, but, he said, "I'm still learning the cell phone."

But at fifty years old, having spent more than half his life in prison, he was looking ahead, affirming a published quote about him: "I made an agreement with myself and with God, that I would put the same energy that I used into committing crimes into helping this community."

Among the people Terrill recruited to Code Tenderloin have been fellow inmates. One employee, Steven Rice, said, while overseeing activities in the new donation and office center on nearby Mission Street, "He was in Soledad with me, and he got out first."

Unlike Terrill, Steven said Del did not intimidate him. "I learned from the Honorable Elijah Muhammad, and he was a little bitty man. So the intimidation factor would never enter into it." Steven, whom nobody would call "little bitty," added, "When I did meet Del, he had the same type of passion that [the] Honorable Elijah Muhammad had." The connection to Elijah Muhammad, Steven said, took place during the thirty-four years he was incarcerated. The message from him and Del: "Start with the people."

Steven continued, "If you don't get to the people, then everything you do is for naught. That's how I see Del. That's why they call him the mayor of the Tenderloin. If he wouldn't have started with the people, he would just be another business owner trying to get you out of the way. It'd be cut and dry. Code Tenderloin is not a cookie-cutter company. Some people have to learn how to deal with that, because you're not being micromanaged. You have to be self-driven. You have to have that passion already in you to do this kind of work. If you don't have that, then it's probably not the job for you."

Steven, like Terrill and many others, was vetted, aided, and promoted by Donna Hilliard. He took a number of Code Tenderloin classes to prepare him for work as a director, someone who oversees managers, who in turn oversee ambassadors, who essentially do outreach. "I went through the whole training." That included Job Readiness Preparation, which had become an eight-week course. His training also included getting a mental health class certification through the auspices of San Francisco's City College. "I did that as soon I got out, day one." And he took a certified community health worker training class. "If you don't understand harm reduction, de-escalation, if you haven't ever had any Narcan training, overdose prevention training, all these things come with the job. Because if you don't have those tools, how are you going to convince somebody else to get a job? I can't just give you a job and you a dope fiend. What are you going to do? Rob the place? But if I take my time with you and can show you the benefits, and we can add that value, now when you look in the mirror, 'Oh man, I feel a whole lot different today.' All that comes into play. Now when I give you a job, you actually are ready."

Steven also works with about forty on-call employees, some living in a shelter or tent. They may be affected by mental issues or substance abuse but are willing to try a day's work. "The on-call list is to give us the opportunity to give *them* the opportunity to slowly and gradually make that change."

Before they get on the on-call list at all, however, Code Tenderloin people such as Steven may approach them and offer a cup of coffee, maybe breakfast, maybe lunch. That leads to a connection and perhaps volunteering, including an invitation to see a Code Tenderloin workplace. Steven continued, as a few yards away visiting UCSF nurses with the Roving Community Health Initiative prepared syringes for vaccinations, "First thing we want to do: come in and look at the activity. 'Put your vest on, come over here and help me. Let's pass out some hygiene kits.' We take them step by step by step. We don't want to just thrust them into anything. Then we'd give them a stipend for working the pop-up, for volunteering."

Steven said such connections also help when, for example, city utility crews need to work where people are sleeping. "If we want to clear this business front, which is one of the things that we do now, I have to give them something to do. I can't just say, 'Hey man, get out of their way.' Oh, no. 'Hey man, how you doing this morning? You all right? We're going to try to clear this area right here. What can I do for you?' I'm going to start that communication. We are like a liaison or a buffer between the business owners and the community. We have to be there, be respected, have a rapport with them in order to make that happen. We offer them incentives to help us do our job, which allows the business owners to thrive, because you want that traffic. You don't want people to be scared to come into your place of business."

"One of our contracts is with SF MTA [Municipal Transportation Agency]," he said, looking both earnest and pleased. Blocks of nearby 6th Street being dug up and marked with orange cones involved a collaboration with Code Tenderloin. "We're out there walking around with the flyers and the hygiene kits, out-reaching, but we're really watching the equipment and things like that. At the same time, the foreman communicates with the team, so they're having a morning huddle, 'We're going to be digging right here.' In that huddle the Code Tenderloin employees get a chance to ask questions." As a result of the collaboration, he said, SF MTA hired two Code Tenderloin people who now have full-time construction jobs.

Code Tenderloin's efforts clearly extend far beyond the initial concept of job readiness training into providing free lunches, clothes giveaways, and street teams including professional nurses who administer COVID and flu shots and clean wounds. Steven mentioned one homeless man, respectful but a conspiracist, ranting about "poison" in COVID vaccines—until one day he pulled up his sleeve to get a vaccine himself. That would not have happened, said Steven, if Code Tenderloin were not "a presence" or if Del and Donna had not created a work environment that said people's needs come first. "You're here to serve the community, period. Self-help starts with us. We have to be right to do the job we're doing. Once we get into that position, all the other things we do just make it easy for us to communicate, to help people. You can't help nobody you're disrespectful to or [who] don't respect you."

CHAPTER 39

TOP RAMEN

"**G**OOD MORNING, GLIDE!" said Del from the church's stage. He was about to give his first guest sermon at San Francisco's Glide Memorial United Methodist Church.

"Good morning, Del!" came shouts from the packed floor and balcony.

Minutes before taking the stage, this summer of 2018, he seemed happy, a bit jumpy and nervous, yet controlled. He had spiffily outfitted himself in a suit and tie, plus pocket square. Friends and family greeted him, hugs abounding, the Glide musicians swinging their horns, two pews set aside for Code Tenderloin supporters. The honor of giving a Glide sermon—called "a talk"—carried enormous significance, as Del would soon attest.

The church's legendary leader, Rev. Cecil Williams, by then re quiring a wheelchair to get around, had been a source of inspiration, compassion, and sometimes comeuppance to Del. It was the Reverend Williams, for example, whom Del credits for turning him away from homophobia.

Today, when Del took the podium forty minutes into the rousing service—Glide runs a tight ship on timing—in typical fashion he made a self-deprecating remark. Gesturing at Rev. Williams, seated among the congregation, Del said how strange it was to be looking not up but *down* at Cecil, then added he had slept in Glide's doorway "many nights."

"Many nights," he repeated softly, "*too* many nights." Reverend Williams famously never turned his back on anyone, as evidenced in two Glide bywords printed on the cardboard fans ushers were handing out: "RADICALLY INCLUSIVE."

Del then offered a prayer. As at other occasions, he focused not on this racially diverse, urban congregation—that day including flamboyantly groomed drag queens, down-and-outers, and at least one woman seemingly "in her addiction," as Del would put it—but rather on the residents of Redding, a largely white city in rural northern California. "[While San Franciscans complain] about the poop on the sidewalks or how long Uber takes to come and get you," Del said, to some laughter, "there's people *right* now, this moment, watching their house burn down." In short, he said, think about the uncontained forest fire. "Quit tripping. Those people up there, they're tripping. I want us to have a prayer for them."

He added, in a rare personal note, "[Pray] for my [relative], who's doing too long in prison. I'm asking the Lord for some of that mercy for him." Del did not name the young man, in prison for molesting young women. Del also prayed for his "very dearest best friend": "[She is] struggling with the hardest part of her life that she'll ever have. She's facing three life sentences right now." He did not name her either, the young woman jailed on charges of arranging the murder of her rival in the marijuana business. If he were not at Glide right now, Del said, he'd be visiting her, as he does almost every Sunday. (A jury later convicted her. She was indeed sentenced to life.)

"Forget the poop," he cried. "There are other things going on in our life. You all know someone that needs prayers. Give it to 'em."

His voice broke as he thanked family and friends present, including his daughter Deleana. "Maybe," he said, looking at her, "this will replace some of those years when you didn't know where I was. If it makes it any better, *I* didn't know where I was." The congregation shouted its understanding. "Thank you, baby," said Del, his tears visible.

Finishing thanks to people involved in the Code Tenderloin job training program, started "by a bunch of us," he put it, he referred to a *San Francisco Chronicle* editorial that morning about the dismal future of minority youth.

Now, warmed up, Del named nearby Tenderloin blocks "a wasteland of our minority youth": "In the afternoons, there's a couple hundred young kids that don't know what the heck to do because no one has given them an agenda. It's for *us* to have given them an agenda. They're out there seven days a week, so *lost*, man. We point at them, 'Look at them out there.' Well, look at us sitting here. We really got to do better." The audience applauded enthusiastically.

As if demonstrating a master class in speech-making or sermon-giving, Del alternated between comedy and tragedy. He mentioned an early Code Tenderloin colleague (with whom he'd had a falling out but reconciled) who urged Del to help a "young lady" of twenty or so, living on the streets, and give her Del's extra room. "I said, 'That's why it's called an *extra* room, because I'm not going to *use* it.'" After the laughter, Del said he finally agreed, adding, "She's still there, four years later." When the applause ended, Del named the woman, Aaniyah Body, an in-home nursing specialist. "[She works] five days a week for seniors and disabled folks, all in the Tenderloin South of Market, some of the worst buildings you could go in. She works ten to twelve hours a day. You know what this little girl does on her off day?" Unpaid, she gets up at five in the morning and goes to her patients, even on a day off, he said, if a client needs a shower.

To the surprise of the congregation and Aaniyah herself, who whispered to the person sitting next to her that she had not dressed for this, Del urged her onto the stage. As the slender woman walked up the stairs, Del wept, shaking his head. The congregation went wild. Then he threw in a dollop of comedy. "She gets up every morning and walks in my bedroom and says, 'Old man, are you still alive?'"

After she returned to her seat, Del the provocateur came forth. "[This area is homelessness] ground zero right here," he pronounced to shouts of agreement. "The most famous homeless man in the world, his name was Jesus Christ. Check the Bible. He was *born* in a homeless shelter.

"We put a lot of time into loving this guy and *praising* him, and we ain't never met him. What about Tyrone outside, who we just met? Are we loving him as much as we're loving Jesus Christ? When you walk by Tyrone, do you speak to him? You just walked through Tyrone's bedroom. If you walk through *my* bedroom you *better* speak to me!"

Del added, to many amens, "It ain't *his* fault he's on that sidewalk. It's *our* fault. We want to pretend the government's in Washington. The government's right here. Those cats just work for us," he said, applause building. "*We're* the government. We got to do it better."

Change the statistics, he enjoined the congregation. Do so one by one. "Go find a homeless person or person in need you can get along with. Do something for him. Encourage him. Offer him referrals. Let him pop in and take a shower. Ain't that big of a deal. It's just water, man. That is Jesus Christ outside."

When Del brought the subject back to the state of the city's minority youth, keeping his tone light, he described what happened when Caroline Barlerin opened Twitter's doors to Del and his students. "I took twelve young African American cats off the corner and put them in Code Tenderloin. These were ex–dope dealers. And they just retired *hours* ago, if you know what I mean," he said to laughs, then described a long struggle to make them walk seventeen minutes to Twitter to learn about job opportunities. "They did not want to go. 'Man, you ain't taking us over here and showing us off in front of these white folks. They ain't going to do nothing for us.' It was like pulling kids," Del said, comically acting out a frantic adult trying to corral a group. "I could pull these two up, these two go in the store. I got to go to the store to get them. Now these two are gone."

Once he managed to get them all to Twitter, Del said, they sat mutely as employees walked by, typing on their devices. "Caroline and her team are trying to engage with my cats. My dudes ain't saying *nothing*. All they want to do is get the *hell* out and back on the other side of Market, where they're comfortable.

"Just when I thought all was lost, three young African American guys with Twitter shirts on pass by." They were also typing on their devices. Del's voice dropped as he described how his kids locked on the three, watched them all the way out the door, then raised their arms eagerly, shouting, "Sir! How can I do this?' I couldn't shut them up!" Del rode the wave. "We need to do that for our kids—we need to let them know they can fit in there," he said, prompting a huge smile from Caroline, sitting in a pew.

Del's final pitch made his voice break. "Get you a passion if you don't have one. Stay with it. Be generous with it. My passion is homelessness. I live and sleep it, eighteen hours a day, seven days a week. Because these are *my* folks outside. Until I could see more of them coming in *off* those streets, I'm going to be out here, man." The extended applause and shouts came louder than before.

Now in complete emotional sync, Del told a story he had related at least once, if to a much smaller audience. It involved something that happened a morning months earlier.

"I says, I ain't feeling it today. I don't want to hear that H word. I ain't going to that damn Tenderloin, first of all. I'm going to stay right here, sit in *my* house. They can do whatever they want to do over there. I was *not* going to deal with homelessness that day. Trust and believe. I said, 'Let me go down and get me some breakfast.' I drive down to the Lucky supermarket. Guess what? There's a homeless dude on this door."

Del gestured, as the congregation burst out laughing: "And a homeless dude on *this* door. I'm figuring, how am I going to get around this? I try my jogger thing, and I can't. I'm seventy. I can't run *real* fast. But I'm running through the door, and the dude grabs me. I said, 'Ohhhhhh, dude! Get back! Get back! I don't want to *hear* that stuff today.' And I didn't say 'stuff.' "He says, 'No. No, brother. I don't want your money. Can you get me a pack of Top Ramen?'"

"Oh. Top Ramen? Yeah, I can get you a pack of Top Ramen. That's easy! I'll take a little break from my boycott today, get the brother some Top Ramen. I go in and don't know where the Top Ramen is because I do not eat Top Ramen. I tried it about ten years ago, and I didn't know until somebody told me there's a little packet of flavoring you're supposed to put in there."

The congregation laughed as one. "I thought it was their preservative. I said, 'Who would eat this cardboard?'"

A clerk directed Del to aisle seven.

"Aisle seven at Lucky's is as long as this church. I said, man, who in the heck eats that much ramen? It's about two hundred different varieties. Now I forgot what brand the dude has asked me to get. I ain't going back outside and coming back in. That's too much on my boycott day. I'm looking at the prices. Six cents, eight cents, fourteen cents. I said, Oh, I'll just get a whole bunch of it. I start grabbing ramen. Now my shopping cart is like this with ramen," Del said, indicating a heap.

"I go to the checkout counter. It's like six bucks. I got a hundred packs of ramen. The lady puts it in two big old bags, and I go out. Dude is still there. I hand him those bags. He says, 'Whose is this?' I said, 'It's for you.' He said, 'This is for *me*?' I said, 'Yeah, man. It's no big deal.'"

Now Del began to weep. "He puts them bags down, and he grabs me." The man cried so long his tears drenched Del's shirt.

During a churchwide hush, Del collected himself before continuing, "He hugged me and he hugged me. And he kept saying, 'Thank you, man! Thank you.' Right at that point, I said, 'No, bro. Thank *you*, man. Thank you, because you brought me back.' I thought I could check out my passion." Applause in the church began building anew. "I actually thought I could check out something that I love more than anything. *He* brought me back."

Del's voice was back to full throttle. "When you do something for someone, you're doing it for yourself."

With that, he thanked the congregation, cheers ricocheted off the stained-glass windows, and the Glide choir, quickly reassembling, broke into "We Shall Overcome."

ACKNOWLEDGMENTS

OFTEN THE FINAL PERSON authors thank in a heartfelt coda is their spouse. I'm reversing that. My husband, Jonathan Brittain Perdue, in numerous ways, is the reason this book exists. I could not have written it without his love. Yes, words and deeds, deeds and words.

Two other people have been extraordinary: my agent, Reiko Davis of the DeFiore Agency (special thanks to a row of women writers, culminating in Elizabeth Rosner, for suggesting Reiko), and my primary editor, Joanna Green of Beacon Press (special thanks to Roxanne Dunbar-Ortiz for leading me to Joanna). Both Reiko, then Joanna, basically reshaped the book, with my secular blessing. Beacon's managing editor, Susan Lumenello, gets my appreciation for her fastidious (and diplomatic) micro editing.

Thanks to early chapter readers: Mary Felstiner, Diana Ketcham, Cyra McFadden, B. K. Moran, Annegret Ogden, and the late Carol Field, Jean McMann, and Diana O'Hehir. Appreciation again to Sheri Prager for transcription care. Thanks to James McGrath Morris for his bracing suggestions. Although Del Seymour introduced me to most interviewees, others—Leah Garchik, Lynn Ponton, and Pam Swedlow—helped too. Grateful thanks to them. For wondrous prepublication endorsements, thank you Fr. Greg Boyle, Dr. Harry Edwards, Prof. Nigel Hatton, Anne Lamott, and Dan Rather. Extended thanks to endorser go-betweens: Shelley Fisher Fishkin, Anne Lamott, and Bill and Sally Rankin. For various forms of helpfulness along this long way, I thank Cara Black, Helena Brantley, Dalton Conley, Judy Dater, Mitch Engleman, Kevin Fagan, Ryan Fox, Lorene Garrett, Leslie Mitchner, Joan Steinau Lester, Andrew O'Hehir, Emilie Osborn, Susanne Pari, Camilla Smith, Tessa Souter, Ellen Sussman, and Rev. Marvin K. White.

Matthew Desmond, whom I have never met, inspired a central tenet in this book: my absence. In his work *Evicted: Poverty and Profit in the American City*, I noticed that although he witnessed virtually every event described, he never referred to himself. In my previous books, I was a presence (if limited), as when interviewing (and re-examining the stereotypes of) elderly German women, American waitresses, and Native Americans. This time, thanks in part to Desmond's example, after my very personal preface there is no I, no me. Basic reason: this is not my story.

Over years of dropping by various Code Tenderloin offices and attending Code TL events, I feel fortunate to have met many of the compassionate volunteers and staff, including Justin DeMartra, Leontine (Miss Tina) Collins, Maria Judice, and, in particular, the friendly-amid-everything-else-going-on executive director, Donna Hilliard. Finally, whether it goes without saying or not, I will say it: I am grateful beyond measure to every interviewee in these pages—Jason Albertson, Josh Bamberger, Caroline Barlerin, Pam Coates, Shash Deshmukh, Sam Dodge, Marie Duggan, Teresa Ewins, Alonzo Fluker, Lovenia Glaudé, Walter Hughes, Terrill Jones, Jo Licata, Jacqueline Mitchell, Steven Rice, Karl Robillard, Sonja Scott, Laura Slattery, Pam Swedlow, and Kathy Treggiari—and especially Del's daughters, Deleana Seymour and Regina Diggs, for their insights offered with noble candor. Beyond any such measure, I thank Del Seymour.

NOTES

PREFACE

1. The statistic comes from San Francisco's 2022 biennial Point-in-Time (PIT) Count, in *The 2023 Annual Homelessness Assessment Report (AHAR), Part 1: Point-in-Time Estimates of Homelessness* (Washington, DC: US Department of Housing and Urban Development, Office of Community Planning and Development, December 2023).
2. *The 2023 Annual Homelessness Assessment Report (AHAR), Part 1: Point-in-Time Estimates of Homelessness*.
3. My first interview with Del took place December 2015. I continued interviewing him off and on into 2023. My interviews with other people in the book began in 2016 and ended in 2023. All primary interviews were recorded and conducted in person, with some telephone and/or email follow-ups.

CHAPTER 1: THE APPROACHING FALL

1. *Storied: San Francisco*, Jeff Hunt, host, September 17, 2020, www.storiedsf.com.
2. Practical Recovery describes itself as a San Diego–based drug and alcohol rehab program; Practicalrecovery.com.
3. Addiction Resource, based in Phoenix, Arizona, offers an extensive array of information and services.

CHAPTER 2: THE TENDERLOIN AND A GOOD NIGHT'S SLEEP

1. Jose Martinez, "San Francisco Overdose Deaths Top 800 in 2023," CBS News Bay Area, January 17, 2024, https://www.cbsnews.com/sanfrancisco/news/sf-overdose-deaths-over-800-in-2023-tenderloin-workers-try-to-reverse-trend.
2. Next Door Shelter, Homeless Shelters Directory, last updated May 15, 2023, https://www.homelessshelterdirectory.org/shelter/ca_next-door-shelter-episcopal-community-services.
3. Christian Leonard, "San Francisco's Shelter System Is in the Spotlight," *San Francisco Chronicle*, September 15, 2023.

CHAPTER 5: THE OFFER

1. "Union Leader Charges Cab Bosses 'Ignoring' Taxi Drivers' Safety," *Chicago Defender*, February 29, 1968.

CHAPTER 6: GRADUATION DAY

1. Disclosure: I helped edit their joint autobiography, *Beyond the Possible: 50 Years of Creating Radical Change in a Community Called Glide* (New York: HarperOne, 2013).

CHAPTER 10: WELCOME (NOT) TO THE LAFD

1. Del credits his data to a 1973 book about the history of racism in the Los Angeles Fire Department, *The Old Stentorians*, by A. B. Hartsfield-Mills.

CHAPTER 12: A DOUBLE END

1. Attempts to verify the dramatic story via the *Los Angeles Times* or the *Los Angeles Daily Journal* have been unsuccessful. Del maintained that shootings in South Central Los Angeles were so common at the time that neither publication would have covered the story.

CHAPTER 16: PROSPECTS OF MURDER

1. Archives from the *Fresno Bee* do not specifically describe a plane crash into a mail truck, but at least three times in 1992 alone the paper printed articles about similar events. "Close Call near Chandler: Plane Hits Power Lines, Crashes in Neighborhood" read one headline.

CHAPTER 22: ADVENTURES IN CRIMINAL JUSTICE

1. Documents in author's possession.
2. David Watson, "Alameda County Judge D. Ronald Hyde Ordered Removed from Bench," *Metropolitan News-Enterprise*, September 24, 2003. The newspaper describes itself as a "Los Angeles daily newspaper focusing largely on law and the courts," http://www.metnews.com.

CHAPTER 24: INVENTIONS

1. "OnStar," *Wikipedia*, https://en.wikipedia.org/wiki/OnStar, accessed January 16, 2024.

CHAPTER 27: CONFRONTATION

1. Newspaper article in author's possession.

CHAPTER 33: HOW TO STOP HOMELESSNESS

1. Trisha Thadani and Joaquin Palomino, "San Francisco's Deadly Failure on the Drug Crisis Is Unfolding Inside Its Own Housing Program," *San Francisco Chronicle*, December 15, 2022.
2. HSH Budget, Department of Homelessness and Supportive Housing, https://hsh.sfgov.org/about/budget, accessed January 25, 2024.

CHAPTER 37: FILLING NEEDS, AND MORE NEEDS

1. Alejandro Serrano, "Job-Training Pop-Up Opens on Troubled Mid-Market Block Where Liquor Store, Smoke Shop Just Closed," *San Francisco Chronicle*, September 20, 2019.
2. "Second Suspect Arrested in Fatal San Francisco Tenderloin District Shooting of Community Worker," CBS Bay Area News, September 3, 2021; "Tenderloin Shooting Leaves 17-Year-Old Dead, Others Injured," KTVU.com and *Bay City News*, June 29, 2021; "SFPD Battling Tidal Wave of Crime and Illegal Drug Sales in the Tenderloin Neighborhood," CBS Bay Area News, May 25, 2021.